THE GREEKS AND THE ENVIRONMENT

THE GREEKS
AND THE ENVIRONMENT

Edited by
Laura Westra
Thomas M. Robinson

ROWMAN & LITTLEFIELD PUBLISHERS, INC.
Lanham • New York • Boulder • Oxford

ROWMAN & LITTLEFIELD PUBLISHERS, INC.

Published in the United States of America
by Rowman & Littlefield Publishers, Inc.
4720 Boston Way, Lanham, Maryland 20706

12 Hid's Copse Road
Cummor Hill, Oxford OX29JJ, England

British Library Cataloguing in Publication Information Available

Library of Congress Cataloging-in-Publication Data

The Greeks and the environment / edited by Laura Westra, Thomas M.
   Robinson
      p. cm.
   Includes bibliographical references and index.
   ISBN 0-8476-8445-8 (alk. paper). — ISBN 0-8476-8446-6 (pbk. :
alk. paper)
      1. Environmentalism—Greece—History.   2. Philosophy, Ancient.
   3. Plato—Views on ecology.   4. Aristotle—Views on ecology.
   I. Westra, Laura.   II. Robinson, T. M.
   GE199.6874   1997   96–39654
   363.7'00938—dc21   CIP

ISBN 0-8476-8445-8 (cloth : alk. paper)
ISBN 0-8476-8446-6 (pbk. : alk. paper)
Printed in the United States of America

∞ ᵀᴹThe paper used in this publication meets the minimum requirements of
American National Standard for Information Sciences—Permanence of Paper
for Printed Library Materials, ANSI Z39.48–1984.

To H. S. Harris, who taught me to love the Greeks

—*Laura Westra*

To Livio Rossetti, for twenty years of friendship

—*Thomas M. Robinson*

Contents

Foreword

Contributors to *The Greeks and the Environment*, primarily scholars whose expertise is the study of ancient Greek philosophy, have been a gift to humanity, since the serious consideration of solutions for environmental problems of any proportion is a matter of universal importance. The contributors are also to be commended for their service to the community of environmental scholars, especially environmental philosophers, who have generally found Greek philosophy not inimical to the resolution of ethical problems but also in some ways, particularly in its emphasis on abstract rationality, responsible for environmental malaise.

Only a few individuals have previously read Greek philosophy to the end of determining how it contributes constructively to understanding contemporary environmental attitudes and behaviors. However, positive interpretations of Greek philosophy remain in the minority. Environmental philosophy is dominated by largely negative appraisals that view Greek thinking more as an obstacle to overcome than a source for constructive thinking.

Viewed against this intellectual background, there are at least four reasons to commend this collection. One has to do with the prestige of origins. By denying any constructive role to the Greeks, environmental philosophy appears to sunder itself from the intellectual roots of philosophy. The risk is that environmental ethics appears to some as more a faddish, momentary phenomenon driven by the press of immediate circumstance than a philosophy driven by the deeper currents of Western civilization. However, the literature of environmental thought increasingly calls for foundational reappraisals, such as reconsidering the basic definition of our humanity or the nature of the good society. Such efforts can only be aided by the serious reconsideration of the original sources of our ideas.

A second reason to commend the contributors involves the cultural function of the classics. Granted, scholars of ancient Greek philosophy sometimes appear to other intellectuals as antiquarians: a closed community of academics who study the past for the sake of the past. Thus the study of the Greeks becomes an end in itself, seemingly serving no purposes beyond those dear to the immediate scholarly circle. Yet in a time of crisis, as many have argued, literate cultures necessarily return to classical texts, for such texts are interwoven throughout the history of effects, that is, the intentional project that is the West, a process carried out by ongoing interpretation and reinterpretation. In this context, the defining mark of a classic text is its potency to enable new interpretations.

Still another reason this volume is timely is suggested by the notion that conversation is the locus of knowledge. Insofar as the conversation concerning Greek philosophy has been "insular"—that is, primarily a matter of specialists talking among themselves—or "closed"—that is, dismissed as a dead letter by specialists working in the area of environmental thought—then seemingly it had little to offer to the cultural conversation about environmental issues. *The Greeks and the Environment* simultaneously serves to bring scholars of ancient Greek philosophy into a larger conversational circle and to announce to environmental philosophers that Greek philosophy is not a dead letter but a conversational topic of potentially vital concern.

Finally, the text promises to bring new meaning and perhaps enthusiasm to the Greek philosophy classroom. Whatever the role the classics once played at elite institutions, today's students are particularly concerned that their core curriculum courses have relevance. Where this book is used as either a required or an elective text, students might more readily come to appreciate that the classic texts are not just the writings of dead white males but are bound up with consequential issues of today.

All these reasons together are consistent with the Socratic admonition to reflect daily upon virtue and the nature of a good society. As many scholars have argued, the Socratic vision underlies the Western intellectual tradition—scientific and ethical. Surely, as the world ventures toward an anthropogenic mass extinction of species and the disruption of biophysical processes, such as the carbon cycle, there is more reason now than ever to reconsider the teachings of the Greeks (and the pre-Platonics as well, as Eric Havelock terms them). As a teacher who has taught a core curriculum section of ancient Greek philosophy for more years than I can remember, and as an environmental philosopher who once dismissed the relevance of Greek philosophy to these times, I welcome this new collection and commend the editors for their efforts.

—MAX OELSCHLAEGER

Part I

Overview

Introduction

Laura Westra and Thomas M. Robinson

Many books and articles on environmental ethics make some reference to the alleged sources of our present environmental crisis and often identify these with either the Western religious traditions[1] or the history of philosophy, or both. The latter's focus is centered on ancient Greek thought,[2] which is then criticized from two perspectives. First, many of those early thinkers are viewed as fundamentally misguided in their understanding of the world and the role of philosophy, in ways that are counterproductive for the possibility of an ethics of environmental concern. Second, those ancient doctrines are taken to represent the basis for many disturbing and inappropriate trends in contemporary philosophy with regard to the natural world.

The present collection is intended to examine some of the evidence for this indictment of supposed Greek philosophy from the environmental point of view. It should not be viewed in any sense as a definitive presentation of all that might be said in an "environmental" defense of ancient philosophy, but we believe that the present group of essays goes a long way toward suggesting provocative new ways of relating ancient Greek philosophy to ecology and environmentalism.

It is worth noting that, as far as ecology is concerned, among those who practice and study it taking the ecosystem approach, the use of one ancient Greek, that is, Aristotle, is routine.[3] But, so far, the ancients, even Aristotle, have not gained much widespread acceptance in the environmental ethics literature, with some exceptions.[4] It is all the more important, therefore, that these thinkers be examined for themselves, by those with the philosophical and historical background to know them best, rather than be simply cited as examples of attitudes and doctrines often presented more for their reinforcement of preexistent negative attitudes than for their own intrinsic value. It is time to view some of these thinkers

3

carefully, giving their positions a fair hearing and examining dispassionately any possible "positive" concept or attitude we might find amongst them on questions of ecology. We should also feel free to speculate whether, had they been faced with our problems (problems that clearly had no existence during their lifetimes), anything present in their thought might not suggest a positive, useful "new" approach.

It is easy to see that the environmental philosophers who cite the negative influence of some of the Greeks do so primarily in an effort to understand the roots of our ecological predicament, rather than to discover anything positive in their work. An example of this attitude can be found in J. B. Callicott's 1989 article, "Traditional American Indian and Western European Attitudes toward Nature: An Overview."[5] In this work, Greek pre-Socratic thought is selectively represented by Leucippus and Democritus and their atomistic and mechanistic universe and by Pythagoras, who is thought to have linked "the order of nature" with the mathematical.

From this point of view, Callicott argues that the Greeks are the primary source of the "nature as machine" metaphor, which views nature as external, alien, scientifically observable, but essentially "other," a thing to be used and manipulated by the only rational beings, humans. He says:

> Modern philosophy of nature might be over simplified, but nonetheless not incorrectly portrayed as a merger of Pythagorean intuition that the structure of the world order is determined according to ratio, to quantitative proportions, and the Democritean ontology of void, space . . . and material particles.[6]

This is discussed as the misunderstanding accepted and compounded by Descartes and "popularized much earlier in Pauline Christianity."[7]

However, this presentation of early Greek thought ignores completely the other side of such thought, starting with Pythagoras. The Pythagoreans were well known in aniquity as vegetarians, not because of ecological concerns, but because of their doctrine of reincarnation, which entailed respect for all animals, since any of these might be housing the souls of departed kin.[8] Further, Pythagoras and Empedocles both recognize our kinship to animals, although they do not say much about plants or other features of natural landscapes. In fact, Pythagorean sects even used barley cakes, honey, or oil, rather than animals, in sacrifice.[9] For Pythagoreans we are made "of the same elements (as animals), and one breath permeates us all."

Many similar arguments can be found in the literature, where a like position is attributed to Empedocles and many others. Democritus even believed that animals were part of a justice system, and hence that they, *like humans* (my emphasis), could and should be killed when "they do harm."[10] Examples could be multiplied to show that the "great divide" between the human and the nonhuman world is by no means a part of all ancient Greek thought. Even the understanding of humans, in such supporters of hierarchy as Aristotle, as "rational animals" supports our integration with nature, if we view the two-part definition as providing equal emphasis on both terms. Aristotle argued for the existence of soul (vegetative, sensitive, and rational) throughout all natural existents.

Callicott acknowledges the difficulties from an environmental standpoint arising from Plato's account of a separate formal "reality," and he sees Aristotelian biology as compounding these problems. In contrast, Westra argues that Aristotelian doctrine can be shown (textually) to support a holistic environmental ethic. Not only are we not "essentially foreign to the hostile physical world,"[11] but we are (a) largely the same as all else that inhabits the natural world; and (b) we are all kin, not only because of similar physiological characteristics but also because of a shared soul, of which only one small part is quite different from the rest of nature.[12]

For instance, the telic unfolding of the universe is something in which we all participate, and the Prime Mover's sustenance of life and movement is something we all share. Aristotle is normally at great pains to start each argument, no matter how esoteric its eventual conclusion, with an examination of what is in nature. This leads a well-known Aristotelian, Martha Nussbaum, to cite an anecdote taken from the *Parts of Animals* and then draw some conclusions that are well supported textually but run counter to Callicott's interpretation:

> In the *Parts of Animals* (1.5) he addresses some students who had evidently protested against the study of animals, and their form and matter, asking for something more sublime. He tells them that this reluctance is actually a form of self-contempt: for they are, after all, creatures of flesh and blood themselves.[13]

Thus, long before Aldo Leopold's "land ethic" (1969), we find a clear unequivocal statement of our kinship to all life, in clear rejection of much of Platonism and—later—of Cartesianism. Nussbaum adds: "We could generalize Aristotle's point by saying that the opponent of the return to appearances is likely to be a person not at peace with his humanity."[14]

I have cited this passage of Aristotle in this volume (see Westra, p. 94) and argued for its significance. Finally, Callicott's attack on "hierarchy" in

Aristotle ignores the fact that a significant group of today's ecologists *also* make use of this concept and refer explicitly to Aristotle, as mentioned earlier.[15] Hierarchies in nature are not simply quaint Aristotelian conceits with deleterious impacts on our approach to nature; they represent instead an important category for a better understanding of ecological processes.

Hierarchies are based on differences, and a recent paper on the topic argues that the differences between humans and animals, like the differences between men and women, or citizens and slaves in Aristotle, may be viewed as part of the "psychic continuum" just mentioned.[16] Thus, they may be understood as functionally supportive of natural processes, in the way that human differences may be supportive of a diverse body politic, both contributing significantly to the thriving of their respective "wholes." Howe argues that as the principle of integrity[17] supports optimum diversity in integrity, not only for the benefit of each ecosystem, but also for the benefit of all species, a similar use may be made of differences (in a positive sense) for the polity:

> What is important for Aristotle, according to Westra, is species survival. Given the notion of *akme,* then we should be able to make the next step, that ecosystems transcend individual species, because species survival is tied with the survival of surrounding species.[18]

We are not sure that we can (or should) attempt to extend the argument from environmental/survival concerns to the body politic, since we might be perceived to be arguing for understanding women or slaves as "different kinds," a position many would find morally repugnant. But we believe we will have better luck with an environmental argument, even though ecological disintegrity clearly was not a problem for ancient Greece. As Howe justly notes, in the *Nicomachean Ethics* (1.6.1096a27) Aristotle addresses the question of the "goods" necessary for happiness, in contrast with Plato's one, universal good. In that passage, Aristotle speaks of the "right locality," in regard to place, as a necessary "good." Howe suggests the translation "suitable habitat," as "the Greek word being used here is *diaita,* which is the term used to describe the habitat of a species of animals."

The relation between some representatives of ancient Greek thought and nature is captured with more accuracy than in many accounts in Max Oelschlaeger's work *The Idea of Wilderness* (1991). He recognizes the pre-Socratics as "the first physicists" and praises Thales for his innovative reliance on "sensible evidence and logic" and Anaximander for his foreshadowing of evolution. But the problem of "natural change," he believes, was central to both Parmenides and Heraclitus. In their effort to address that issue, Parmenides argues for the first time for the unity of all that is, and Heraclitus, in fact, conceives the good life as essentially "the maintenance of the natural order."[19] Moreover, for the first time, we find in Heraclitus ethics and physics "formally interwoven." In Oelschlaeger's words: "Heraclitus's claim was that only by understanding the natural order of the world, and accommodating their own actions to it (the *Logos*), could human beings achieve a good, ordered and balanced life."[20] In fact, the commonality of all that is, even its organic unity, is a prominent part of pre-Socratic thought and an important step toward an environmentally sound moral understanding.

Another clear example of an environmentally sound idea arising from the ancient Greek world lies in something that we have largely lost in modern times, that is, a strong sense of repugnance for human *hybris*. An important and often-cited book by biologist David Ehrenfeld addresses the question of our misguided and overconfident approach to global "management" of nature. Its title, *The Arrogance of Humanism*,[21] anticipates the author's argument, and it stands in stark indictment of our current pretensions to control nature rather than act in concord with it.

A more complete and detailed discussion of "Greek philosophy" can be found in Eugene Hargrove's *Foundations of Environmental Ethics* (1987).[22] After an accurate presentation of early pre-Socratic theory, Hargrove turns to Heraclitus and Parmenides. He argues that Heraclitus is appropriately focused on change, but Parmenides' emphasis on a world that is "without beginning, indestructible, unshakable, endless" Being was harmful to any philosophical consideration of nature as such.

But this interpretation is likely to convince only on a Berkeleyan interpretation of Parmenides' poem, and that is very implausible. The poem is not about the identity of Being and thinking, but rather about the real as knowable and the real as opinable.[23] The real as knowable is the real simply *as* real and viewed exclusively in its totality; the real as opinable is the world of particulars that is the object of our sense perception. As such, the world that is the object of such perception will almost certainly be that living, breathing world in which most Greeks of the day believed, which "grew" (10.6) to its present state and in which the "goddess who steers all things sent female to mingle with male and male with female" (12.5–6). If it is a world that is forever the object of opinion, not knowledge, this no more inhibits investigation into, and appreciation of, it than does the cosmos investigated in Plato's *Timaeus*, the "most likely account" of which reveals it as being a richly cohering, living unity that constitutes the most perfect world that the Demiurge, given the constraints of matter, could possibly have made.

After an introductory essay by Anhony Preus on some ancient ecological myths and metaphors, John Rist writes an essay that combines strong claims with a cautionary note. In this essay John Rist makes it clear that current controversies surrounding environmental issues were not in the forefront of Greek consciousness, not least because the degradation of the environment with which we are now so familiar was simply not in evidence at that time. On the other hand, he points out, Plato in particular elaborated a metaphysical, moral, and political set of ideas, preeminently in the *Republic*, that would have served as an excellent foundation for a sound theory of environmentalism, based as they were on the assumption of an objective value system from which nothing (including, one must assume, the environment) could be excluded as irrelevant or inapplicable.

Tress also argues that it would be too simple to trace contemporary environmental concerns immediately to the Greeks. There is an area in which much modern thought and the views of Plato and Aristotle overlap, and that is in their generally holistic approach to our understanding and appreciation of nature. Where they differ is in the philosophical basis for the holism, the Greeks arguing from an overtly teleological stance, and most moderns, influenced by Darwinian postulates, from an empiricist and materialist one.

Other scholars in this volume who look at Plato are Mahoney, Adams, and Goldin. Mahoney's point of departure is Carol Merchant's threefold taxonomy of ethical approaches—the egocentric, the homocentric, and the ecocentric—and the current tendency to understand Plato as being more obviously inclined toward the first two rather than the third on the grounds that, for Plato the dualist, the universe of sense perception was *ex hypothesi* of a lower status than his higher-order universe of Forms. Mahoney responds by arguing that the peculiar brand of dualism espoused by Plato is in fact fully compatible with a holistic view of the material world that has much in common with views espoused by environmentalists. And the supposed egocentricity involved in his doctrine of human *eudaimonia* ("happiness") involves in fact a commitment to the view that one's own good will always involve the promotion of the good of the broader whole. On these grounds, he concludes, Plato has a fair claim to be called *eco*centrically inclined, despite general perceptions to the contrary.

Adams, in her essay, lays stress on the picture drawn in the *Timaeus* of an organized and coherent universe that is in all respects, down to the smallest biogical detail of the animal and plant kingdom, the best that the world's Demiurge could make, given the constraints imposed by the laws of matter. It is a world of living creatures, including ourselves, that is itself a living creature, and Plato makes it clear in his argument that the good of this living creature is only achievable when all of its parts, like the parts of any other living creature, operate in harmony and cooperation. As such, the argument is not overtly "ecological" in aim, but it would clearly serve as the basis for a sound and defensible environmental ethic.

Like Rist and Adams, Goldin is convinced that to attribute an overt and specific environmental ethic to Plato would be inappropriate. But he also feels that there are places in his writings that suggest "insights important to ecological thinking." One such passage for him is to be found in a little-read dialogue, the *Critias*, in which Plato seems to suggest that the over-harvesting of timber in the lands surrounding Athens has led to an overall decline in the ability of those lands to sustain life. This seems to show a strong awareness of what human intervention can do to the environment and can be legitimately viewed as a fairly natural outcome of the view of the universe as a single living creature that Plato had drawn in some detail in the immediately antecedent dialogue, the *Timaeus*.

Four scholars in the volume, Westra, DeMarco, Shearman, and Matthen, concentrate their attention on Aristotle. The burden of Westra's contribution has already been described. For DeMarco, Aristotelian "form" can and should be construed ecologically if we are to understand the functioning of natural wholes (something notoriously hard to do on current interpretations of Aristotle, which discover ample evidence in his writings of the functions of *parts* of animals but never once of an animal as a whole) in such a way as to avoid what he calls "the extremes of individualism and holism." Such an approach, he argues, allows him to accommodate without difficulty evolutionary change at the level of species, in which a new kind of life form "will live and live well so long as its character is a virtue, that is, so long as its definitive good is a successful ecological function in context. This function is the 'end,' the definitive good of a being that is its active substance, as Aristotelians knew already; in evolutionary work, this ecological function is the primary object of selective forces and the sum of the creature's adaptations."

Shearman, taking as his point of departure Stephen Jay Gould's article "The Golden Rule," finds an Aristotelian basis for the way in which "the scientific investigation of nature has been linked with achieving a good human life" and has on this basis justified the preservation of species diversity. But Aristotle's views on the matter, he argues, go much deeper than that. For Aristotle all living things participate in the divine insofar as they are able; the divine attribute of immortality, for example, at any rate at the level of species, is achieved by reproduction. Given this quality, it is part of virtuous activity, and the joy that goes with virtuous activity, to respect them all as a source of beauty and wonder.

For Matthen, Aristotle is not the "localist" he is often taken to be, though some of his statements, such as the one that events that seem to bring about the demise of races are merely "small changes of brief duration," seem to have that cast to them. On the contrary, Aristotle took the universe to be an organic whole, not unlike an organism or living body, and such a holistic view brings him close to the environmentalist camp. But a weakness in his theory was his assumption that the universe's unchanging form is the cause of its stability. On this view, environmental change, even major environmental change, will always be simply local and never able to affect the whole.

The volume concludes with two essays on ecological thinking and later Greek philosophy. Holland argues that the supposed anthropocentrism of the Stoics has been overstated and that their fortitude, and more generally their attitude to pain and happiness, could well be put to use in our thinking about the environment. And Blakeley offers reasons that Plotinian philosophy does not entail, as many believe, an overall depreciation of the world around us, but rather opens up the possibility of a mystical unity with the cosmos that "raises the prospect of a very distinctive ecological or environmental ethic."

I

Some Ancient Ecological Myths and Metaphors

Anthony Preus

This essay is a rapid introduction to the study of ancient ecological myths and metaphors; my goal is to situate more precise arguments in a larger context. The myths, models, and metaphors mentioned here include Eden or the Golden Age, Human Dominion, Noah's Ark/ Deucalion, Cosmic Justice, Cosmic Cycle, Vegetarianism, and *Autarkeia*.

Garden of Eden/Golden Age

The myth of the Garden of Eden expresses belief in a previous period in which everything—and especially the ecological arrangement—was perfect; that time no longer exists, because there was some sort of disaster, possibly caused by human activity, resulting in the present undesirable ecology. We all know the biblical version; classical Greek poetry and philosophy had an analogous myth, that of the Golden Age. Plato in the *Statesman* talks of the reign of Cronos as one in which "savagery was nowhere to be found, nor preying of creature upon creature, nor did war rage nor any strife whatsoever. . . . They had fruits without stint from trees and bushes; these needed no cultivation but sprang up of themselves out of the ground without man's toil."[1]

Eden or Golden Age stories tell us a good deal about their authors and the cultures from which they derive, and there are normative consequences of such myths. For example, one might be motivated to live *as if* one were in the Garden of Eden: follow a vegetarian diet, or actively pursue nonviolent solutions, for example. Kant's "Kingdom of Ends" is a highly intellectualized version of the "Peaceable Kingdom" of eighteenth-century Christian mythology. So, too, Socrates in the *Republic* describes a primitive society with a vegetarian diet: "reclined on rustic beds strewn with bryony and myrtle they will feast with their children, drinking of their wine, garlanded and singing hymns to the gods in pleasant fellowship, not begetting offspring beyond their means lest they fall into poverty or war. . . . Living in peace and health, they will probably die in old age and hand on a like life to their offspring."[2] Glaucon objects that this will be a "city of pigs," though Socrates replies (372a) that it is in fact the "healthy city."

The essential elements of an Eden story are present here: an initially healthy state of humanity lost through a human defect in character; no serpent here, nor marital negotiations, just Glaucon's desire to have chairs and tables, and a diet that includes meat. There begins acquisitiveness, there begins a way of life that exceeds the capacity of the land to sustain, for "we will need cattle in great numbers if they are to be eaten" (373c). Thus we are driven to acquire our neighbors' land, having abandoned ourselves "to the unlimited acquisitiveness of wealth, disregarding the limit set by our necessary desires." That is the origin of war, the origin of the necessity to have an army, and the origin of a difficult struggle to achieve a just society, as it is told in the *Republic*.

Human Dominion

A closely related myth, yet logically distinct from that of the Golden Age, is that of human dominion over the natural world. In the biblical version, God asks Adam to name all the animals in Eden—dominion of reason; when Eden is lost, survival becomes a struggle in which human beings attempt to establish a dominion of power.

The theme of dominion over nature has, of course, inspired many writers; in early myth we see the theme in the labors of Heracles. Philosophically, it reappears notoriously in Aristotle's *Politics* 1: "Plants exist for the sake of animals, and the other animals for the good of humanity; the domestic species both for his service and for his food, and most of the wild ones for the sake of food and supplies of other kinds. . . . If nature makes nothing without a purpose or in vain, it follows that nature has made all the animals for the sake of humanity. Hence even the art of war will be by nature an art of acquisition that is properly employed both against wild animals and against such of humanity as, though designed by nature for subjection, refuse to submit to it, inasmuch as this warfare is just."[3]

I don't believe that this passage gives us Aristotle's final word on ecological relationships, but it is a particularly eloquent and disturbing expression of an ecological attitude that became dominant in the modern era, with consequences we all must live with. A straight line can be drawn from this passage to Herbert Spencer's "survival of the fittest" and late nineteenth– and early twentieth–century social Darwinism. One may argue in reply that authority implies responsibility; Aristotle himself recognizes that human activity may have deleterious effects on the environment. He tells, for example, of the extinction of the scallop in the Pyrrhaean Strait due to a combination of a long-continued drought (which made the local water saltier than optimal for the species) and the "dredging machine used in their capture."[4]

Noah's Ark

A third sort of myth is the Noah's Ark story: that of an ecological disaster followed by a new beginning. Noah's Ark stories are said to have developed in the Mesopotamian region because the Tigris and Euphrates occasionally flooded so disastrously that it seemed to the inhabitants that the only place left out of the water would be Ararat. But other peoples have such stories—even Native Americans. The Hellenic version was the story of Deucalion and Pyrrha; although it is not as developed as the biblical version, it has some interest. When there was a great flood, Deucalion and Pyrrha managed to float off in an ark and land on some mountain or other in the Greek world.[5] A charming aspect of the biblical version is that Noah saves the various species of animals by taking along a pair of each kind in his ark. That part is not reproduced in the Deucalion and Pyrrha story, for the Greek couple regenerate humanity, not only as parents of the race (as Noah is the ancestor of the various races in the biblical version)—for Deucalion and Pyrrha are parents of Hellen, the eponymous ancestor of the Hellenes—but also of other people, who were generated from stones Deucalion and Pyrrha threw over their shoulders after being told by Themis to "cast the bones of their mother behind them." The earth as mother of all is, of course, an important and frequently encountered ecological image.

The presence of the various animal species in Noah's ark and their absence from the ark of Deucalion and Pyrrha lead to contrasting taxonomical attitudes. Plato and Aristotle, despite the theory of forms and the idea of permanent essences, did not expect to find a countable set of natural kinds—the number on the ark; there can be borderline cases, kinds can shade into each other. In modern taxonomy, influenced by the image of Noah's ark, it took a long time to shake the notion that the compendium of zoological specimens would exhaust the possible discoverable kinds.

The myth of Noah's Ark inspires a kind of zookeeping that takes Noah as a model. Faced with the extinction of many animal species due to the ecological disaster of the unlimited spread of humanity in search of arable land, the best we seem to be able to do in response is to take a few individuals from their natural environment to preserve them in the arks of our zoos and preserves, in the (probably vain) hope that they will be able to survive the human deluge.

The Cosmic Cycle

Anaximander and Cosmic Justice

Pre-Socratic philosophy is full of ecological myths and metaphors. When Anaximander is quoted as saying that "they give justice and reparation to one another for their injustice in accordance with the arrangement of time,"[6] a range of possible interpretations opens up for us, some of them ecologically important. The famous Nietzschean interpretation of Anaximander, that the very coming into being of entities is itself the injustice for which they pay with their reciprocal destruction, is an example. The idea is that the universe as such is in some sort of long-term steady state such that disturbances to the equilibrium bring some sort of compensatory reaction. Recent commentators, like Charles Kahn,[7] find in Anaximander a concept of an order of nature that emphasizes periodicity, or a cosmic cycle.

Heraclitus and the Cosmic Cycle

The cosmic cycle is indeed a favorite theme of pre-Socratic philosophers (as of many ancient thinkers). Heraclitus is famous for his version of the notion of cosmic retribution, suggesting a cyclical pattern: "For souls it is death to become water, for water death to become earth; but from earth water comes into being, from water souls" (B36). "The world, the same for all, neither any god nor any man made; but it was always and is and will be everliving fire, kindling in measures and extinguished in measures" (B30). Heraclitus *embraces* the strife—"War is father and king of all"—and encourages people of ability to strive to be the best, to be leaders; even if they eventually will pay for their injustice (as Anaximander puts it), they will in the meantime have actually existed. Heraclitus, unlike some of his nineteenth-century admirers, did not frame that goal in terms of an attempt to dominate nature, however. *We* read stories like those of Heracles' contests with the Nemean Lion or the Hydra as parables of humanity's attempt to dominate a recalcitrant nature, but for Heraclitus, "Thunderbolt steers all things," for "Adult human beings are called foolish by the gods as children are called foolish by adults."[8]

Empedocles: Love and Strife, Impassioned Vegetarianism

Empedocles developed the idea of a cosmic cycle into a detailed account of both generation and destruction:

> I will tell you a two-fold story. At one time they grew to be one alone from being many, and at another they grew apart again to be many from being one. Double is the generation of mortal beings, double their passing away: one is born and destroyed by the congregation of everything, the other is nurtured and flies apart as they grow apart again. And these never cease their continual change, now coming together by Love all into one, now again all being carried apart by the hatred of strife.[9]

Empedocles envisages a cyclical process between two unstable extreme conditions. In the victory of Strife, the universe is a sphere of totally separated concentric spheres of earth, water, air, and fire; each of the elements is by itself, not blended with anything else. As Love gains the ascendancy, the elements come together in proportionate and organized wholes, and complex entities, such as living things, are generated. The continued ascendancy of Love brings together disparate elements into a systematic whole, until there is a total blending of all the elements in the Sphere of Love. As Strife gains the ascendancy, things tend to fall apart into their constituent elements until everything is separated out again.

As Hippolytus reads Empedocles,[10] this double cycle, which we take to be described in the poem *On Nature*, is intimately tied to the religious and normative theories that we associate with the poem *Purifications*. Human souls are, according to Empedocles, fallen angels, punished for their crimes by being forced to live in each of the elements for a period of time: "Ether pursues souls to the sea, the sea spits them up onto the threshold of earth, the earth into the rays of the bright sun, and the sun hurls them into the whirls of the ether; each receives them from another; all hate them."[11] Hippolytus goes on to say that Love would want souls to achieve unity, but this punishment is the work of Strife; so "Empedocles urged his followers to abstain from all living things, for he says that the bodies of animals are the dwelling-places of punished souls."

At some point in the cycle, there is a Golden Age, an Eden: "Among them was no god Ares, nor Tumult, nor was Zeus king, nor Kronos, nor Poseidon, but Kypris was queen. . . . With foul slaughter of bulls their altars were not washed, but this was the greatest defilement among men: to bereave of life and eat the noble limbs."[12] Sextus Empiricus conveys much the same story about Empedocles, saying that Pythagoras and Empedocles claim that there is a fellowship (*philia*) not only of human beings with each other but also with irrational animals. "For there is a single spirit which pervades the whole world as a sort of soul and which unites us with them. That is why, if we kill them and eat their flesh, we commit injustice and impiety, inasmuch as we are killing our kin. . . . Empedocles somewhere says, 'Will you not cease from ill-sounding slaughter? Do you not see that you tear at one another in the carelessness of your thought?'"[13] "Alas that the pitiless day did not first destroy me before I contrived with my lips the terrible deed of eating flesh."[14]

So with Empedocles we have a development of the idea of the cosmic cycle together with the idea of a former Eden leading to an impassioned plea for a vegetarian way of life. Dominion over nature is, for Empedocles, illusory; treating animals as if they were put here for our use is ultimately doing the work of Strife, and we will pay the penalty for our injustice.

Plato: *Autarkeia*

The idea of a cosmic cycle reaches its highest expression in Plato's *Timaeus*. Notably, the physical universe as crafted by the Demiurge is totally self-sufficient, "its own waste providing its own food" (33c), "for the creator conceived that a being which was self-sufficient would be far more excellent than one which lacked anything" (33d). The ideal of self-sufficiency is more than a logical consequence of the notion that the universe is, after all, everything, and there is nothing outside it from which it can draw.[15] *Autarkeia* becomes an ideal for human activity, an idea with obvious ecological consequences: the inhabitants of the first society of the *Republic*, the so-called "city of pigs," live peacefully with their neighbors fundamentally because their way of life is self-sufficient.

Yet for Plato we cannot achieve true *autarkeia* through our own initiative; we need the cooperation of the gods, who, as he argues in *Laws* 10, function like "physicians defending the body from the onslaught of disease, or farmers anxiously apprehending recurrent seasons of danger for their crops, or overseers of flocks and herds" (906a). When *pleonexia* invades the body, "it is called disease, when found in seasons and whole years, pestilence, while in societies and politics it shows itself under the designation of injustice" (906c). And with the help of the gods we can avoid *pleonexia* in all its forms.

Aristotle

Aristotle has little use for the myth of the Golden Age, and it's easy to see why. For Aristotle the best environment for a human being is a polis in which one can function as a deliberative citizen, a polis that offers leisure for philosophical contemplation. Primitive societies satisfy only the bare necessities; the fully developed state is an achievement of the history of social organization.[16]

Further, Aristotle makes little use of the notion of a periodic destruction of the human race, as symbolized by the stories of Noah and Deucalion. He says, for example, that the flood of Deucalion was a local event.[17] But he does not deny that there are in some sense cosmic cycles: "just as winter occurs in the seasons of the year, so in determined intervals in some great period of time there comes a great winter and with it an excess of rain."[18] So, too, rivers come into existence and perish—"neither the Tanais nor the Nile has always been flowing"[19]—and the sea advances in one place, recedes in another.

In general, if something *can* go out of existence, or come into existence, it quite likely *will* do so; since the rotation of the heavenly spheres governs generation and destruction, those processes tend to occur cyclically: "In all animals the time of gestation and development and the length of life aim naturally at being measured periods. By a period I mean day and night, month, year, and the times measured by these, and also the periods of the moon. . . . It is the aim of nature to count the coming into being and the end of animals by the numbers of the higher periods, but nature does not bring this to pass accurately because matter cannot easily be brought under rule and because there are many principles which hinder generation and decay from being according to nature, and often cause things to occur contrary to nature."[20]

Once in a while, Aristotle shows that he has the notion of a great cosmic cycle as a kind of background assumption: "while probably each art and science has often been developed as far as possible and has again perished, these opinions [concerning the gods] have been preserved like relics until the present."[21] But the notion of a cosmic cycle does not get cashed out into a normative theory in Aristotle's system; unlike the

Empedoclean system, the Aristotelian does not use the cosmic cycle as an argument to persuade us to abstain from meat; rather Aristotle expects that whatever exists is there for our use, and the cosmic cycle and our relationship to it will roll on as it will.

An ecological notion that *does* have a significant influence on Aristotle's normative position is that of *autarkeia*, or self-sufficiency. He assumes that the *eudaimon* life is self-sufficient,[22] and so, to make a long story short, the theoretical life is best because it is most self-sufficient.[23] When Aristotle talks about happiness in the *Rhetoric*, he says that it can be defined as "prosperity combined with virtue" or *autarkeia* or "the secure enjoyment of the maximum of pleasure" or "a good condition of property and body, together with the power of guarding one's property and body and making use of them."[24] But *autarkeia* depends on the combination of internal and external goods, plus good luck.[25]

2

Why Greek Philosophers Might Have Been Concerned about the Environment

John M. Rist

In fact, Greek philosophers were not concerned about the environment, for the obvious reason that they could not see it as threatened. The environment was not viewed as a problem, and indeed was scarcely recognized as "the environment." Greek cities were doubtless often dirty, foulsmelling places threatened by disease, such as the notorious plague at Athens at the beginning of the Peloponnesian War so graphically described by Thucydides. And they may at times have sprawled. But they had few factories, no cars or modern industrial pollution, no plastics or man-made radiation, no noise pollution from airports, and they covered a very small area of the earth's surface. Outside the cities lay vast tracts of thinly inhabited countryside, crossed by occasional roads and paths between villages and generally feared (not without reason) by townsmen.

The Greeks were rarely "romantic" about the countryside, and a Roman emperor who took his court to the top of a mountain was regarded as more than a little eccentric. Greek society was largely urban; the countryside was a place for hicks, who would in the classical period be romanticized even less frequently than their surroundings. Civilization was in the cities, and the countryside, whether wild or cultivated, could largely be left to itself—so long as it could supply the minimum necessary foodstuffs. It was underpopulated, often infested by wild beasts, and alien to "civilized" life. Satirists might praise its rustic virtues, especially the chastity of its women, but they preferred not to live there.

There was worse still: rural space was inhabited by divine or demonic powers, in springs, groves, and rivers; its trees and buildings were liable to be struck by lightning from Zeus. Much of the Mediterranean coastline was often infested by pirates and malaria, and—some briefly peaceful Roman times excepted—the beach life of modern urban refugees looking for sun and sex away from the rat race of the Eternal City was virtually unknown in classical antiquity. The ancient Greeks knew of a hostile rural environment two thousand years before the coming of that process of the "demagicization" (*Entzäuberung*) of the earth documented by Max Weber for the ages of the Protestant Reformation and early modern scientific progress.

Yet it is in that still god-soaked and, as they often saw it, "god-awful" countryside that the seeds of a concern for the environment—had one been necessary—might have been discovered. For despite man's fear of nature, the gap between men and animals, plants, groves, streams, and lakes was comparatively narrow. Descartes's view that animals are a sort of machine would have been unthinkable; beliefs that men might be reincarnated as beasts, or had been beasts already, were taken seriously within several philosophical traditions, notably by Pythagoreans.[1] Even atomists like Epicurus are better described as vitalists. It is mistaken to ascribe materialism in the modern acceptance of that word to any Greek thinker. Though "moral dualism"—in which the body and matter are seen as evil or as the sources of evil—is well known to ancient philosophy, the dualism of mind and matter as understood in post-Cartesian times is not.

This is an essay about method, about useful and less than useful ways of appropriating ancient thought to the service of modern problems, specifically to problems of environmental ethics. When I assert that Greek philosophers were not concerned with the environment, I am not saying that, had environmental problems been brought to their attention, they would not have been concerned with them. I am saying that such problems were not brought to their attention, indeed that they could not have been brought to their attention, because environmental problems had not been identified as such. This distinction is important, because it is a feature of the history of philosophy in general and of ethics in particular that one may be obliquely discussing a problem, assuming answers to a problem, or proposing theories that would be helpful to those who have identified a problem, without having identified that problem oneself. Thus, characters in the Homeric poems talk about wanting things (and wanting people, as in the opening passages of the *Iliad* we find Achilles and Agamemnon wanting to enjoy the same slave girl) long before anyone formulated the concept of willing or talked about a faculty of will; and it was common knowledge that not everything wet could immediately be identified as water long before Aristotle proposed a distinction between substances (such as water) and qualities (such as wetness).

In considering such matters, the avoidance of anachronism is not merely a matter of pedantry. The identification of a philosophical problem *as a problem* changes the way that problem is discussed, allowing new solutions and at times precluding earlier ones. If we apply such a method-ological principle to the attitude of Greek philosophers to the environ-ment, it would seem to follow that we cannot very usefully pick out those bits of their theories that might seem more "environmentally friendly": papers like "Plotinus and the Rain Forests" are unlikely to be successful if they merely concentrate on those odd texts of Plotinus—there must be very few of them—in which he says nice things about trees or discusses *in passing* the nature of agriculture. To consider whether there are resources in the thought of Plotinus or of any other ancient philosopher by which we might make progress on problems of environmental ethics, we shall less profitably consider detailed philosophical claims, such as a belief in reincarnation (especially if such claims are philosophically and scientifically suspect). More helpful might be a consideration of Plotinus's *"mentalité,"* or at least of the more basic Plotinian principles: those princi-ples to which Plotinus himself would appeal, or on which he would fall back, if an environmental problem *as such* were brought to his attention. We have already alluded to one such principle: his belief (shared by the overwhelming majority of "premoderns") that the world itself should be understood vitalistically, not merely mechanistically. Indeed it has often been suggested that the replacement of an admittedly shadowy vitalism by mechanism was one of the driving forces behind "modern" man's sci-entific contempt for the universe: a contempt that said that the world should no longer be feared, respected, or worshiped, but that it should be owned, with the right to its use and abuse firmly in its owners' power—in the voyeuristic postmodern imagery, that it could be raped.

This paper will therefore try to identify certain principles, preferably at the broadest possible level of generality, in ancient philosophical thought: principles not dependent merely on apparently bad science but strictly ethical and metaphysical in nature. I shall suggest that such principles are not necessary if we are merely fighting to achieve the public-policy goal of an improvement in environmental conditions among which we live on this planet—not necessary, that is, if we are to see ourselves merely as pro-pagandists for the good and the beautiful rather than the fast and the loose in environmental ethics, but essential if we are to be able to *justify* our more generous positions philosophically rather than remain, at best, the proponents of what Plato would call "true opinion," at worst, merely promoters of what we happen to like and have chosen to promote.

It will thus become apparent that in environmental ethics, as in ethics more generally, if we want to justify our position by the appropriation of ancient (and medieval) wisdom, we shall have to pay a metaphysical price that we may not like. But without justification for our theories, and especially for our environmental theories, we shall look like mere senti-mentalists to those mechanistic adversaries who care for little beyond themselves and their own lifetime. Sentiment, as Oscar Wilde put it, is emotion you don't have to pay for.

An enriched portrait of ancient wisdom on such matters might be available if we declined to restrict ourselves to philosophical texts as such, but I shall not venture onto those wider waters to any significant extent, not only because of my own ignorance but because it is the philosophers, not the general public, who think seriously about the crucial matter of the *justification* of right belief.

The narrower subject of this essay, then, is quite properly not "Were the Greek philosophers interested in the environment?" but "Why might Greek philosophers have been interested in the environment had the environmental problems faced by our contemporary world been brought to their attention?" For consideration of moral and political questions arises in practical contexts. Plato and Aristotle worried about factionalism and civil war because factionalism, civil war, and the loss of a sense of civic unity threatened the existence of the communities in which they lived. Environmental damage did not threaten the Greek polis; it threat-ens the modern nation-state and global village. It has therefore become an urgent topic for modern moral philosophers. Our question is: Has Greek philosophy any untapped resources that might be helpful to modern environmentalists? Do the settled attitudes of Greek philosophers to the universe in which they lived offer us any comfort in our own struggle against those of our contemporaries with little or no concern for the envi-ronment, even when they are financially and socially in a position to con-tribute to solutions of massive environmental problems?

We have already touched upon certain ancient attitudes that might at least encourage respect for the environment had it seemed necessary. But as we have seen, these attitudes are not only largely religious in their nature; in some of their commoner ancient forms, they would seem to depend, for those of us who live after the *Entzäuberung*, on outdated sci-ence. Nevertheless, claims about such possible entities as a World Soul or divinities living in groves or springs depend not only on outdated science but more fundamentally on continuing, though much controverted, meta-physical beliefs. Most ancient thinkers accepted some version of a meta-physical picture of the world in which nature is seen hierarchically. In that hierarchy what is alive in the strictest sense is at the top. But life itself is higher up the scale than the inanimate or at least (since I have suggested that vitalism underlies much ancient thinking) than what displays less advanced forms of life and approximates to what we would call the inanimate. It was the common view of Platonists, Aristotelians, and Stoics alike that mental life is the highest form of life. Such hierarchical claims may be defective in at least three ways: the ordering of the hierarchy might be misunderstood; the notion of hierarchy itself might be mistaken, though some or all objects in the world, or the world itself, might be of intrinsic value; or nothing at all might have any value unless we, or some of us, decide, perhaps under the delusion that we can identify our actions as those of wholly rational agents, that we can create (rather than identify) such value. Needless to say, such latter claims seem to rest on the undefended assumption that rational agents, if any, are themselves in possession of intrinsic value; they are not only rational but, as such, "good."

In a typical ancient view, men are more important than animals, animals than plants, plants than stones or the "four elements" of which, according to some, the whole sublunary universe is ultimately composed. But man was rarely seen as the highest being in the universe or the best example of a creature endowed with mind. Plotinus thinks that the Gnostics are arrogant for giving man too high a place in the universe *(Enneads* 2.9.5). Atheism in the strict sense—positive nonbelief in the existence of a god or gods—was very rare in the ancient world. Few philosophers and fewer ordinary people would have subscribed to it. Plato in the *Laws* thinks it a phenomenon so unusual that it can be more or less discounted.

One of the advantages of theism, in almost any form, is that it helps to restrain the ceaseless desire of human beings to reconstruct the world exactly as they, or some of them, choose to reconstruct it. For if each man's life is limited to his seventy-odd years or so, and if there are no objective values beyond those that human beings choose to contract or adopt, the environmentalist has a hard time. That is why he likes to throw out words like "sacred" when speaking of the universe or of our own planet; he likes to pretend that there are values beyond those that he chooses to create. The ancients had the advantage over him in that they usually believed that such values are part of the furniture of the universe. In the short run, as we have seen, that did not endow them with much concern for the environment; in the longer run, it gave them a theoretical framework in which concern for the environment might, if necessary, have been justified.

We may identify a paradoxical situation: Ancient thinkers evince little overt concern for the environment, while normally possessing a mental universe in which they have the resources for justifying such concern, while we moderns often exhibit concern for the environment but have few theoretical resources on which such concern can be grounded. I leave aside such minority, often vaguely Thomistic views—unfashionable at least in the post-Christian West—as that whereby we are allocated our planet by God, not to be absolute lords and masters, but stewards of an inheritance to which none of us individually or collectively has complete title.

Notice, however, that the paradoxical situation to which I have referred is not limited to environmental issues, for environmental ethics is, after all, a branch of ethics in general, and its contemporary difficulties merely reflect the difficulties of modern ethics as a whole. The fundamental problem with which we are at present concerned is the issue of whether there are objective standards in ethics, or, to put it otherwise, whether moral judgments are cognitive or noncognitive, and if they are cognitive, whether the facts to which they refer are, in the last analysis, the creation of man, groups of men, or simply human individuals. The implications of this problem for the environmentalist are serious, for dependent on his resolution of it is his ability to argue his case on moral, metaphysical, or merely prudential grounds. But no environmentalist, for example, who talks about integrity in the natural order should delude himself or others that the word "integrity" is value free or that the case he constructs around it is merely a prudential case.

Let us pursue the matter further with reference to the first principles of any possible theory about an obligation, or at least a moral obligation, to be concerned about the environment. On what kind of principles could any nonprudential argument for environmental protection be based? Here are a number of suggestions, with possible counterarguments:

1. The physical universe is beautiful and should, if possible, be left that way. Certainly large parts of the physical universe may be called beautiful, but by what standard? All the old objections to objective values in ethics apply (perhaps in spades) in aesthetics. As Mackie, whose book on moral philosophy begins "There are no objective values," continues: "The claim that values are not objective, are not part of the fabric of the world, is meant to include not only moral goodness. . . . It also includes non-moral values, notably aesthetic ones, beauty and various kinds of artistic merit."[2]

2. Acts of vandalism and philistinism directed against natural objects, as against works of art, are degrading and damaging to those who perform them. But here again, the argument is either a covert appeal to objective values (some kinds of character and characteristics are not only unpleasant to deal with but are actually wicked), or it is based on a kind of conventionalism (we agree that some behavior is

wrong in that it makes us in some way antisocial), or it reduces itself to a prudential judgment (the world would be better for all of us, including myself, if we agreed not to tolerate such behavior).

3. The most common approach, and the most attractive, would involve a claim something like that made by Rawls that if we could imagine a group of people reasoning behind a veil of ignorance about their own future (ignorant, that is, about their future health, social position, talents—perhaps, some would add, about their sex) they would, if they were rational agents, agree that certain sorts of behavior would best follow a rational path.[3] Such sorts of behavior would include an attitude of respect for the environment.

It might be objected that this is mere prudentialism, but that is not quite the case, for two reasons: First, our supposed rational agents are not reflecting on their own good in what in real life might be some privileged circumstance. They cannot therefore allow their privileged circumstance to influence their judgment. Second, Rawls's thesis depends on the view that fully rational arguments just are moral arguments.

But this approach also suffers from two basic flaws, one formal and the other practical. Its formal flaw is that it attempts to extract the content of moral behavior from one of its formal conditions, that is, its rationality. Part, but only part, of this weakness is that it assumes the sub-Kantian habit of taking universalizability as not merely a necessary but a sufficient condition of the moral judgment. (Kant himself does not do this insofar as he "restates" his account of the categorical imperative to include the certainly nonformal requirement that persons are privileged in that they are always to be treated as ends, never as mere means, a thesis that appears to be an unacknowledged survival of some form of Christian theology.)[4] But there is also the practical flaw involved in talk of the "veil of ignorance" and other such devices to ensure impartial rationality. This is not merely the point that *in fact* no one ever lives in such conditions, but more seriously the doubt as to whether beings living in such conditions would be human beings at all. For it is to be doubted not only whether human beings could ever want to live in this way, but much more seriously whether they are capable of living in this way. The point has recently been expressed clearly by Nagel,[5] and all the more effectively in that as a would-be reformed Kantian he should find it (and to a degree does find it) destructive of the sort of position he himself wishes to espouse: "What lies beyond our current understanding is not adequately captured in the idea of a set of questions we do not yet know how to ask. It may include things that we or creatures like us could never formulate questions about." Admittedly, Nagel is not referring here to the capacity for specifically moral reasoning, but there is no reason similar concerns should not be serious in that area as well.

It might even be the case that although no argument could demonstrate the existence of objective values, such values nonetheless exist and the moral world is only intelligible *on the working hypothesis* that they exist. Indeed, in my earlier implication that much work in contemporary environmental ethics is not philosophy but political advocacy guided by high-minded ideals lurks the suggestion that advocates often make an assumption of objective values, though they dare not hang their case upon it either because they cannot themselves *explicitly* admit it or because they know that in the propaganda war in which they are engaged, their credibility will be undermined, if not destroyed, if they can be tarred with "discredited" metaphysical or religious claims.

The situation of the modern environmentalist who wishes to *justify* his behavior, to give an account of his first principles, is dire in a way somewhat similar to that of the modern antiabortionist: both have to justify abandoning what seems prima facie to be convenient behavior (polluting someone else's land or destroying someone else's existence) in the pursuit of some other goal and at the price of various forms of personal hardship, especially loss of money. What both have to argue is not only that it makes sense to act in the interest of others but that such sense *entails* a responsibility to do so. But responsibility is not a scientifically measurable notion, and if I cannot mount metaphysical arguments for its "reality," I shall usually find that hard-line opponents can dismiss me as a sentimentalist, a bleeding heart or tree hugger. For to my plea about the environment, "What about future generations?" comes back the answer, "I shall be dead by then," and, in an adaptation of Epicurus, "After death the future is nothing to us."[6]

Modern man's environmental plight is to be attributed not merely to his technological capacity, not merely to his reliance on post-Cartesian dismissals of the nonhuman world as material that he can use as he sees fit, that he can use or abuse; more basically, it can also be attributed to his loss of the notion that each man is not merely an individual but *also* a member, not merely of the community of the human race, but of something wider than the human race. Such lost views took the form not only of the idea that we *could* be such members but that to a degree we *must be* such members and that, if we are to flourish, we *ought to be* such members. In effect, a person who struggled to liberate himself from such membership could be seen as acting self-destructively, even suicidally.

If, however, we at last return to antiquity, we find, as we have seen, that there is little overt concern with the environment. That, as we have also seen, is because those philosophers who thought of the moral life as some kind of "soul making" or "person making"—Plato above all, but to some extent Aristotle and the Stoics—did not include threats to the environment among threats to the moral project in which they were engaged. Had they done so, they would have wished to restrict threats to the environment. Yet it would not be difficult, if we were to transport Plato to the late twentieth century, to show him that threats to the environment are indeed threats to the moral and political project in which he is engaged. Furthermore, I would argue, it would not be difficult for him to maintain that the resources are indeed available within his own philosophical repertoire to propose not merely a pragmatic and prudential concern for the environment but also a moral concern in the strong sense of "moral" in which he would want to talk about the moral virtues (justice, courage, self-restraint, and the rest) in general.[7]

Suppose Plato wanted to include within the education of his philosopher- kings in the *Republic*, or of his less ambitious lawgivers in the *Laws*, a teaching that we must respect the environment. He would have two possible approaches. First, he could argue that since the external world is (at least sometimes) beautiful, it reflects the omnipresence of the Form of Beauty, is thus capable of inspiring us, and thus should be respected or at least managed in such a way as to preserve its beauty as well as possible while putting higher beauties and their goods in a preferential position. And there is of course no doubt that in Plato's sublunary universe, if we leave the gods aside and concentrate on physical objects (compounds, in whatever sense, of form and matter), the most beautiful object is the soul of the beautiful young man or, better, for the judge who is not himself the teacher, the beautiful soul of the older man (such as Socrates) who can teach the young.

So the first way Plato would approach environmental questions would be to ask: Would the preservation of nature help or hinder the soul in its quest for moral excellence? At first this might not seem to be a very promising approach. Plato's dialogues, with the important exception of the *Phaedrus*, are all set, not in the countryside, but in the city, for reasons that we sketched at the beginning of this paper. And in the *Phaedrus* itself Socrates looks slightly uncomfortable in his rustic surroundings, which Plato quickly associates with the forced allegorization of the story of the rape of Orithyia by Boreas, the north wind. Such rhetorical and mythological fantasies are little to his taste, and insofar as the Greek countryside might encourage them, he would see adequate ground for further suspicion of it.

But Greeks, and certainly Plato, are very capable of appreciating and depicting natural beauty without becoming sentimental or romantic about it. The question he would want to ask, when confronted with the massive destruction of the environment that is a feature of the modern world would be: Is exposure to such destruction liable to make us morally better or worse? And there is little doubt that he would believe that it makes us worse, for he has, he thinks, an objective standard, the Form of the Good, by which he can measure correctly, and not in some fallible way depending on the fallible judgment of a man or a group of men picked at random, what makes the soul better and what makes it worse. In the central books of the *Republic* there are attacks on "banausic" activities, activities of craftsmen who in bad working conditions necessarily deform the human body and narrow the vision of the human soul to the immediate and the trivial. Such people, he thinks, cannot philosophize. It would hardly take long for a man of Plato's acumen to recognize that engendering a world in which, at its worst, we have to endure catastrophes like Bhopal or Chernobyl is not going to help those living (or rather surviving) under their shadow to lead the philosophical life. For Plato certainly subscribes to a view like that summed up by Aristotle at the beginning of the *Politics* (A.1252b29-30) that although cities are first established for the sake of life, for mere survival, there is a sense in which their justification for continuing over time is their unique capacity to generate the good life— that is, the life where a man has the opportunity in a congenial community to develop his highest capacities to the greatest degree that the ordinary circumstances of his life as a responsible citizen will allow him to achieve.

Thus, confronted with modern environmental threats, Plato would certainly appeal to legitimate prudential considerations, for he would be the last to say that a citizen should have no concern for the existence and well-being of future generations of citizens; to the contrary, he would wish to promote their chances of living in a clean and healthy environment. But Plato's appeal would be not only to prudence plus a sense of responsibility (the latter being a notion, as I have argued, that cannot convincingly be claimed to be merely prudential). He would also appeal to the maintenance of genuine beauty in physical objects, a beauty that can, to a degree, be evaluated, as Plato himself offers an evaluation of it in Diotima's speech in the *Symposium*. Even if the would-be philosopher first uses the physical beauty of his boy love as a path towards love of Beauty himself (thus in one sense, but not perhaps, as we shall see, a serious sense, defying Kant's dictum that we not should use our fellow humans as means), there is no indication that he loses interest in the boy as he ascends to an evaluation of more than human beauty in the Form itself. Indeed, one might argue (and perhaps Plato might argue, citing the case of Socrates) that it is only when one sees the immeasurably greater beauty of the Form that one can appreciate how, in his limited perfection, the boy really is beautiful. (If that is so, Plato's theory would resemble Augustine's view that it is only by recognizing that human beauty should not be worshiped as God's beauty that we can form a proper—that is, a nonidolatrous—appreciation of the beauty of the boy—in Augustine's case more likely of the girl—at all.)[8] At any rate, in the *Symposium* itself, where Socrates is clearly represented as the ideal philosopher in love with Beauty, his concern for those who are starting on the philosophical road seems no more diminished than it is in every other Socratic dialogue: everywhere he goes, Socrates tries to make "beautiful" people better in their souls.

Recall again why Plato would want to balance two goods—the good of making human souls, human individuals, better, and the good of respecting goodness and beauty, to an appropriate degree, wherever they might be found. Here is where Plato's insistence that Goodness is an objective, cognitively recognized reality stands him in good stead. With reference to the Good, he will not say that the universe is merely to be used and abused (after all, he still retains the old view that it is god-drenched, as we have seen), but he has a measure by which he can begin to determine how and where "less" beautiful things should be sacrificed, or at least not promoted, in the interest of that which—if it behaves decently—is higher (i.e., man), but which, if it behaves badly, is deserving of the greatest and severest penalties.

A further advantage of Plato's objective measuring rod is that he will not put off his opponents, as ecologists so often do, by being unable to determine whether a healthy man is more important than a healthy dog (fearing the designation of speciesist—that term that finally reveals the folly of refusing attempts to evaluate the cosmos and its contents into some kind of objective hierarchy and that, when invoked, seriously damages more thoughtful ecological efforts).

So it seems that it would not be so difficult to persuade a late-twentieth-century Plato (or, for that matter, an Aristotle or a Zeno of Citium) that environmental ethics should be taken seriously, and that, regardless of whether you have a concern for the human race in general, and in particular for those who live outside your own polis, you should still be concerned with the environment as a whole, both because the whole environment is a concern to every Platonic citizen and because the principles of environmental respect are such as to promote, rather than impede, the improvement of the citizens of the polis itself.

Such considerations point to a further fundamental difference between most ancient and much (though not all) modern political science and political philosophy, one that we cannot entirely omit, since it would be virtually the unanimous view of the ancients that unless one subscribes to it, then public policy over the environment is likely to be rather ineffective. With the exception of the Epicureans, Cynics, and Skeptics, philosophers from Socrates on accepted the generally held thesis that it is the duty of literary figures, and certainly of philosophers, in the words of Aristophanes (*Frogs* 1009–1010), to make the city better. And since the city consists of its citizens, so it is the proclaimed aim of the city itself to educate its citizens, or even the wider Greek world: Pericles spoke of Athens as being the school of Hellas. Thus it was a major function of the Greek city actively to promote the moral well–being of its citizens. Of course, if one compares an ancient city with a modern state, it is immediately apparent that the educational resources of the ancient city (with virtually no capacity for bureaucracy or even an effective police force) not only left the aims and dreams of such governments far beyond their reach but concealed the fact that if there were to be any sort of effective state machine for promoting the virtue of its citizens, it could very readily get out of hand, as our experience of the "virtuous" Robespierre and St-Just showed so clearly in the French Revolution.

Among actual Greek cities the most serious attempt to organize citizen virtue was certainly made in Sparta and other Dorian communities, but the philosophers regarded these attempts as well intentioned but hopelessly inadequate because of the overrestricted concept of virtue (reduced more or less to courage and military prowess) that the Spartans claimed to promote. Nevertheless, few ancient theorists would have evinced any sympathy for the modern view that the state, being in many respects at odds with the individual, should be allowed to restrict him, or even to guide him, just as little as possible. Insofar as modern liberalism is normally tied to some form or other of individualism, the state is seen ideally as a mediator between competing individualisms, not favoring any particular side, or moral position, or ideology, except insofar as it might find it necessary to do so in the interests of a minimally essential degree of law and order. As it is often put, the state (in direct contrast to the ancient polis) sees its role as the maintenance of a level playing field for as many competing players as it can accommodate. In such a society concern about the environment will take its place among other goals, good, bad or indifferent, that struggle for success in the national marketplace.

Such a struggle is officially viewed less as an attempt to make the citizens better than as the means by which an individual, or a set of individuals bound together as a pressure group, may try to persuade a majority of active voters—if we are in a democracy—that their product is more in the private interest of the rest of the population than is the product, say, of the arms trader or manufacturer of nuclear reactors. Thus the state, through its practices and official representatives, is supposed to minimize its "interference" in the private and supposedly individualized (but often merely homogenized) lives of its citizens. Above all, it is not supposed to argue that a policy of ecological protection would contribute to the moral virtue of the citizenry, for the lawyer for a logging company would soon rise to his feet to say he does not need to be lectured paternalistically about the sort of moral improvement his customers and/or the Canadian people need. It is true that the ancients had much less reason than we do to fear bureaucracy; they had seen so much less of its abuses. On the other hand, they usually knew much better than we do that the notion that individuals are moral atoms and that each of us has the right to carve his own way "provided he does not hurt someone else" (when it is often difficult, and certainly contentious, to determine whether someone else is being hurt) is far from a self-evident truth. More and more, we give the benefit of the doubt in such cases to the individual; we fear his rights to do as much as possible of what he likes will be infringed. The ancients, lacking at least this sort of concept of rights, would be much more prepared to ask whether this man's "right" makes him or others morally inferior and whether certain profitable actions, such as "raping" the rain forests, are good for the moral well-being of the responsible agents and of the wider communities to which they belong.

But the ability of the ancient thinkers to reflect in this way depended not merely on their nearness to nature, not merely on the fact that they were not seeking a neutral state but wished the state to promote the virtue of its citizens, but also on the overriding fact, discussed above, that they believed that there are objective values to which they might appeal in restricting the crazily inflated claims to individual (or to interest-group) rights, individual (or interest-group) freedoms from restraint, and maximum tolerance for any kind of moral claim provided that its social damage can never be *demonstrably* proved—which, of course, it virtually never can be. Above all, then, many ancient thinkers could justify a concern for the environment in terms of a morality based on objective values, and at least Plato was prepared, in the *Republic*, both to try to show that such claims and tactics are objectively reasonable and to point unflinchingly to the moral anarchy that must ensue (and in fact does ensue in our own contemporary discussions) if he fails.[9] And Plato would be the first to say that if we cannot show that a serious concern for the environment follows from the general relationship between morals and metaphysics, then even if it is "right," its advocates, as we suggested earlier, will remain just that: advocates, people, in Platonic language, possessed not of knowledge but merely of true opinion. And in Plato's view, true opinion is shaken by the wind.

3

The Philosophical Genesis of Ecology and Environmentalism

Daryl McGowan Tress

Ecology, the study of the relationship of living things to one another and to their environment and the influence of man on this ecosystem, and ecology's activist extension, environmentalism, the organized efforts to protect the natural environment from destruction by human beings, have emerged as major forces in our era. The term "ecology" was coined in the nineteenth century by the German Darwinian Ernst Haeckel.[1] Now in the twentieth century, scientific studies of the interdependence of living things and their natural surroundings comprise a major subdivision of biology, and these studies often document the varied dangers posed to nature. The consequent attempts to protect the natural environment and to educate the public about the vulnerability of the natural world, especially in the face of threats to it from the human domain, are a familiar part of contemporary life. Recent science, it would seem, has revealed, on the one hand, the interconnections and interdependence of the elements of the natural world and, on the other hand, the danger for nature of the products of modern science and technology.

One might be led to think, therefore, that ecology and environmentalism represent specifically recent efforts—that is, new biological discoveries about the interconnections of nature as well as the new dangers nature faces from the modern world. This view is largely correct, I will suggest. Nonetheless, as we know, an awareness of "nature" is hardly a new occurrence. The study of *physis* and *kosmos* is a central preoccupation of ancient Greek philosophy and science and, for that matter, of premodern—that is, pre-seventeenth-century—philosophy and science in general. Indeed, in choosing the term "ecology" to designate the science of nature's interconnections, Haeckel turned to the Greek for the words *oikos*, "house or home," and *logos*, recapturing the Greek idea of nature as an "earth household." The term "ecology" is a cue to an early Greek philosophical insight into nature as a structured whole and functioning home for human beings and other living things.

Ecology, then, so closely associated with contemporary science and public policy, is a reminder, by way of its etymology, of a premodern conception of nature. In the premodern, classical view, natural entities form an organized, regular, hierarchical system of great beauty. Nature as a whole is eternal or everlasting (Aristotle) or, to the extent that it has come into being, was perhaps planned or designed by a beneficent intelligence (Plato). This natural system, along with the creatures within it, is a source of marvelous interest and important guidance for human beings. We note, for example, Aristotle's pleasure in the observations and activities of natural history (e.g., *Parts of Animals*) and Plato's use of the planets' orderly rotation as an instructional image for the human soul (e.g., the *Republic*). In Greek philosophy, nature is regarded as operating according to its own inherent principle of motion and rest; in living organisms, this principle is called *psyche*. Nature itself is sometimes—as in Plato's *Timaeus*—viewed as "ensouled" and thus as an intelligent living organism.

This organic classical scheme is in decided contrast to a modernist scientific view, which had its beginnings around the seventeenth century.[2] The emphasis of the new physics was mechanical; science and philosophy during this era brought about the "mechanization of the world picture."[3] The new physicists and philosophers of this era believed the physical sciences would explain the world in terms of quantifiable forces and universal laws.[4] Within the prevailing view of the new physics, nature came to be viewed, not as an ensouled living creature integrated within itself, but as a working machine with indifferent, replaceable parts. The effects of this turn in the study of living things from philosophically based natural history to a mechanical model have been a major influence on the science well into the twentieth century.[5]

In light of this general contrast, it might seem all the more the case that ecology and environmentalism favor a return to a classical model of nature as a living home and reject the modern mechanical-reductionist model that subsumes the biological domain to that of a quantitative physics. I would like to examine this apparent connection and ask, To what extent *does* contemporary ecology represent a return to a classical conception of nature? Do ecology and environmentalism really have their roots in Plato's and Aristotle's—or a broadly identified "classical"—philosophy of nature, or are the influences of the classical in fact rather limited?

Despite the important similarity between the classical view and contemporary ecology in their shared conception of the living holism of nature, there are grounds to wonder about the extent to which classical philosophical conceptions of nature serve as the ground of today's ecology and environmentalism. Two major and relatively recent developments in intellectual history serve as the basis for questioning whether ecology and environmentalism can trace their lineage directly back to Plato and Aristotle. The first of these is the scientific-philosophical shift that occurs in the nineteenth century, away from "essentialism" and its vestiges after the seventeenth century and toward *time, history,* and *process* as basic to the study of nature.[6] This turn in biology is most conspicuous in Darwin's important evolutionary theory. The new emphasis on process is definitive for the science of biology and especially for ecology, creating a great divide historically in biology with respect to what preceded Darwin. The second intellectual shift that raises questions about ecology's roots in classical views of nature also makes its appearance in the nineteenth century, and it too can be found in Darwin's work: the importation into the study of nature of the modern political and economic framework of power, relying heavily on notions of competition, domination, exploitation, and powerlessness. While, after Darwin, the notions of competition and struggle for existence become central to biological thought, including ecology, the uses and abuses of power are not part of classical studies of nature in Plato and Aristotle.

In both these respects, then, distinctively new conceptions—or new applications—of process and politics significantly shape the study of biology as we know it in the twentieth century. For convenience, I will refer to them as "late modern" notions. These late modern conceptions of the nineteenth century differ from the classical (and are, arguably, anticlassical) *and* differ as well from "early modern" mechanics, as will be seen. I suggest that, despite ecology's similarities with classical views of nature and *kosmos,* the more significant impact on contemporary ecology and environmentalism derives from early modern mechanics together with late modern politics and process thought. Thus, my thesis is that while the classical influences exert themselves in ecology and environmentalism, most notably in the recognition of nature's holistic interconnections, these influences are mediated and sometimes superseded by other, later intellectual developments.

Employing these admittedly broad categories of classical, early modern, late modern, and contemporary ecology, one can identify the contrasts between the classical philosophical outlook and contemporary ecology by examining three main tenets of modern ecology and environmentalism:

1. The recognition of the *connection* of living things on earth, and their dependence on one another and on the nonliving components of the planet.

2. The recognition of the *value* of the natural world.

3. The conception of the *fragility* of nature, along with an obligation human beings have to protect it from danger.

Let us examine these points in greater detail.

Nature's Interconnectedness and Interdependence

Recent ecology and environmental movements rest on the notion of ecosystem (a subunit of the biosphere), the concept that nature in its biotic and abiotic parts should be recognized as an interconnected web of relations. Despite some differences among the experts about a definition, there is a consensus that "ecosystem" refers to a network of biotic and abiotic interdependences that function adaptively.[8] Plato and Aristotle, like many contemporary ecologists, recognize extensive and unique sorts of connections among living things and the environment. For example, in the *Timaeus* Plato speaks of the *kosmos* as a bounded organism that contains innumerable wholes within it, all subject to input and output vis-à-vis their environment. These wholes are all complexly organized by the forethought of the Demiurge and form a larger, living system. Also, in the classical view, nature's system is a hierarchy; for example, in the *Timaeus* birds, reptiles, and wild beasts derive as lower forms from (morally fallen) human beings, and in *Generation of Animals* Aristotle posits a scale of animals based on the criterion of vital heat.

In contrast to Plato and Aristotle, for the early modern seventeenth-century philosophers and scientists under the sway of the new physics and mathematics, the universe was lifeless, and notions of uniquely organic connections could be dispensed with, given a universally applicable mechanical paradigm. According to a mechanical view, linkages within or among creatures are mathematical *as such*.[9] We might note that the early modern model, like the classical, views nature as a stable system in that nature's changes are regular and orderly, but the modern model accounts for this by way of the universal laws and forces of physics rather than by the uniquely organic form of living systems as in the classical scheme.

Recent ecology's basic concept of ecosystem as a web of living interaction clearly marks a departure from early modern mechanism and in that departure looks rather like the classical model. But the fundamental insistence in ecology on the importance of temporal effects and adaptive processes, along with ecology's metaphor of a nonhierarchical "web" or "network," makes it significantly different from a Greek philosophy of nature. Whereas, for example, Aristotle's *kosmos* involves stable species, the ecological view of the interconnection of living entities and the environment is primarily a view of the process of change deriving from an evolutionary framework, that is, from a framework within which transformation (usually via adaptation) and diversification (usually via random mutation) of populations are the fundamental realities of nature. Ecology and evolutionary theory are closely and strongly tied together so that, Ernst Mayr writes, "Many of Darwin's discussions and considerations would be quite appropriate for a textbook of ecology."[10] Indeed, the linkage between ecology and evolution is such that the two can be merged and Darwin's theory spoken of as "essentially ecological" because "ecologists are concerned with how organisms adapt to their environment in order to survive."[11] Three points should be noticed:

1. Ecology's ecosystem is composed of dynamic populations rather than species; that is, it is an interconnected web of changes, both internally (in type) and externally (in territory, geographically).

2. Understanding the ecosystem's dynamics in an evolutionary context requires that the system be viewed as processes driven significantly by random events (e.g., climatic changes, introduction of new predators, and declines in food sources, etc.), rather than by providential design or final causality.

3. The ecosystem's survival is always at stake, more or less urgently, so that adaptation to the changing threats to that survival is necessary, at the peril of the ecosystem's demise or extinction.

In these three respects, the contrast with the classical view is plain. Aristotle, for example, is not an evolutionist, as we know; for him, living entities are stable kinds rather than changeable "populations." Aristotle and Plato explain the internal stability of living kinds by virtue of the permanence of their forms. The form or *psyche* provides the entity with an intrinsic aim (i.e., "that for the sake of which"; the resources for its accomplishment may or may not be available). The form or the permanence of the *psyche* and the stability it engenders ground the classical claim that nature and natural types are everlasting and not threatened with annihilation (*Ti.* 41a–b). Furthermore, for both Plato and Aristotle, natural entities are hierarchically interconnected; nature is not simply a collection of competing or more or less equivalent organisms, as in at least some ecological philosophies.[12] The hierarchical ordering in the classical view derives, once again, from the inherence of *psyche* or form and its different grades in plants, animals, and humans.

The Recognition of the Value of the Natural World

Basic to the contemporary ecological and environmental movements is the idea of nature's value. Nature's value is asserted by some to be intrinsic, by others to be instrumental. As Arne Naess posits as the first principle of his "Platform of the Deep Ecology Movement": "The flourishing of human and non-human life on Earth has intrinsic value." And, he continues, "The value of non-human life forms is independent of the usefulness these may have for narrow human purposes."[13] While Naess holds that all natural entities have inherent value, some other ecologists and environmentalists maintain that nature's value is instrumental and is ultimately in the service of human interests and needs.[14] Whatever the basis, the value ecologists and environmentalists attribute to the natural world remains the justification for the programs of action or reform to preserve nature that they advocate or undertake.

With the scientific revolution and the new philosophies of the seventeenth century came a new regard for the natural world. For example, Bacon's call for the conquest and control of nature derives from a voluntarist interpretation of the world's creation, according to which the world is as it is simply because of God's will. Nature has no inherent meaning or purpose on this view, and the full "responsibility for conveying meaning and purpose to the world [rests] entirely on the human person, the only creature endowed with purposiveness."[15] Bacon's thinking and the general early modern attitude toward nature are sometimes regarded as the model rationalization for the exploitation of nature. But the attitudes even here are not simple and unambiguous; a thorough investigation, for example, of the details and context of Bacon's proposals in the New Atlantis regarding farms, natural lands, parks, and zoos and the importance he attached to "diversity"[16] would be needed to give a fair and accurate picture of his sensibility and that of the age.[17] What we can say in brief is that the early modern attitude *has come to be perceived to have been* one of diminished respect for the inherent value or meaning of nature, in connection with its new emphasis on human power, purposes, and needs. This shift, it is said, led to, or at least permitted, the eventual exploitation of nature's resources. And here we notice, no doubt, the sources of the serious differences between contemporary "deep ecologists" and "utilitarian ecologists": the utilitarians are perceived as affiliated with a modernist mentality that some ecologists regard as the very source of the ecological crisis, while the deep ecologists, in attributing intrinsic value, are perceived as affiliated with the classical and as mystifying what must be managed as a practical political and scientific problem.[18]

Plato and Aristotle appreciate the value of the natural world and recognize our moral relation to nature. Plato's *Timaeus* stresses the inherent goodness of the *kosmos* and the things within it, and Aristotle writes of the beauty of natural entities in *Parts of Animals:*

> Having already treated of the celestial world . . . we proceed to treat of living creatures, without omitting, to the best of our ability, any member of the kingdom, however ignoble. For if some have no graces to charm the sense, yet nature, which fashioned them, gives amazing pleasure in their study to all who can trace links of causation and are inclined to philosophy. . . . We therefore must not recoil with childish aversion from the examination of the humbler animals. Every realm of nature is marvelous . . . so we should venture on the study of every kind of creature without distaste; for each and all will reveal to us something natural and something beautiful. Absence of the haphazard and conduciveness of everything to an end are to be found in nature's works to the highest degree, and the resultant end of her generations and combinations is a form of the beautiful. (*PA* 1.5)[19]

Nature is a marvel and a form of the beautiful for Aristotle, to be studied and respected as an end in itself, in contrast to Bacon's modern attitude that subordinates nature to human purpose. And Aristotle indicates in this passage the reason for nature's beauty and intrinsic value: directedness toward a telos is found to the highest degree in nature. The early modern philosophies and sciences, in contrast, deny final causality; this difference accounts in large part for the great divide between the ancients and the moderns. Contemporary ecology, insofar as it lays claim to being a modern science, also must forswear teleology, and in so doing, it significantly distances its outlook from the classical. Indeed, as noted above, ecologists tend either to assert the value of nature as a first principle that cannot or need not be demonstrated or to argue nature's value as a means to our human ends. Either way, Plato's and Aristotle's teleological mode of appreciating nature's worth is bypassed, as ecology is more closely tied to the requirements of modern scientific methodology and its rejection of finality.

The Conception of the Fragility of Nature, and the Human Obligation to Protect It from Misuse

A familiar note of crisis regarding nature's vulnerability prevails in much of the ecological and environmental discourse of our time. Nature is a fragile web of relations, and much that man has produced technological-ly in the name of progress over the last hundred years or so is destroying, or threatening to destroy, the planet's ecosystem.[20]

The idea of "nature in peril" is surely not part of the early modern peri-od and the age of discovery. That era was forcefully impressed by the rich bounty of nature and the ways that newly developed human techniques might artfully transform nature to make it all the more wonderful. By the nineteenth century, however, the earlier picture of nature's simple avail-ability for man and his needs had become a grimmer portrait of nature in the writings of Malthus, which importantly influenced Darwin and other evolutionists.[21] Malthus, writing deliberately against the optimism about human progress expressed by Enlightenment writers such as Condorcet, told of a world in which conflict was inevitable. Darwin, integrating Malthus's ideas, saw nature as a landscape upon which there is continu-al, relentless struggle for survival in the face of ever changing and diffi-cult circumstances. Darwin's late modern theory differs in several respects from the more optimistic earlier modern outlook:

1. Nature is rife with the struggle for existence, rather than being a sta-ble, law-abiding whole as in the prior modern view. The process of natural selection, by which organisms survive that are best able to compete or adapt, is deeply embedded in nature, operating on every level, that is, on populations and on individuals.

2. In nature as understood by Darwin, needed resources are scarce rather than abundant, in contrast with Bacon's view.[22] This scarcity guarantees continual competition among individuals and among populations.

3. Chance—rather than design or providential creation or laws of nature—is foremost in determining the working of nature, given conditions that change constantly and rather arbitrarily. We know that as late as the nineteenth century, evolutionary theory's rejection of "design" was a radical departure.

In the classical philosophical treatments of nature by Plato and Aristotle, one does not encounter the idea of "nature imperiled." For them, powerful bonds maintain the order of individual living entities; these bonds are of various sorts, but the most important no doubt is *form*. Because of the power of form, or *psyche*, combined with the action of the telos, there is no crisis in the world's maintenance and continuity, according to Plato and Aristotle; neither one sees nature and its basic order as "endangered."[23] Consequently, in their view, human beings do not (and could not) have a special responsibility for preserving or reordering nature. In Plato's *Timaeus*, for example, anything approaching such responsibility sits with the Demiurge, or possibly with the lesser gods; that is, it is a matter of divine rather than human responsibility. For Plato and Aristotle, the responsibility humans have concerns conforming to nature rather than preserving it, contemplating the magnificent and stable order of nature and patterning our souls after its orderly forms (or the Forms nature exhibits). Efforts to save the *kosmos* or to correct nature's patterns make no sense in the context of their thought.[24] We might say that nature as a whole—that is, insofar as human creatures must be considered a part of the whole—will be perfected to the extent that we human beings bring ourselves into harmony with our own and the *kosmos*'s divine order.

Having now examined the later sources of ecology's and environmentalism's principle of nature's vulnerability, in contrast to the classical view, what remains to be shown is how, among ecologists and environmentalists, man comes to be seen as having a special responsibility for nature's endangerment and for its protection. A study of the history of Darwin's influence (including the ensuing debates about the extent to which human beings should be regarded as subject to the same laws of natural selection as all other organisms, or whether instead humans were extrinsic in some way to nature and its laws), along with other important intellectual and social currents in the nineteenth and twentieth centuries, would be needed to demonstrate the reasons for this shift.[25] We can speculate briefly that several factors were involved: the increasing erosion of trust in a religious worldview that assigns responsibility for the creation and maintenance of the world to the divine, rather than to the human; the ascendancy of political programs such as socialism urging man to take responsibility for the public world; technological advances that seemed to assure man that he could take charge; and mounting evidence of the downside of technology and the damaging consequences of industrialization. Whatever the precise reasons for the change, however, there remains the significant difference between classical views of nature's well-being as self-perpetuating or divinely ordained and the contemporary ecological view that assigns to fallible human beings responsibility for an endangered nature.

Conclusion

The classical views of Plato and Aristotle share with contemporary ecology and environmentalism an appreciation for the many interconnections in a holistic natural world. Despite this shared notion, we have seen that the classical views of Plato and Aristotle differ markedly from contemporary ecology in several important respects. The bases for their holistic views are different: From the classical point of view, nature's unity is the result of *psyche* and formal and final causes. Ecology, on the other hand, explains nature's interconnection by way of an evolutionary framework and modern material causality. Furthermore, their characterizations of holism differ: From the classical perspective, nature is a stable, everlasting whole of (more or less) stable kinds arranged hierarchically. Ecology views nature and natural entities as shifting populations in a benign, non-hierarchical "network" of relations, forced into a constant process of struggle for survival—a struggle that now is primarily against the damage inflicted by human beings. And while ecology and environmentalism share with classical philosophy a deep respect for the intrinsic value of nature, their views diverge about the responsibility for the maintenance of nature's integrity. In all these respects, the influences both of modern materialist science and late modern process-thought and politics are significant, and they mark the underlying influences of classical philosophy on ecology and environmentalism with a distinctively modern and late modern impress.

Part II

Plato

4

Platonic Ecology, Deep Ecology

Timothy A. Mahoney

It can be argued that the very idea of Platonic ecology[1] is absurd for two reasons. First, Plato seems to be the archetypal dualist who denigrates the material world as a second-rate imitation of an ideal, immaterial world. Second, if we situate Plato's ethics within Carol Merchant's[2] three-fold taxonomy of ethical approaches—egocentric, homocentric, and eco-centric—it seems to be egocentric. Dualism and egocentrism are patently inimical to ecological consciousness. Thus no sound approach to ecology can be based on Plato's philosophy.

This position cannot be summarily rejected, because there are certain Platonic texts that seem to support it. But there are other important texts that must be included in any overall assessment of Plato's thoughts bearing on ecological matters. I shall argue that as we see this more comprehensive picture emerge, we see the outlines of Platonic ecology take shape as well. Furthermore, I claim that this Platonic ecology provides a distinctive and fruitful approach to environmental thinking, an approach that has important affinities with today's "deep ecology" movement.[3]

The essay is divided into two main parts. In part 1, I consider the charge of dualism. First, I examine the texts that undergird this charge, and I conclude that there is little doubt that Plato is a dualist. However, I argue that Plato's particular brand of dualism is not inimical to ecological thinking. In fact, Plato's conception of the spatiotemporal world—he claims it is a single living organism in which the good of every individual is intimately connected with the good of every other individual as well as with the good of the whole—exhibits the kind of holism which is attractive to many of today's environmentalists, especially those associated with deep ecology. Furthermore, one can view Plato's theory of Forms as an attempt to counteract the kind of shallow, egocentric, anthropocentric, and merely conventional value structures that many philosophers, especially deep ecologists, identify as the fundamental source of our environmental crisis.

In part 2, I consider the following arguments in support of the claim that Plato's ethics is a species of egocentrism. Some claim that Greek thinkers in general are egocentric because their ethical thought centers on *eudaimonia*, that is, happiness. In addition, some assert that it is obvious from the *Republic* that Plato is a paradigm of an egocentric approach to ethics. Finally, others argue that Plato supports a "contemplative ideal." But such a blatant disregard for one's "this worldly" responsibilities is certainly egocentric.

In the course of addressing these arguments, I will present a different view of Plato, one that better represents his thought as a whole. Plato believes that reason allows one to come to know oneself and others as parts of an organic universe rooted in eternal goodness. This realization is genuine self-knowledge that causes one to reconstitute one's conception of *eudaimonia*, or the truly happy human life, so that promoting the good of this greater whole becomes the center of one's concern. This anticipates another important claim of deep ecology: human well-being is embedded in the broader well-being of nature as a whole. Hence Plato's ethics should be regarded as ecocentric within the context of Merchant's classificatory scheme.

My overall conclusion is that Plato's philosophy has significant affinities with today's deep ecology. Furthermore, Plato demonstrates that neither dualism nor an emphasis on achieving one's own true happiness is inimical to profound ecological concern.[4] Thus Plato provides an approach to environmental philosophy that is well worth our consideration today.[5]

Dualism

Plato and Platonism in general are best known for what is often called the "Theory of Forms."[6] Plato and Platonists assert that the spatiotemporal world does not exhaust reality. In fact, the orderliness and intelligibility of the spatiotemporal world are actually dependent on another realm of non-spatiotemporal entities that are eternal, not subject to change, and grasped by the mind alone. Thus the spatiotemporal world is in some important sense secondary to, and derivative from, this other realm, the realm of Forms. Finally, it seems that one has genuine knowledge only of this realm of Forms; one's cognitive relationship with the spatiotemporal world (which Plato sometimes calls "opinion") is of lesser quality.[7]

Plato often uses sharp language to contrast the two worlds. A few examples should suffice. First, one of the most famous such passages is the cave analogy in the *Republic* in which Socrates[8] compares objects in the spatiotemporal world with mere shadows cast on the wall of a cave before captives who know no better than to take them for reality.[9] This analogy echoes the equally famous line analogy in which the spatiotemporal realm is presented as the image of the higher realm that contains the Forms.[10] Second, in the *Symposium* the beauties of the body are found on the very lowest rung of the ladder of beauty, at the top of which is the Beautiful itself, that is, the Form of Beauty that exists beyond the realm of physical bodies, space and time.[11] Third, the strident antiworldly tone hits a crescendo in the *Phaedo*, the dialogue that depicts the final hours of Socrates' life. Socrates claims that the philosopher disdains the body because it interferes with reason's attempt to grasp the pure reality of the Forms. One must try to purify oneself of the body, its desires and sense perceptions, in order to remain centered in one's soul alone so that one can commune with the higher realm of the Forms.[12]

These passages demonstrate that Plato conceives of the spatiotemporal world as dependent on, and inferior to, the realm of Forms. Such a dismissive view of the natural world seems to be utterly opposed to the gravity with which environmental issues—issues fundamentally rooted in the natural world—must be taken by anyone with serious claims to be an ecological thinker. It appears that on the evidence of these and other similar passages one should reject curtly the very notion of Platonic ecology. But this would be a hasty conclusion.

Even in the *Phaedo*, perhaps the most otherworldly of Plato's dialogues, there are indications that the spatiotemporal world is good and valuable, even if its goodness and value are derivative from the realm of the Forms. In recalling his first encounter with the thought of Anaxagoras, Socrates describes how excited he was to hear that Mind (*Nous*) directs, and is the cause of, everything, including the spatiotemporal world.[13] If Mind rules all things, then it would arrange all things for the best, both for each individual and for the collective whole.[14] This is a continuing theme in Plato's dialogues: Mind—represented by gods who are depicted as archetypal rational beings[15]—rules the spatiotemporal realm.[16] Plato claims that the beauty and the orderliness of the natural world reflect the skillful governance of the gods.[17] The greatest of Plato's dialogues dealing with nature, the *Timaeus*, describes the natural world as a work of reason[18] made on the eternal model of a single living organism that contains all other organisms as integral parts,[19] so that the natural world is itself a single living organism.[20]

Plato presumably believes that the universe is an organism because the relation in an organism between the good of the parts and the good of the whole is one of mutual entailment: the parts are so intimately related to one another that the existence, characteristics, and well-being of each is intrinsically tied to the existence, characteristics, and well-being of the other parts and of the whole organism.[21] Consequently, an organism represents the maximal harmony among all of the parts and the whole.[22] Thus, even though the natural world is inferior to the realm of Forms, the natural world is good precisely because it reflects the goodness and harmony of that higher realm as closely as is possible in the spatio-temporal realm. The natural world has this constitution because the god who fashions it desires that it be as good as possible.[23]

There is not so much a contradiction as a difference in emphasis between this favorable view of the world and the "anti-" spatiotemporal-world passages examined earlier. In some passages Plato emphasizes that the natural world is flawed and genuine evil exists in it. Nevertheless, he also claims that the natural world is good because it participates in the Forms. In other passages, he emphasizes the Forms themselves because he wants to stress his fundamental belief that genuine values are rooted in realities that transcend the limits of ourselves and our shallow, shortsighted understanding of the world. This fundamental belief is another important parallel between Plato's view and that of deep ecology.[24] Thus Plato is committed to the claim that genuine values cannot be reduced to individual desire or human preferences,[25] to the results of social agreements[26] or any human decision,[27] or, most generally speaking, to attributes of spatiotemporal objects or events.[28] The distinction between the Forms and the spatiotemporal world represents Plato's rejection of the claim that human actions should be dictated by egoism, anthropocentrism, or mere convention. Thus Plato agrees with another of the central claims of deep ecology: human actions must respect the value of the natural world, a value that it has independent of its human inhabitants.[29] This brings us to our examination of the claim that Plato's ethics is egocentric.

Egocentrism

The claim that Plato's ethics falls into Merchant's egocentric category[30] can be supported in at least three ways. First, Greek ethical thought in general is egocentric because it centers on *eudaimonia*. Second, Plato is a paradigm of an egocentric approach to ethics. This is obvious in the *Republic* in the way in which Socrates responds to the challenge of

Glaucon and Adeimantus. Socrates acquiesces to their suggestion that the relative values of justice and injustice be judged by reference to *eudaimonia*. Is the just person happier or unhappier than the one who is unjust (1.361d)? Third, Plato supports a contemplative ideal: the ultimate in personal happiness is achieved by "fleeing from this world"[31] in order to spend one's time in contemplation of the Forms. Such a blatant disregard for this-worldly responsibilities is certainly egocentric.

These arguments raise three questions, each of which I will consider. First, is Greek ethics in general egocentric because it focuses on *eudaimonia?* Second, is Plato's version of eudaimonistic ethics in the *Republic* egocentric? Third, does Plato have a contemplative ideal? To these three questions we must add a fourth: what is the connection between Plato's ethics and his conception of the natural world described in the first section?

The first argument is that Greek ethics in general is egocentric because it focuses on *eudaimonia*. J. Annas, in what is probably the best single recent work on Greek ethics, notes the "charges of egoism made against ancient ethical theories because of their eudaimonistic form."[32]

The Greek word *eudaimonia* does not correspond exactly to the English word "happiness," but this is probably the best overall translation.[33] Perhaps the most important contrast between the two terms is that the term "happiness" is more *rigid*[34] than the term "*eudaimonia*." As Annas notes, "the notion of happiness is more bound up with the notions of felt pleasure and experienced satisfaction than the ancient concept is."[35] One might illustrate this difference as follows. It is coherent to claim (as the Stoics did) that the virtuous person who experiences all sorts of calamities, including prolonged torture, is not robbed of his or her *eudaimonia*, but it is virtually nonsensical to claim that the virtuous person who experiences all sorts of calamities, including prolonged torture, is not robbed of his or her happiness. The Greek concept does not exclude from consideration felt pleasure and experienced satisfaction, but at the core of the concept of *eudaimonia* is living the best life possible, whatever one decides after thorough reflection the content of such a life should be. Consequently, it is quite possible that one could decide that the content of *eudaimonia* is living a moral life because morality is intrinsically valuable.[36] This being the case, we should reject the claim that Greek ethics is egocentric because it is focused on *eudaimonia*. With this clarification of the concept of *eudaimonia* established, we can turn to the second question.

Is Plato's particular version of eudaimonistic ethics egocentric? In support of this claim, some commentators point to the way Socrates defends justice in the *Republic*. The Greek conception of justice as the social virtue that deals with the proper treatment of other people approximates our conception of morality. Socrates accepts the suggestion of Glaucon and Adeimantus that the relative values of justice and injustice be judged by reference to *eudaimonia*: is the just person more or less *eudaimon* (happy) than the one who is unjust?[37] This seems to imply that one should be moral (just) only if morality (justice) contributes to one's happiness (*eudaimonia*). And it is precisely this implication that commentators find egocentric.[38]

But the earlier examination of the conception of *eudaimonia* suggests that a different interpretation is possible. The challenge of Glaucon and Adeimantus is to demonstrate that morality (justice) is so intrinsically valuable that it must be included as a component of *eudaimonia* (happiness). I submit that if this is the correct interpretation, then the way in which Socrates defends justice does not imply that Plato's ethics is egocentric in any important sense. Let me call this the nonegocentric interpretation.

The way Glaucon and Adeimantus state the challenge is compatible with the nonegocentric interpretation. They ask Socrates to explain the nature of justice and injustice and the intrinsic effect of each on the soul when the extrinsic rewards and consequences of each are left out.[39] To emphasize this demand, Glaucon challenges Socrates to defend the claim that the just person is more *eudaimon* (happier) than the unjust person even when: (a) the just person reaps none of the extrinsic rewards of seeming to be just, but suffers all the bad extrinsic consequences of seeming to be unjust; and (b) the unjust person reaps all of the extrinsic rewards of seeming to be just but suffers none of the bad extrinsic consequences of seeming to be unjust.[40] One can understand this challenge in the nonegocentric way. Glaucon and Adeimantus want Socrates to demonstrate that, because of its intrinsic value, justice is such an important constituent of *eudaimonia* (happiness) that one should be just even when being just results in the sacrifice of other seemingly important constituents of one's *eudaimonia* such as pleasure, health, wealth, etc.

Socrates' response[41] to this challenge supports the nonegoistic interpretation. He argues that being just (moral) is actually the same as achieving the preeminent aim of genuine human *eudaimonia*.[42] A summary of his argument runs as follows. It is obvious that people differ in the particular content that they ascribe to happiness; for example, some aim primarily at power, others primarily at pleasure. Let us say that this difference in content gives rise to different versions of happiness.[43] The various versions differ either because of a difference in the aims they include or because of a difference in the priority they assign to these aims. Collectively, the objects of desire of each of the three parts of the human soul—reason, spirit, and appetite—represent the set of possible human aims.[44] In books 8 and 9 Socrates ranks different versions of happiness with reference to the preeminent aim of each. Socrates gives priority to the aim defined by the objects of reason's desire—the acquisition of knowledge of the Forms and the propagation of goodness—because only reason's desire can be fully informed by an understanding of genuine values, an understanding that reason has in virtue of its knowledge of the Forms.[45] Because of the organic nature of the universe, a human best propagates goodness by contributing as much as possible to the well-being of whatever natural whole he or she is a part. But this is simply another way of describing what it is to be just, according to Socrates.[46] So one should be just because being just is the achievement of what is most important for genuine human happiness.

Certainly there are many points at which one might wish to challenge the argument.[47] But it is plainly misleading to characterize Plato's approach as egocentric. His approach rests on the claim that any acceptable conception of human happiness should make contributing to the welfare of others a central element. From the perspective of ecological values, this suggests that we should go beyond thinking of respecting the environment as a mere duty. We should refashion the very notion of the human good life to make the furtherance of the welfare of the environment a central element of human happiness. This seems to be another important parallel between Plato and the deep ecologists.[48]

We can now turn to the third question: Does Plato have a contemplative ideal?[49] The *locus classicus* of the advice to "flee from the world" occurs in the "digression"[50] of the *Theaetetus*. There the otherworldliness and seeming impracticality of the philosopher are emphasized, even lauded.[51] Socrates explains the philosopher's attitude as follows:

> But, Theodorus, it isn't possible that evils should be destroyed; because there must always be something opposite to the good. And it isn't possible for them to be established among the gods; of necessity, they haunt our mortal nature, and this region here. That's why one ought to try to escape from here to there as quickly as one can. Now the way to escape is to become as nearly as possible like a god.[52]

Several interpreters see this passage as the preeminent statement of Plato's contemplative ideal: we should flee from this world, and take refuge in the divine world where we contemplate the Forms just as the gods do.[53] The problem with this interpretation is that Socrates does not say that one becomes like a god by contemplation; rather, "to become like a god is to become just and pious, with intelligence. . . . A god is by no means and in no way unjust, but as just as it's possible to be, and there's nothing more like a god than one of us who becomes as just as possible."[54]

Here and in other assimilation to god passages,[55] justice rather than contemplation is specified as the most salient aspect of likeness between human beings and gods.[56] I think Plato's point is the following. The flight from the world by which one assimilates oneself to God is to transcend our merely perceptual knowledge of the natural world in order to come to an understanding of the realm of the Forms. In understanding the realm of Forms, one emulates divine understanding, and one also understands the "image" of this realm, the natural world. But to stop at the mere contemplation of the Forms would be to fall short of the assimilation of which humans are capable. As we have seen, God does not merely contemplate; God satisfies the rational desire to propagate goodness by shaping the universe as a whole. Thus humans must emulate God by action as well as by understanding. This is why assimilation to God is aptly characterized as "becoming just with intelligence." This is no contemplative ideal that counsels people to abandon their responsibilities. On the contrary, one flees the world in the sense that one must surpass the shallow conceptions of the world and value that most people maintain so that one gains a genuine understanding that allows one to return to the world and play one's proper role in it. This is another important affinity between Plato and deep ecology: the fundamental source of our difficulties is a mistaken worldview.[57] This brings us to the fourth question: What is the connection between Plato's ethics as described in this second section and his conception of the natural world as described in the first section?

In this second section I have emphasized the rational aspect of human beings, the aspect that brings humans in touch with the more-than-natural realm of Forms and the actions that ensue. Another way of looking at human happiness emphasizes the "natural" aspect of human beings. As we saw in the first section, according to Plato the natural world is a single living organism in which the well-being of all the parts is harmonized. As part of nature, each human's well-being is coordinated with the well-being of nature as a whole: to pursue one's own good is the very same thing as to contribute to the good of the whole natural organism. To attain one's own good, one must contribute to the good of the whole of which one is a part, that is, one must be just.[58] Because humans are rational beings, they can understand the true character of the spatiotemporal world and how their well-being is enmeshed in the web of the well-being of the world as a whole. That is, humans can understand themselves and their own good as natural beings.[59] This is why for Plato "doing one's own task" is the definition both of justice and of *sophrosyne*,[60] a virtue that includes both self-knowledge and self-control.[61] When one comes to genuine self-knowledge, one understands that justice is in one's self-interest, so that true self-control is also justice. Thus, according to Plato, whether one considers the problem of human well-being from the perspective of humans qua rational beings, or from the perspective of humans qua natural beings, the answer is the same: human well-being requires acting justly, that is, making one's contribution to the good of the natural world.

Still, one might object to the basic claim of this second section: that Plato's ethics focuses on the natural world. He devotes little space to ecological issues per se; only once in the dialogues is there any mention of the fact that humans can destroy their natural environment.[62] Instead of centering on nature, his ethics centers on the individual and on political arrangements.

But it is not clear that the particular subjects Plato emphasized imply any neglect of the importance of the natural world. Although there was some ecological destruction in Plato's time, the extent of this destruction and the power of human beings to affect their environment was much less than it is today. The primary field for human activity was much more circumscribed than it is today, and Plato's writings reflect this. Because ecological issues were not as pressing as they are at present, it also would have been much more difficult to excite interest in such issues than it is today. If Plato wished to capture the attention of his audience, he had to address the ethical issues that most engaged them, and this is what he did. Of course, it is impossible to follow Plato in all the details of our current discussions. But Plato's fundamental ethical and metaphysical outlook provides a sound basis for ecological thinking today. We should not be blinded to this fact because he himself does not emphasize ecological concerns.

In addition, when discussing Plato's ecology, one should not neglect to point out Socrates' approving remarks in book 2 of the *Republic* concerning what Glaucon disparagingly calls "a city of pigs" (2.372d).[63] This "city of pigs" seems to be a prototype of a simple, small-scale social arrangement of the sort that many ecologists would urge as an antidote to the typical social arrangements of today's industrialized countries. Socrates claims that this simple city is the true city, a city that is healthy just as an individual is healthy (372e–373a). But Glaucon rejects it because it has too few conventional consumer goods (372d–373b). Consequently Socrates introduces what he characterizes as a "feverish" (373a) and "swollen" (373b) city to satisfy Glaucon's lust for consumption. The echoes of contemporary discussions are remarkable.

In this section I have argued that Plato's ethics not only sets human beings within the larger context of the natural world but also makes contributing to the good of the natural world the central focus of human happiness. Consequently, it is misleading to characterize Plato's ethics as egocentric or even as anthropocentric. On the contrary, Plato's ethics is an excellent example of a truly ecocentric ethics.

Conclusion

Plato demands responsible action in this world, action informed by both genuine values and a conception of the natural world as a single living organism of which one is an integral part. Such an understanding provides a paradigm of authentic ecological consciousness that is even more relevant to us today than to those in Plato's time because of our vastly expanded capabilities for changing our environment. Of course, we cannot follow Plato slavishly. But we should recognize his thought as an ancestor of today's deep ecology. Perhaps most interestingly, Plato demonstrates that dualism and an emphasis on achieving one's own true happiness are not incompatible with profound ecological concern.[64]

5

Environmental Ethics in Plato's *Timaeus*

Madonna R. Adams

In the *Timaeus*, one of his later works, Plato presents an amazing project: a cosmology intended to explain the origins of the universe, including human life, and an ideal vision of human social and political life based on the principles of that cosmology. The work is ambitious.[1] In seventy-five pages, Plato attempts to integrate metaphysics, physics, and ethics into one coherent account, offering a model that draws on concepts from the fields of astronomy, mathematics, physics, biology, anatomy, physiology, music, and medicine. The scope and complexity of the text are evident to the first-time reader, and the work continues to engage scholars from diverse disciplines in lively debate.[2]

My thesis is that Plato's *Timaeus* is of interest for environmental ethics (a) because certain of its principles recur in current reflection, (b) because it offers a carefully constructed model that gives us an opportunity to examine some critical questions that any such project raises, and (c) because it provides a context within which to consider whether or how these issues are addressed or resolved in our present models.

What I wish to do is, first, to give an overview of Plato's cosmological myth, its purpose and principles, and his analogical method of reasoning; second, to show how Plato applies these to the cosmos and to the human being, considered as a microcosmos, and the implications for environmental ethics; third, to point out how his cosmology also suggests a model for thinking about the political/social sphere and how we can apply this model to environmental ethics; and last, to discuss two critical issues that emerge in reviewing Plato's project.

Overview

The Design of the Timaeus

The *Timaeus* falls into two sections: a long prologue, about one-eighth of the text (17–27), and a cosmology proper (28–92).[3] The cosmology takes the form of a monologue by the main speaker, Timaeus, after whom the dialogue is named. In the prologue we are told that Timaeus's speech is to be the first in a trilogy. Timaeus, an expert in astronomy and an experienced statesman, is to provide an account of how the universe came to be, up to and including the origins of human beings. The second speaker, Critias, is to describe the life of the citizens of the ancient, ideal Athens; and the third speaker, Hermocrates, is to show ancient Athens engaged in a heroic combat that saved the civilized world from domination by Atlantis, a corrupt superpower. The *Timaeus* contains only the first, long speech, but it is clear from Plato's introduction that the cosmology is to provide the context for understanding the principles of human, social, and political life. From the outset, then, the cosmology is part of a larger project that has as its goal the description of human life and moral achievement. This will be of interest in our discussion of environmental ethics.

Timaeus's account of the universe is given in the form of a myth. How seriously should the Timaean myth be taken? If it is only a myth, how does it differ from myths to be found in all ancient cultures? One difference is that while Timaeus's account contains mythological elements and symbols, it is a philosophical myth. Its structure and arguments rely on philosophical, mathematical, and scientific concepts. Plato was heir to the tradition of the nature philosophers (pre-Socratics) and their attempts to present the principles of nature speculatively,[4] and he was alive to the issues of his contemporaries concerning theories of nature. He was also an accomplished mathematician. The cosmology employs abstract mathematical constructs, as do our current methods in physics, biology, and medical science. Although his central ordering cause is a divine figure, called a demiurge (*demiourgos*), and there is mention of the work of other, lesser gods, this is a cosmology rather than a cosmogony that would account for the world symbolically in terms of genealogies of various deities.

Of special interest is the design of the cosmology, which rests on an analogy between the ideal, the cosmic, and the human spheres. This analogy provides the formal causality of the account. The dialogue suggests a fourth analogue, that of the political sphere. This analogue is never directly presented but is implied by the dramatic elements in the dialogue and reinforces the underlying ethical intent or purpose of the whole.

Causality in Plato's Cosmology

Plato's cosmology has four structural features that are like four support beams in the foundation of a building. These provide the basis for Timaeus's account of the universe, which has three levels: the macro level of world soul and world body, the micro level of the human soul and body, and the political sphere. These structural features make the cosmology a logically complete model because they explain the universe in terms of the four classic types of causality that Aristotle later called the final, efficient, formal, and material causes.[5] It is clear from the text that Plato understood how each type was needed. It is also clear that even though this was a speculative venture, given in the form of a story, it was carefully reasoned and that Plato considered it more probable than others, no doubt referring to other theories with which he was acquainted (29d; 48d). I will discuss the epistemological status of the account later. Here I will outline the functions of these four primary structural features in the cosmology—the Demiurge, the Ideal Living Creature, the Receptacle, and Necessity—and suggest the significance of each for environmental ethics.

The Demiurge. Timaeus presents the formation of the universe as the work of a divine artisan to whom he refers by several different names. The most distinctive is that of *demiourgos,* or demiurge. The word has an interesting history and comes from two root words: *demos,* referring to the people, from which we derive the word "democracy," and *ergon,* meaning a work or action, from which we derive the word "ergonomic," used of office furniture. "Demiurge" connotes a public or civic functionary as well as an artisan who has a productive role in a city. This Demiurge is not a creator in the strict sense of one who makes something from nothing but literally an artisan who creates something new out of preexisting materials. This will be Plato's model for the work of guiding the political community.

Timaeus asserts that this artisan is good and the best of causes (*aristos ton aition,* 29a6) and that he can produce only what is the best and most beautiful. What is the function of the Demiurge? In addressing this question, Plato's interest lies, not in explaining the absolute origin of matter, but rather in explaining why the universe exists as we know it, namely, as a beautiful and ordered whole, or cosmos. By asserting that the Demiurge, the maker and shaper of the universe, is intelligent and good, Timaeus can assert that the world, his product, is ordered, intelligible, beautiful, and good. This implies that the world has causes that function with some regularity and therefore that we can understand it, since knowledge requires a grasp of the causes of a process or change. It also implies that in Plato's model, the universe is posited as good in itself, a goodness not contingent upon, or bestowed by, human beings. As a cosmos, it is essentially good and beautiful quite apart from its usefulness to us. The figure of the Demiurge, then, serves two functions. Within the cosmology, the intention of the Demiurge fulfills the functions of a *final* cause by his goal of making the world the best of products, and the Demiurge himself serves as an *efficient* cause or agent for the formation of an ordered universe.

The Living Animal. The second structural feature is called the Idea of the Living Animal. It is the cosmic paradigm—its blueprint, as it were. Timaeus depicts the Demiurge as an artist who seeks an inspiration or model for his masterpiece. The model to which the Demiurge looks is one of Plato's Ideas. In Plato's metaphysics, the Ideas are ideal, intelligible forms, self-subsistent, perfect, eternal, and unchanging, such as the Idea of Beauty in which all beautiful, visible things are said to participate. The Idea that the Demiurge selects, one that is unusual in Plato's work, is that of the Living Animal, which, as an ideal form, contains in itself all possible forms of visible living beings.

The Greek word for the Living Animal is *zoion,* from which we derive the words "zoology" and "zoo." The choice of the ideal Living Animal as the model for the universe means that the cosmos will be seen as a living, organic whole, a plenum. It is a biological rather than a mechanical construct, and in the cosmology it serves as a formal cause at both the macrocosmic and microcosmic levels. It also reinforces the claim made above that the phenomenal world, which in Plato's view cannot claim to be the ultimate good, does have positive, derivative goodness because it images the order, harmony, and goodness of unchanging being. These two claims—that the world is an organic whole and that it has independent value—are central to discussions of environmental ethics.

The Receptacle. The third structural feature is called the Receptacle. At times Plato refers to it as space, or place, though it does not coincide with our contemporary concept of either. What is its meaning? Like Heraclitus,[6] Plato sees that everything material is in flux. No physical body is stable from one instant to another. Even as we say "this" or "that," the object to which we refer is already being transformed (49e). Modern physics, with its understanding of subatomic structures and energy fields, confirms this. Yet the universe as a whole perdures. We conceptualize this by saying that change occurs *in* the universe, for every generation, change, or alteration that comes to exist must do so somewhere, in *some place*. Plato meets this logical demand through the concept of the Receptacle. The Receptacle is a logical construct required to speak about a material universe. Strictly speaking, it is not a "place," for the universe itself cannot be said to be somewhere, some*place*: there is nothing that contains it or sets boundaries for it.

The notion of the Receptacle is really a metaphysical concept that expresses a mode of being. Like Plato's Ideas, the Receptacle is eternal and indestructible. Like the Ideas, and unlike the objects, copies of the Ideas, it is not perceivable by the senses. Unlike the Ideas, which never receive anything into themselves, the Receptacle receives all material objects. Plato calls it the foster mother and nurse of all that exists. Unlike copies of the Ideas, it never enters or leaves anything else but provides a "home for all created things" (52).

The Receptacle has another important property. It is represented as constantly moving with a shaking motion, causing a dynamic interaction of all the elements in the universe. This sustained motion is necessary to prevent *stasis*, that is, a polarization that isolates like elements from other elements. If allowed to occur, this polarization would destroy the cosmic process. Taken together, then, the paradigm of the Living Animal and the description of the Receptacle present a universe that is an interactive, interrelated whole both at the level of discrete organisms and at the level of their constitutive elements.

How is this relevant to environmental ethics? Plato's model under- scores the essential transitoriness of all perceivable objects, including our- selves, while it emphasizes the character of the cosmos as a process that endures. It reinforces the concept of the cosmos as a Living Creature (*zoion*) and all of nature as interrelated and interdependent. And it shows that understanding of the nature of the cosmos comes not simply through our senses or immediate experience but through an effort to grasp its principles with our minds.

As human beings we are in a peculiar position. We recognize at the same time our dependency in the universe and our agency. Exactly what that agency ought to be in a universe that is both dynamic and evolution- ary is difficult to determine, but according to the *Timaeus*, such determi- nations must be rooted in attention to, and respect for, the principles of the universe itself.

Necessity. Timaeus calls the fourth structural element Necessity (*ananke*). This term refers to the irreducible properties of matter (material cause). The universe is a cosmos, but its form, beauty, and order are contingent upon the nature of matter. Timaeus acknowledges this when he states, in figurative language, that form can only be imposed on matter by "persuasion," a metaphor taken from the political sphere. That is, the form of any object, natural or artificial, is conditioned by matter and the properties of matter. For example, a carpenter working with a particular piece of wood has to take into account its properties: age, grain, knotholes, hardness or softness. The wood limits or conditions how it can be cut or shaped. A technician building a computer has to understand the properties of her materials in relation to magnetic fields.

With respect to environmental ethics, Necessity represents a limit notion that shows human agents in a cooperative relationship with the material world and the irreducible properties of all material beings, including their own human nature. It also establishes a paradigm for the ordering of the social/political sphere to which I will return.

In summary, the Demiurge and the other three structural elements supply the four basic causes or principles of explanation for the cosmos. The Demiurge as an artisan functions as the efficient cause of the universe, and his purpose as its final cause. The ideal Living Creature functions as a formal cause, and Necessity, the a priori condition of matter, as the material cause. It is on these principles that Timaeus bases his description of the nature of the cosmos and of the human being as a microcosmos.

Cosmos and Microcosmos

The Cosmos

Timaeus's cosmos consists of a world soul and a world body. Together they form the perfect image of the Idea of the Living Animal.

World Soul. World soul is a principle of motion and intelligence, and the account of its formation provides a model for these functions and illustrates how Plato embodies ideal qualities in the description. In a complex passage, Timaeus pictures the formation of soul as the work of the Demiurge, who, like an artist, composes the soul out of equal portions of three ingredients. He calls these by abstract terms: "being," "the same," and "the different," to indicate their philosophical meaning. Of each of these, one part is indivisible and eternal, and the other divisible, like that found in bodies. He divides this mixture of ingredients again and again according to a mathematical formula based on ratios and recombines them in various measures based on complex proportions.

The Demiurge then forms this "material" of world soul into two circles rotating on the same axis in opposite directions. He calls the outer circle the "circle of the same," and the inner circle the "circle of the different." Finally, he subdivides the inner circle to form seven other circles, representing the orbits of Earth's solar system and sets them to move in various orbits at different speeds but in proportion (35–36), like a kind of dance (40c).[7] This elaborate design accounts for the diversity of types of motion in the universe and the harmony of the cosmic system as a whole through the subordination of the motion of the different to the motion of the same by means of the principle of proportionality.

What is the purpose of this account of world soul? First of all, it establishes the principle of proportion and ratio as the basis for the movement and intelligibility of the cosmos. Here circular motion is taken as paradigmatic, because movement in a circle can continue eternally without a change of place. Figuratively speaking, this is a kind of "rest," and so reflects for Plato the unchanging and perfect character of eternal being (34a–b).[8] The circular paths of the various stars and planets sustain the cycles on which time and growth and regeneration on Earth depend. In this way Timaeus portrays the cosmos as a unified system whose beauty lies in the way it maintains balance amid dynamic change, "a moving image of eternity" (37d5).[9]

The second function of the world soul is that it provides an epistemological model that explains the difference between opinion and knowledge. In this model, reason concerned with the sensible world is identified with the soul's movement in the circle of the different, which generates true opinion. Reason concerned with the intelligible world is identified with the soul's movement in the circle of the same. The point is that when reason applies itself to information perceived through the senses, which is constantly changing, it may arrive at true opinion. But to arrive at scientific knowledge, reason must abstract from the particulars in order to grasp the underlying causes and first principles on which science depends.

These two functions of world soul serve as a model for explaining the twofold function of human intelligence as a principle of knowledge and as a principle of order for human life with its diverse emotional and physical needs and desires. It also establishes a cosmic paradigm as the criterion for human life and activity.

World Body. In explaining the constitution of world body, that is, the material nature of the universe, Plato uses a geometric model in which he posits that the basic form of matter consists in two triangular structures: the right-angled isosceles triangle and a specific kind of right-angled scalene triangle that consists of half an equilateral triangle. These triangles have mathematical properties that allow for combinations from which other plane and solid figures can be constructed. According to Plato's hypothesis, it is such formations that differentiate the primary elements. The primary structures are not visible to the eye except in aggregates, but they are responsible for the properties of what is visible (56c). What is the relevance of this model?

By his hypothesis that elemental matter consists in two types of triangles, Plato is accounting for the basic unity of what exists. We have a solidarity with other beings, for we are in some sense of the same "stuff." By saying that every object is explainable in terms of the combinations of elemental triangles, he is accounting for the diversity of things, their form. The emergence of any recognizable element or body presupposes form. Form is what gives a thing its specific nature and its intelligibility, for intelligibility depends on some type of structure or pattern. Finally, by explaining the structure of matter in terms of ratio, he asserts that order and beauty are found in the very constitution of matter.

In summary, like a living being, the cosmos is a unified system based on proportion. Its beauty lies in the way balance is maintained through dynamic change based on intelligible structures. World soul and world body together form an organic whole. It is a beautiful image of the ideal *zoion*, or Living Animal, and provides the model for the microcosmos.

The Microcosmos

Taking the macrocosmos as a model, Timaeus describes the human being as a microcosmos constituted of soul and body.

The Human Soul. In order to account for the complex intellectual, emotional, and physical capacities of human nature, Timaeus explains human soul according to a threefold division after the model of soul in Plato's *Republic* (4.435–42). There is an immortal soul or principle that the Demiurge makes according to the same pattern as world soul, only of ingredients of lesser purity, and there is a mortal soul fashioned by the lesser gods (*Timaeus* 41c–d). The mortal soul has one part that is a principle of emotional life and shares in the rational, and one part that is a principle of growth, nutrition, and reproduction and is nonrational (69c–d). The immortal, intelligent soul has the same two functions as world soul: it is the source of rational activity, that is, knowledge; and it is the principle of order and harmony. Like the cosmos with its diverse movements, human beings form a microcosmos of diverse tendencies and needs arising from their complex, embodied nature. Harmony in this microcosmos, as in the macrocosmos, depends, not on a cessation of motion or desire in any one part, but on the integration of all these powers through well-balanced activities. And here the role of reason in human life is primary.

The Human Body. Plato completes the paradigm of the microcosm with a description of the human body, whose structure reflects the threefold division of soul. The head, designed like a sphere—the form of the cosmic Living Animal—is depicted as the seat of reason, judgment, and self-direction. The region of the heart is the seat of the spirited element that shares both in reason and in instinctive feelings; for example, we get angry because we *perceive* an injury or wrong. The lower torso is the seat of nonrational appetite that must be directed by rational judgment in order to preserve due proportion in the various human functions and the very capacity for rational judgment. For example, excessive indulgence in food and drink may cause illness and immediate or gradual impairment of good judgment.

This series of analogies makes Plato's purpose clear. He portrays a human being as a microcosmos, constituted by the same principles that govern the cosmos. He does this in order to show that human life is subject to, and should be guided by, these principles, that the "ought" is grounded in the "is." What ought to be the case in human life, however, is not obvious to the senses, in spite of the fact that deviation from this model immediately affects experience. Genuine understanding must be gained through knowledge of the world and its true nature. How do we gain such insight? In two ways: First, by scientific knowledge about the cosmic whole. Insofar as this is achieved, we understand better who and what we are. Second—and there is a twist here—the very scientific understanding we seek depends on our ability to make good judgments, to notice, we might say, what is there. But this in turn requires that we already have some sort of balance in ourselves. To take an example, what is it in us that has allowed us to create a polluted environment, from which we ourselves suffer, without "noticing it" until recently?

The answer in the *Timaeus* is that imbalance in the microcosmos, which consists in a disorder or excess in such human emotions as fear, anger, or the desire for pleasure, disrupts the circle of the same, that is, reason and judgment regarding human experience and the world around us. Such disorder affects our very ability to perceive and judge a thing according to its true nature. An ecology of the human person is the basis for correct

judgment about the world, and this personal integration is an achievement requiring understanding of the principles of health. These principles
are articulated in Timaeus's analysis of health and disease, and they are
based upon and illustrate the same cosmic paradigm.

Health and Disease. Plato gives a holistic definition of health as a well-
functioning of the whole being that is achieved and maintained through
a principle of balance or proportionality among its diverse functions. His
analysis of its contrary state, disease, with its physiological, psychic, and
social causes, and their relationship to one other, clarifies this definition.
A few of his examples may illustrate:

- If the appetites of the rational soul are too impassioned, a wasting of
  the body occurs; for example, picture the pallid skin of the
  researcher who never exercises.

- If the emotion of anger, which is a natural response to perceived
  wrong or injustice, is sustained through prolonged disputes and
  conflict, private or public, such controversy and unabated competition inflame and overwhelm the body, causing "rheums," *rheumata*
  (88a5). Here Plato accurately diagnoses a cause of what we call
  stress-related disease and notes that this is not well understood by
  most teachers of medicine (88a). Such a connection between sustained anger and some rheumatic disorders has been confirmed by
  contemporary research.

- If the body is too strong for the soul and the soul is weak in intellectual power, the physical appetites overcome the interest in knowledge and cause dullness and ignorance or, as in the case of an excessive pursuit of pleasures, overwhelm reason and judgment.

The basic principle is evident:

For, as we affirm, a thing can only remain the same with itself, whole and
sound, when the same is added to it, or subtracted from it, in the same
respect and in the same manner and in due proportion, and whatever comes
or goes away in violation of these laws causes all manner of changes and
infinite diseases and corruptions. (82b)[10]

The initial cause of disease may be physical, psychic, or social, but in any
case, the dysfunction results from a lack of balance.

According to Timaeus's account, moral good and evil also depend directly upon the quality of the relationship between soul and body and are defined with respect to that relationship. A healthy relationship engenders virtue, and its contrary engenders vice. Moral ill results from an imbalance between body and soul or from a bad education. For example, sexual excess may be due to ill disposition of the body, that is, disease, or to an imbalanced desire of the soul. Either may result from poor social upbringing. A good character, on the other hand, is one in which balance and integration are obtained through choices that are based on and reflect the principles of the cosmos (88d). What does this mean in practice? The principle is proportion, and the prescription for establishing and maintaining it is the pursuit of activities that balance each other.

> There is one protection against both kinds of disproportion—that we should not move the body without the soul or the soul without the body, and thus they will be on their guard against each other and be healthy and well balanced. And therefore the mathematician or anyone else whose thoughts are much absorbed in some intellectual pursuit must allow his body also to have due exercise, and practice gynmastics, and he who is careful to fashion the body should in turn impart to the soul its proper motions and should cultivate the arts and all philosophy if he would deserve to be called truly fair and truly good. And the separate parts should be treated in the same manner, in imitation of the pattern of the universe. (88b5–d1)[11]

To sum up, the human being, like the Receptacle, is the subject of diverse movements. Just as the irregular movements in the Receptacle are ordered by the Demiurge through the regular motions of world soul, so the individual must order his or her own being in imitation of the Demiurge by harmonizing the motions of rational and nonrational soul. And just as the rhythmic, shaking motion of the Receptacle sustains the interaction of the various components in the universe with one another, so the human individual must maintain balance in the human organism through activity. In a passage that reads like an article from a current health magazine, Plato states that "moderate exercise reduces to order" (*katakosmei*, 88e1–3).[12] A sick body should not be aggravated by the use of pharmaceuticals (*pharmakeuon*, 89b1)[13]; rather, disease should be managed by regimen, "as far as one can spare the time" (*schole*, 89c8).[14] The correlative training of the mind, referred to in 89d–e, is detailed in the *Republic*, book 7, and in *Laws*, where each stage of development and education, from fetal life to preparation for highest civic office, is carefully mapped and a rationale provided along similar lines.

Health and Ecology. Plato's model of health and disease has direct application for environmental ethics. Recent knowledge and experience have forced technological societies to attend to the intimate organic relationship between human life and the larger ecosystem on which it depends for air, water, food, and life. Given this fact, Plato's model of health and disease extends to our relationship with the ecosystem and requires that human activities be directed so as to maintain harmony in this system of which we are a part. This in turn requires as a minimum that human beings not disrupt this balance by their excesses or choices.

Plants and Animals. In the cosmology, Plato mentions plants as living beings lacking in locomotion and subject like all animals to cosmic principles (77a–c). But apart from being a source of food, they receive no special consideration.

The origin of animals is dealt with only in a highly mythic-moral manner and in conjunction with the origin of women. In stark contrast to contemporary sensibility, Timaeus states that the soul of a male human being who does not achieve moral excellence in life is reincarnated first as a woman. The animals living in the air, earth, or sea represent further types of moral deficiency or degradation. Plato's antifemale bias, rooted in a defective biology, is inescapable. However shocking we find this, the reduction of female nature and of all animals to types of deficient moral states demonstrates that Plato's primary interest in the cosmology lies in the ethical sphere. To be complete, the cosmos, in imitation of the Ideal Living Animal that contains in itself all living things, must include animals. But since animals have no ethical agency, they appear only as a necessary completion of the account and are treated in a way that reinforces its ethical message. While the treatment of women raises serious problems in interpreting Plato's philosophy, it is anachronistic in terms of our present knowledge and does not in itself undermine the argument in the rest of the cosmology.

Leaving these issues aside, what Plato has traced through the speech of Timaeus is a complete model for human life based on a cosmic paradigm: the human being presented as a microcosmos. I suggest that there is one other analogue implicit in Plato's grand scheme, the city interpreted as an organic, living being after the same cosmic model. This representation and insight into the city emerge from Plato's project. For our purpose here, I will touch briefly on how the design of the cosmology provides a basis for this vision and on some implications for environmental ethics.

The Polis as a Living Creature

The formal design of the cosmology rests on an analogy between the ideal, cosmic, and human *zoia*, but in Plato's use of his material, this analogy also serves as a basis for an ethical vision of human society. It does so by suggesting a fourth analogue, that of the political *zoion*. This analogue is never presented directly but is evoked in dramatic fashion. These dramatic features extend the analogy and its application to society. Here are some of the analogies it suggests.

The word Plato selects for the maker of the cosmos, "demiurge," is a term that refers to public function in the city. The persona of the Demiurge models the qualities and aims of Plato's ideal philosopher-ruler of the *Republic*. Just as the Demiurge looks to the Ideal Living Creature as a model when forming the cosmos, so should the rulers of the city-state look to the cosmic *zoion* in guiding the city, the political *zoion*. Just as the cosmos is an organic model constructed on the principle of proportionality, so is the just city an organic unity in which each member fulfills his function for the common good. In this analogy the "just city" reflects the organic harmony of the cosmos.

The Receptacle, which includes all that exists in the universe and is the condition for their coming into being, also serves as a model for the city in which human beings are born and develop and which, especially for the Greeks, is the condition for human existence. The constant swaying motion of the Receptacle that prevents *stasis*—that is, a polarization of like elements—models the function of the polity. *Stasis* is the Greek term for civil war, which occurs when like-minded groups become isolated from those who differ from themselves and set themselves over against one another. This destructive situation is precluded by the continual harmonious interaction that the city is meant to provide. The terms Plato uses to refer to the Receptacle—mother, country, home, nurse, place—carry deep political connotations for the Greeks.

The last structural feature, Necessity, which stands for the irreducibility of the properties of matter, is dealt with by the Demiurge not by force but by persuasion, so that all the moving forms of being participate and reflect as far as possible the qualities of proportion, balance, and order. In like manner, persuasion, not force, is the key political instrument for securing a well-functioning society, one that recognizes the diversities and innate individualities of its primary elements, the citizens, who are by nature dynamic, intelligent, and self-directing and who must be drawn into participation in the common endeavors of the society.

These dramatic elements give the political analogue a presence in the cosmology by which Plato indirectly, but effectively, proposes a vision of human society as part of a cosmic whole. As such, like the individual microcosmos, it ought to be directed by the same principles. Some practical implications for environmental ethics follow from this model.

For Plato, a healthy and virtuous polity is one that is in harmony with, and directed by, those who understand the principles of the cosmos. It is the role of government to support such a context. Just as individuals are responsible for maintaining their health in the ways outlined above, the citizens and their representatives are responsible for doing the same in the political sphere. We know that there is a reciprocal effect between the human community and the ecosystem, and furthermore, as Marx makes clear, that human activities, lifestyles, and ethical assumptions are very much features of the economic system. Decisions about public affairs, then, would need to attend to such relationships and look not only to harmony within the human community but with the environment as well. Since the economic system both shapes, and is shaped by, political institutions, Plato's paradigm of the political unit would logically extend to responsibility for the impact of technologies on the environment.

In short, Plato's cosmology offers a model for understanding the social and political dimensions of human life and the principles by which the political sphere should function. It is an ethical model of what individuals and society ought to be and ought to try to achieve, by imitating the Demiurge and ordering their human activity in a way that reflects the "thoughts and revolutions of the universe" (90d1–2), thus creating a human "cosmopolis."[15]

Plato's cosmology is an ethical project both in intention and in structure and contains features that may apply to an ethics of the environment. I wish to consider two questions that emerge in considering the *Timaeus* from such a perspective: What is the sense of the phrase "environmental ethics"? and What is the epistemological status of environmental argument?

Two Critical Issues

The Meaning of "Environmental Ethics"

What is the sense of the phrase "environmental ethics"? Like all other living organisms, we are not only affected by our environment, but we inevitably affect it. However, there is a major difference between human and nonhuman species. The activities of nonhuman species serve to sustain the interactive and interdependent web of life. Bees pollinate flowers as they collect nectar. The life cycle of the tiny coral creates giant reefs that form the basis for intricate ecosystems of sea life. Beavers build dams for their own use and thus create niches for other species. The activity of the human species has the capacity to disrupt this intricate balance.

We cannot objectively harm the cosmos as a whole, because we can neither create nor destroy it as such, but we can drastically alter numerous eco-balances in our present global system and terminate life forms that took millennia to develop. Since evolution is not a reversible process, nothing that we know shows that a life form that we terminate will ever emerge in the same form after it has been destroyed. Furthermore, we can drastically affect the very conditions needed for life in general. Although it is theoretically possible, from the fact of the emergence of our own planet and the life forms it sustains, that such a system could emerge somewhere else in the cosmos, given the right conditions, nothing assures us that these conditions will be replicated so that another equally rich system will inevitably occur. Finally, while we cannot extinguish the processes of the cosmos, we can disrupt conditions of life on earth in such a way as to harm ourselves, exterminate our species, or so genetically alter it as to change its fundamental identity, just as we can continue the process of gene manipulation to create new types of life forms—plants, animals, and, theoretically, perhaps even other forms of intelligent life.

It seems to me, then, that when we speak of environmental ethics, we are focusing, or attempting to refocus, our understanding of the larger dimensions of what it means to be a human being, reexamining the foundations of our value systems with respect to other life forms, and determining what we as intelligent and sentient beings ought to do or avoid in relation to the natural world of which we are a part, especially in an evolutionary universe. This understanding is inevitably concerned not only speculatively but also practically with human life and its quality, survival, and responsibilities. Environmental ethics, then, is intrinsically anthropocentric in motive, though not with respect to its subject matter or conclusions. This is Plato's perspective on the cosmology. His ultimate goal or concern is to portray human life as it ought to be lived and to ground these principles in the nature of the universe.

Epistemological Status of Environmental Argument

If we want to claim that human beings should or should not act upon, or interact with, the environment in specific ways, what is the basis for that claim? Increasing knowledge of consequences of human actions (global warming, reduction of rain forests) gives us information. But how does that information entail a mandate for changes in human behavior? Plato's framework gives us two lines of argument, one empirical and anthropocentric, and the other speculative and metaphysical.

If we argue on the basis of human survival, which also requires the survival of plant and animal life, then our argument is anthropocentric. Damage to the ecosystem at our hands is not Plato's concern. But what we ought to do with our information is given in principle in the *Timaeus*. At present we know that disruptions in the eco-balance threaten our lives. This order must be preserved if we are to survive in our present form. In his treatment of disease, Plato asserts that the balance within the microcosm depends on integrating the various dimensions of our being. Insofar as we understand that we have an organic relationship with the environment—air, water, food—and that the disruption of this relationship follows from certain actions, then on Plato's reasoning, we "ought" to harmonize our activities, choices, and lifestyle in keeping with natural balances.

If we wish to argue on the basis of the positive goodness and unique worth of planet Earth, however, then the basis of our argument must be metaphysical and not merely instrumental. It must rest on some premise other than the factual claim that radical shifts in our ecosystem endanger our species and that system. It would involve some measure of hypothesis such as: the cosmos is good and beautiful in itself. Such an argument will be essentially inductive. That is, our conclusion may be correct, but it remains in the realm of probability, since we have no further ground or first principle, apart from the cosmos itself or a religious argument, on which to base this claim.[16]

Here Plato's framework is instructive. He sees the limits of demonstration, and it is for this reason that he calls his cosmology a "likely story." The phrase has two senses. It can mean both a myth or account based on analogy (on like relations between different types of being) and one that is probable. Both senses apply to the cosmology. It has an analogical structure based on the likeness between different levels of being, and in more than one passage, Plato, in the mouth of Timaeus, affirms that his account is one that is highly probable.[17] By using the phrase, "likely story" in this latter sense, Plato shows that he is aware of the epistemological limits of such a project, namely, that he (like ourselves) is not in a position to demonstrate the ultimate origins of the universe. We cannot answer deductively questions such as why there is a universe in the first place or whether the universe as material reality is eternal, because we are reasoning from effects to causes and cannot demonstrate the cause of the universe itself.[18] What we can do is learn to understand what is the case and how the diverse causes *within* the universe produce specific types of changes. Because Plato knows that it is impossible in principle to demonstrate scientifically the origin of matter or the existence of the universe, and because he holds that we cannot have scientific knowledge about something in constant flux like the material world, he uses the form of a myth. This allows him to undertake a hypothetical description of the principles of nature that can be argued coherently without requiring deductive proof that neither he nor we can provide.

Within the inevitable limits of such a project, however, Plato's *Timaeus* is serious, and its structural features represent principles that recur in one form or another in much of cosmological theory. It seems to me that if we, like Plato, wish to attribute intrinsic value to the cosmos on account of its beauty, order, and integrity, we must inevitably acknowledge that this is itself a first principle that we accept as such.[19]

Plato's cosmic model may be inadequate for our purposes,[20] but the first principles it embodies are not. They emerge from close observation of the cosmic system and from the experimental knowledge, central in much of ancient medicine, that human nature is a microcosmos that functions on these same principles. As a mathematician he recognized order in the cosmic process and saw that order, understood as organic harmony, was essential for human health and good character, as well as for vigorous and peaceful polities. In Plato's model, the causality is understood as moving in one direction: human beings are inferior to the great causes of the universe and dependent upon its first principles in all dimensions of life. As intelligent beings, they are free to respect the principles of nature or to disregard them, but they are not able to escape the consequences of their choices that, of necessity, follow.

Plato's hypothesis is thus not arbitrary. Principles of health and disease, virtue and vice, have experimental bases. The development of true judgment about the cosmos and human nature derives from the foundation of a sound human ecosystem. We know from our experience that people and communities who live close to the natural world tend to be better attuned to the affinities between the physical, emotional, and intellectual dimensions of life. Their own lifestyles based on harmony with the natural principles provide them with both a refined perception and judgment of the human and outer worlds of nature and an integration of the two, just as Plato's account explains.

Plato understands that our view of the cosmos has direct implications for human life and self-understanding. He sees human beings as part of a cosmic whole and wants to locate a model for ethics based on the first principles of that natural order. He recognizes that human beings live their lives with some sort of perspective and wants to affirm the kind of perspective that will lead to integrated human and social existence. Stories are powerful. Geologian Thomas Berry has argued persuasively that what we are reaching for in our present global and cultural change is a common story, one that is able to fulfill the function of the religious stories of all traditions, but that must also include what we know scientifically about the world.[21] Plato's account affirms a positive view of the cosmos that engenders a sense of respect, awe, and joy, all of which seem to be essential for a complete human response to the natural world and to our human reality. By embodying the principles of ethics in a cosmic story, Plato not only describes, and even *pre-*scribes, but, perhaps just as important, motivates with a vision that inspires.

6

The Ecology of *Critias* and Platonic Metaphysics

Owen Goldin

Plato cannot be said to have been an ecologist. That is to say, his biological studies did not attend to the relations between living beings and their environment. Our evidence for Plato's biological thought is almost exclusively found in the *Timaeus*, which considers particular living beings as images of Form. Each living being is a copy of the Form of some particular animal, and all of these forms are parts of the Form of Animal (or Living Being) as such, of which the cosmos as a whole is said to be a copy (30c–d). Each of the copies is a body vivified by soul, whose proper motions are the regular cyclical motions of thinking (36d–37d, 42e–44d). Human beings are teleologically organized to allow these cyclical soul-motions to occur with as little bodily interference as possible (47a–e). All other living things are understood as deformed versions of humans (42b–d, 91d–92c). Those humans who attend unduly to things of the body have their souls reincarnated in bodies that render the cyclical motions of thought even more difficult. Such reincarnated humans are the other animals and plants. No attention is paid to differences in nutrition and other life processes, nor to how success in these areas depends upon differences in habitat.[1]

Each living thing apparently has a twofold purpose. First, it is to be as adequate an image of its ideal pattern as possible. Second, its soul must participate in the circular motions of intellect in as undisturbed a manner as possible. In both cases, the telos of each being is exclusively internal to each being as such. That is not to say that what one living being does may not have the effect of being to the advantage of another. Obviously, this sometimes occurs, as when a person feeds a horse. Does this happen on a universal level, as part of the natural order? Nothing that Timaeus says commits one to the view that the welfare of any of the parts of the cosmic animal depends on that of any other. We are missing even the strongly

73

anthropocentric hierarchy of Xenophon's *Memorabilia* 4.3, according to which the whole natural world is designed and established by the gods to serve human purposes.

But although it would be an overstatement to say that Plato was an ecologist, there are passages in his writings that show insights important to ecological thinking. My focus here is on a passage in which Plato apparently suggests that the overharvesting of timber has led to erosion in the lands around Athens and to a general decline in their ability to sustain life. This passage seems to show an awareness of the interdependence between human activities and the health of the land that is without precedent in ancient Greek thought. It is worthy of close attention in order to determine exactly what Plato says and does not say. Once the passage is understood on its own terms, in its own context, it is not inapprpriate, I think, to consider how the insights expressed by Plato might find a place in his metaphysical thought.

The *Critias* immediately follows the *Timaeus*, which begins with Socrates' summary of a discussion, said to have occurred on the previous day, in which the nature of the best polis was discussed. His discussion follows the main lines of the discussion in the *Republic*, with the rule of the philosophers left unmentioned (17c–19a). Socrates reiterates his desire to see his creation in action, taking part in some great battle (19b–20c). At this point Critias indicates that he has heard an ancient tale about the heroic exploits of Athens in its battle against Atlantis. It so happens that Athens at that time conformed to Socrates' account of the best society. Thus the static, ideal image of justice sketched by Socrates can be seen to come alive through the telling of a historical story in which the society is concrete, given a determinate place in space and in time.

Critias's story is preceded by the grand metaphysical cosmogony of Timaeus. Unlike Socrates' community, that of Critias is embodied and is subject to the variability and imperfection that mark all embodied being. Accordingly, Critias's account requires the metaphysical background of the account of Timaeus, which explains what it means to be embodied and the problematic relationship that soul has with the body in which it finds itself.[2]

Critias begins his account by describing the natural environment of ancient Athens. In accordance with the introductory account of the *Timaeus* (22d–23b, 25c–d), this land is said to have been subject to periodic torrential floods, which wiped out all inhabitants except the illiterate mountain dwellers, and thus ancient Athenian history is said to have been lost to all but the Egyptians, who are spared such disasters.

In spite of such periodic devastation, Critias affirms that the Athenians are under the direct care of the gods. He tells us that different gods were allotted different land areas, not, as conventional myth has it, on account of the way their various quarrels turned out but on account of the intrinsic characteristics of the various land areas (109b). Athens, a land conducive to the development of wisdom and the arts, is accordingly allotted to both Athena and Hephaestus.[3] These are deities of the traditional Greek pantheon, but they have been purged of moral failure, in accordance with Socrates' reformation of religious myth in the *Republic,* books 2 and 3. Insofar as it is these deities who are said to have created and cared for human beings, they correspond to the lesser deities of the *Timaeus,* who carried out the wishes of the Demiurge in creating the various kinds of animals that the world contains (41a–d).[4] But unlike these deities, they have the further role of directly steering human souls, guiding human conduct. Perhaps they are representations of the cosmic soul, personified for the rhetorical necessities of patriotic myth. If this is so, we again see one of the teachings of the cosmological myth of the *Timaeus,* that human life is rightly led by having the motions of the human soul be in accordance with those of the cosmic soul.[5]

But how is this divine providence to be reconciled with the natural disasters said to wipe out all but uncivilized human life? Apparently there is a brute necessity to the workings of the physical world that renders unstable and impermanent the accomplishments of Athenian civilization.[6] Thus, the power of divine providence is limited. Again, in the guise of a historical account, we see a poetic expression of one of the teachings of the metaphysical cosmogony presented by Timaeus: the directive force of soul can only go so far in ordering and limiting bodily reality.

Critias continues his description of the natural environment of ancient Athens by extolling the excellence of the soil:

> That soil was of surpassing excellence, and this allowed the land at that time to feed a great army, which was free from working the soil. The following is significant evidence of this excellence. What soil remains is a match for the soil of any land, in bearing large quantities of all sorts of crops, and in being good pasture-land for all animals. But at that time, the land not only gave us fine things, but gave us a great abundance of them. (110e–111a)

Both the early Athenians and the land on which they dwell are said to have natural virtue. At least on the literal level of the myth, the first Athenians came from this very soil; no doubt the excellence of the soil was to a large extent responsible for the native excellence of the people. We have seen that it is this characteristic of the land that allows it to be particularly fitting for it to be assigned to the care of Athena and Hephaestus.

But Critias has something else in mind when he indicates the native excel-lence of the Athenian soil. For a farmer, "good soil" is soil that is fertile, allowing one to achieve both quantity and quality in the harvest. Without an account of the nutritional composition of good soil,[7] excellence of soil would need to be taken as a given, not further analyzed in terms of the chemistry of the *Timaeus* or in any other way.

At any rate, Critias is here pointing out that, in the beginning, the land was the kind that an ideal community would require. The Athenians would not be limited to subsistence farming, since the land could sustain a sizable population of citizens free from working the earth. Critias indi-cates that what soil there is in the area is still of this high quality.[8] The loss, albeit severe, has been in quantity alone. Nonetheless, it should be point-ed out that even this casual observation calls into question the extent to which the Athens of the time of the dialogue could support the ideal com-munity. Without the capacity to support itself from its own lands, it, like the feverish city of the *Republic* (373d–e), would need to take others' lands. Critias's remarks seem to indicate that contemporary Athens could never meet the standards of Socrates' ideal community.

Critias's comparison between the land then and the land now indicates an awareness of the dependence of the well-being of humans, and the liv-ing things on which they depend, on an uncertain and unstable state of the land as such. But what are the causes of the land's degradation? Critias's answer is complex:

> Now since many huge cataclysmic floods have occurred in the last nine thousand years (for these events were that long ago), the earth that erodes during these times and events leaves no deposit worth mentioning, as it does in other places, and it is always carried away, spiralling into the depths of the sea. So, as in the case of small islands, the remaining lands (compared to those back then) are the bones of a body ravaged by disease, with all of the soft fat[9] earth having wasted away, leaving behind only the earth's ema-ciated body. But then, when the land was still pristine, today's mountains supported high hills, and what we call the Stony Plains were full of rich earth, and in the mountains there was a good deal of timber, of which there are clear indications even now. Some of the mountains can sustain only bees these days, but it was not long ago that they were wooded, and even now the roofs of some of our largest buildings have rafters cut from these areas and these rafters are still sound. There were also many tall cultivated trees, and the land offered a vast amount of pasture for animals. What is more, the land enjoyed the annual rain from Zeus, not lost, as now, when it flows off of the bare earth into the sea. Rather, much of it was retained, since the earth took it in within itself, storing it up in the earth's retentive clay, releasing water from the high country into the hollows, and supplying all regions

with generous amounts of springs and flowing rivers. That what we are now saying about the land is true is indicated by the holy sanctuaries, which are situated where this water used to spring up. (111a–d)

The blame for the degradation of the soil is laid first on the regular cataclysmic floods and the peculiar topography of the area around Athens. It was these same floods that periodically wiped out wisdom and ancient history. Through contact with Egypt, lost learning was renewed. In contrast, lost soil could not be regained, because the floods washed away the soil into the irretrievable depths of the sea. In other areas, eroded soil is simply deposited elsewhere and provides new rich and fertile grounds for farming. But around Athens the old soil was supported by a steep rocky framework, with no lower framework to retain the eroded soil before it slid into the sea. This is why the land around Athens is by and large rocky and bare.

Critias then presents two pieces of evidence for the past abundance of good soil. First, he points to some rafters that still do a fine job of supporting the roofs of some of the larger buildings around Athens. Although these rafters evidently came from trees in the mountains, there are no longer any trees of such size in those parts. The implication seems to be that the mountains no longer have enough soil to sustain such trees; this is why the evidence that such trees existed is evidence that there was once more abundant soil.

Critias indicates that during his time one finds a number of sacred sanctuaries, traditionally established in verdant areas, by springs and streams, where there is no water at all. One can infer from this that areas that are now dry and rocky were once able to retain water, which flowed into underground caverns and welled up as springs. These springs are now absent, because the soil which contained the underground waters is gone. All that is left is the bare rock, from which the water runs down directly to the sea.

From the point of view of today's ecology, the implication is obvious. The rise of Athens coincided with massive deforestation of the mountainsides. There were two consequences of the loss of root structure. First, water could not be taken up into the biomass. Second, there was nothing to keep the hillsides from eroding away.[10] The floods, the distant memory of which Plato is reporting, may well have been caused by this erosion. There is no evidence, though, that Plato recognizes a causal link between the deforestation and the floods.

But not all erosion occurs through mudslides and violent flooding. Plato apparently recognizes a causal connection between the deforestation and a less sudden form of erosion, for Critias remarks that there were forests in the mountains not long before his time. The mountainsides must have been covered with timber at a time after the last flood, for otherwise the last flood would have washed away the buildings whose rafters provide evidence for the old forests. It follows that even after the last cataclysmic flood, there was enough soil to sustain a forest. Likewise, the sanctuaries to which Critias refers would have been washed away by the latest floods. Their survival is another indication that the soil, which had once retained significant amounts of water, had washed away on account of human activity. Plato sees that deforestation contributed to the degrading of the land itself.[11]

So there is some support for ascribing to Plato a recognition that the welfare of the human community depends on that of other living beings and that this, in turn, depends on human prudence concerning the consequences of what is done to other living beings. No larger moral is drawn, but it is remarkable to see in Plato even a glimmer of this central insight.

Plato is one of the great synoptic thinkers; he is always well aware of the implications that one of his theses has on the others. Though Plato nowhere takes up this issue, it does not seem out of place to speculate on the relation of his ecological insight to his metaphysics.

We return to the metaphysics of the *Timaeus*. The prospect of widespread environmental degradation might seem to call into question the stability of the order of this cosmic organism. But Timaeus makes clear that the Demiurge is making the cosmos an explicit exception to the principle that anything that comes to be (or is subject to the flux of becoming) also passes away. The living animal as a whole is a single, self-regulating organism that is not to suffer degradation or decay (32c–34b). The living cosmos is, was, and always will be as good a copy of the ideal animal as is possible.

This means that any environmental degradation must be local, temporary, or both. Ecological decay would be analogous to the sort of political decay discussed in the *Republic*, books 8 and 9, and is presupposed by the story of Athens and Atlantis that is the context for Critias's remarks about environmental degradation. Humans flourish and best exemplify the ideal of humanity when their lives are located in the sort of political structure that Socrates had outlined. But such a structure itself is subject to the flux and perishing that permeate bodily existence. A good society will inevitably decay into something worse. Likewise, on the merely biological level, human beings and, for that matter, forests flourish best given certain conditions. But these conditions, too, are impermanent, on account of both the natural instability of land forms (making them apt to be washed away by naturally occurring floods) and the foolishness and shortsightedness of humans, impelled as they are to do many things, such as cut trees for timber, in order to meet the demands of the body.

There is a bit more to say here. The Greeks were familiar with the mythical notion of a long-ago past in which the land was verdant, offering its fruits in abundance and providing the setting for an ideal human life. It would have especially reminded them of Hesiod's Golden Age (Hesiod *Works and Days* 129–47). The contrast with a Golden Age was the mythical basis on which Lucretius presented the idea of a senescent world, losing its vitality and fertility as part of a natural process of dissolution (*De Rerum Natura* 2.1157–68, 5.782–836). The *Timaeus* gives the earth more credit than that. But in another work, Plato, too, toys with the notion of a Golden Age and a world that no longer offers its bounty as it did of old. In the *Statesman*'s Myth of the Reversed Cosmos, world history is divided into alternating eons. During one, the world is directly controlled by a divine Demiurge. During the other, the cosmos is left to its own devices, its motion and order derived from its own thinking, dependent on its memory of the previous order (271d–e, 272d–273e). As is the wont of embodied souls, memory becomes progressively more muddled, and the world becomes ever more chaotic, until the cosmos threatens to be lost in chaos. It is at this point that the Demiurge again steps in. During the era of the direct control of the god, the earth gives its bounty without stint; since this is not the case now, human beings require the arts, including agriculture and, the Stranger hints, perhaps philosophy itself (271e–272d).

A full interpretation of this myth cannot be given here. For the present let it suffice to say that, questions of dating apart, the myth of the *Statesman* and the cosmology of the *Timaeus* share a number of turns of phrase and metaphysical teachings.[12] This has led to the view, promoted by the Neoplatonists but not without its contemporary adherents,[13] that the alternating eons mythically represent intelligible order and intransigent Necessity. The era of direct divine control is a representation of what the world would be like if it were a perfect copy of the Forms. But this is impossible, for such a world would be bodiless; indeed, it would be the intelligible world itself and could not have the status of a copy at all. The increasing disorder in the world is thus a mythical image of the imperfection of any bodily thing. It is this imperfection that is responsible for the human need to toil in order to survive, at the expense of the perfect continuous motions of the intellect.

Accordingly, the decay of the earth and the difficulty one has in relying on the earth to supply material necessities are not found in some particular historical era but are permanent features of the realm of Becoming. The progressive decay of the lands around Athens can be seen as the result of soul's falling short of wisdom. The nature of body as such is responsible for the fact that the world soul cannot perfectly direct the body of the world. Thus we have periodic catastrophic floods. Likewise, human beings inevitably err in regard to what is to their benefit as embodied beings. Thus we have deforestation and the erosion that results.

What, then, would be the Platonic perspective on ecological healing? Can the forests around Athens ever grow back? Can Athens have the abundance of fertile land it once possessed? If the nonliteral reading of the *Statesman* I have suggested is correct, any hope for healing through divine intervention would be vain. Ecological as well as political decay is to be considered as the result of inevitable imperfection and perishing in the realm of Becoming, which, as a whole, must be taken to be as beautiful and perfect an image of Being as is possible. Plato's attitude toward political reform would signal his probable attitude toward ecological healing. Plato is a pessimist about politics. A healthy political community requires the unlikely combination of wisdom and political power (*Republic* 540d–e, Letter 7 326a–b). Nonetheless, though Plato himself despaired of ever being the agency by which such political reform can come about, his continued interest in political questions, as well as his continued involvement in the lives and education of his own students and associates, shows that he did not lose all hope of improving the flow and flux of human affairs. Likewise, Plato would most likely despair of a perfectly healthy earth. But here, too, there is no reason to doubt that Plato would have taken it to be the part of a decent person to improve things by taking whatever steps he can.

Part III

Aristotle

7

Aristotelian Roots of Ecology: Causality, Complex Systems Theory, and Integrity

Laura Westra

> ... and being is better than non-being, and living than non-living—
> for these reasons there is generation of animals. For since the nature
> of such a kind cannot be eternal, that which comes into being is eter-
> nal in the way that is possible for it.
> —Aristotle, *De Generatione Animalium* 3.1.731b30–33

My work on ecosystem integrity has centered on the scientific approach of complex systems theory, on which many current policy studies are based. Other studies also use Aristotelian language and concepts to express new ideas in science. An Aristotelian has no trouble recognizing some of these ideas and concepts; "natural hierarchies," "excellence," "optimum function," "goal-directedness," and "well-being" are all concepts familiar to both ecosystem science and Aristotelian scholarship. This essay will attempt to render explicit the meaning of some of these concepts and to trace their roots, after first presenting the understanding of ecosystem integrity in current scientific and philosophical terms.

It has become progressively more unacceptable and socially incorrect to appeal to moral absolutes, whether in philosophical debates or in a policy forum. To do so appears regressive, oppressive, and totally out of step with the postmodern world we inhabit. The only well-founded appeals, it is believed, are based on an ever increasing variety of individual rights. However, while that particular modern thrust has led to a number of good things for most of us, it has also sanctified any and all individual choices, simply because they represent our preferences. When the *summum bonum* could no longer be appealed to, although we gained in many ways, we also lost, singly and collectively, an important dimension of our moral and spiritual selves.

Current environmental threats, too numerous to mention, have served one useful purpose: they have forced us to rethink our interrelation and accept once again a communitarian perspective. Moreover, even the "community" is now a global one; since our regional or national communities are proving insufficient when faced with global threats, we are having to relearn to consider ourselves cosmic citizens. Problems such as ozone-layer depletion, deforestation, or toxic pollution can no longer be addressed or redressed by individuals, groups, or even nations in isolation. Even ideal pollution laws in Windsor, Ontario, would not serve to ameliorate the hazardous conditions of air and water without equal legislation in Detroit, Michigan.

Thus, we find increasingly in legislation and mission and vision statements of various countries and institutions a call to restore or protect ecosystem integrity. We have been forced to reinstitute a holistic perspective (at least in some regards) and to admit the need for categorical rather than preference-based principles. (The Montreal protocol [1989] on the ozone layer, and the biodiversity treaty of Rio [1992] are two examples of this admission.) The protection and restoration of ecosystem integrity is another example of a holistic, global, binding goal. It is also a moral goal, in the sense of demanding compliance before calculations of individual or group preferences.

I have argued that integrity is a value capable of grounding a categorical imperative.[1] Being life-supporting, Ecosystem Integrity carries implications similar to those we find in interhuman moral doctrines for the absolute value of life. Since the latter is the basis for all rights and utilities (except in special cases such as those, for example, involving holding particular religious beliefs), it remains either explicitly or implicitly foundational for all moral doctrines. I do not propose at this time to defend integrity as a moral as well as a prudential goal; I will simply offer my definition, then trace the Aristotelian roots of my argument.[2]

In my earlier discussion of the links between Aristotelian doctrine and both ecology and environmental ethics, I excluded any discussion of the Prime Mover, since I believed that the full articulation of Aristotelian thought, including the doctrine of Prime Mover, would render my work too narrowly theological in scope.[3] Recent work by R. Ulanowicz and by Sarah Broadie, however, has shown me that my work on integrity is open to discussion and revision in light of new philosophical and scientific insights. In view of this, I plan first to reopen the argument for the exclusion of the Prime Mover, re-present some previous Aristotelian insights, and change certain things I no longer take to be accurate views on Aristotle's position. Next, I will discuss several Aristotelian concepts that appear in modern form in the science of ecology and are sometimes used to support arguments in environmental ethics. Third, I will present another argument taken from Aristotle in support of a specific approach in environmental ethics, that is, the biocentric approach.

The "Ascendency Perspective" and the Activity of the Prime Mover

If my argument for the moral force of integrity in its Aristotelian context, as used in the "principle of integrity" (PI), can be accepted, it is important that integrity's own roots and definition be open to reexamination. These include (a) its identity as separate from that of the concept of "ecosystem health"; (b) the question of Aristotelian causality, including its formal and final aspects; and (c) the role and function of the Prime Mover and its relation to life-support systems. When these aspects of the relation between integrity and Aristotelian thought are reviewed, new and fruitful conclusions will emerge.

Some of the claims made for the concept of integrity, including its difference from that of ecosystem health, have clear Aristotelian roots. To say that something possesses integrity implies that we are viewing something as unitary, and this has been one of the major claims of the recently accepted ecosystem approach, of which the value of integrity is an integral part.[4] But these scientific questions have no parallel in the understanding of unity in the writings of Aristotle, where the link between the two concepts is not often made. In the *Metaphysics (Metaph.)* Aristotle makes some claims about unity that are relevant. He says, for example, "The nature of unity must be the same for all categories" (*Metaph.* 1053b24), and in so doing offers us a definition that is usable for any subject matter. Elsewhere he says, "To be one (*to heni einai*) is to be indivisible, being essentially a particular thing distinct and separate in place or form or thought, or to be whole and indivisible; but especially to be the first measure of each kind" (*Metaph.* 1052b 16–18, trans. Tredennick). According to this definition, in order to ascribe integrity to an ecosystem, we do not have to be able to call a system exclusively "a particular thing, distinct in place," as philosophers of science, such as Shrader-Frechette, require; it is enough to view it as separate in "form or thought," "whole," and "the first measure of its kind." These characteristics, when joined, are certainly sufficient to make a whole one entity, rather than a heap of unrelated entities.

But there is yet another feature of this sort of unitary whole that is an unmistakable aspect of integrity: the fact that whatever acts as one in regard to function represents a unity, without need to specify precise size and limits. R. Ulanowicz[5] and others offer examples of an ecosystem acting as a unity. This can be made clear without even considering a whole organism and thereby reopening debate with supporters of the Gaia hypothesis or of animistic or vitalistic theories. If we consider instead a hand, this is indeed part of a whole, but it does not need to be viewed as having a soul or being a thinking, purposeful organism in order to have a function that is unique to its kind. A hand is still a hand no matter what its size, shape, or age; it needs, however, to be alive and basically undiminished, although it can miss perhaps parts of a finger or two and still retain its function. But it is no longer one if it is separated from the organism or divided into pieces.

Hence, if one values the function, one must necessarily value the integrity or the undiminished structural unity on which such function depends. Emphasis on function, however, is emphasis on activity, motion, and change. Aristotle's theory accepts and emphasizes motion and change in some specific ways, primarily in the passage from potentiality to actuality, as well as through all forms of causality, material, efficient, formal, and final.

A difficulty arises if one tries to trace connections between Aristotle and ecology by reference to the paradigm of complex systems theory, in that no complex system is static or fixed in form through time. As Ulanowicz says, "very few systems we encounter are at thermodynamic equilibrium and most certainly no living system."[6] This is an important problem that needs to be addressed, since Aristotelian science is usually viewed as flawed because it does not appear to accommodate evolution; the change and motion it acknowledges are intended simply to bring a potential organism to its preestablished (and basically unchanging) actuality, according to a progressively self-perfecting form, but not as a tool for altering the form in response to other changes.

This aspect of Aristotelian theory is so basic that it is difficult to envision another interpretation of his thought such that it might permit the inclusion of some evolutionary theory. In order to do this, it will be necessary to reexamine some other aspects of Aristotelian causality. At first sight, this may appear an attempt to reconcile irreconcilable theories, that is, complex systems theory and Aristotelian doctrine. The notion of live organisms coming to be precisely what they were meant to be appears to be far too deterministic to fit complex systems. For these systems are "open," and so not compatible with a "deterministic reality."[7] Furthermore, speaking of an "open" universe, Ulanowicz says: "In accounting for the reasons why some particular event happens, it is often not possible to identify all causes, even if one includes all levels of explanation. There will always remain a small (sometimes infinitesimal) open window that no cause covers."[8]

Appealing to Popper, he terms the forms that are immanent in each organism "propensities" that "keep reality from dissolving into total randomness."[9] Aristotle's individual entities, by contrast, move from potency to actuality, and this actualization can and will occur, provided nothing happens to prevent it.

But for Aristotle, too, the form of an organism's precise actualization can be anticipated only up to a point. A human embryo will develop only into a human being; but we cannot be sure whether the ensuing being will eventually be a Socrates or a Sophist, an Alexander or a coward, a healthy, well-developed human or a deformed, unhealthy one. Aristotle would in fact agree with Ulanowicz when he says that "there is no such thing as an absolute probability. All probabilities are contingent to a greater or lesser extent upon circumstances and interfering events."[10]

Are things more fixed and determined, however, in another sphere, that is, that of the planets and "fixed stars"? Aristotle views this sphere as the highest and most rational; it is the realm of "the mutual attraction of heavenly masses for each other," and it is kept in place eternally through final causality and the activity of the Prime Mover. Aristotle views its motion as predetermined through time and dependent on the Prime Mover, whose primary activity and function, according to accepted scholarship, is to contemplate itself. This eternal existence, in turn, causes the movement of the various heavenly bodies through attraction or love on their part. This standard interpretation, it is clear, cannot be used in a scientific or historical context. Nor is the Aristotelian conception of the role of forms sufficient to underpin the scientific realities of complex systems: formal causality and universal laws understood as immutable through eternity are not enough.

When we consider open systems, we need to go beyond physical forces and consider "propensities" as "inherent in a situation." The "situation" comprises such things as climatic changes, various forms of interaction among entities, and systemic feedback, including mutualism. Hence neither unchanging formal causality nor the unmoving final causality ascribed to the Prime Mover by accepted Aristotelian scholarship is appropriate to the actual interactions and development that new science discloses. According to new theories, science always maintains "some plasticity or indeterminacy," thus eliminating mechanistic and fully deterministic explanation and rendering it obsolete.[11]

But indeterminacy without complete randomness entails *creativity* of some sort, which—I have argued, speaking of Plotinus—can be seen as the highest form of activity, both human and divine.[12] In the words of Ulanowicz:

Taken as a unit, the autocatalytic cycle is not simply acting at the behest of its environment, it actively creates its own domain of influence. Such creative behavior imparts a separate identity and ontological status to the configuration above and beyond the passive elements that surround it. We see in centripedality the most primitive hint of entification, selfhood and id. In the direction toward which the asymmetry of autocatalysis points, we see a suggestion of *telos,* and intimation of final cause.[13]

For Aristotle, everything within the universe is telic, and the Prime Mover represents the culmination and source of final causality. So the next question must be, Is there anything that can be said to minimize the standard interpretation of the Prime Mover as being static, unchanging, and rigidly determinant and permit us to re-present Aristotle in a more scientific perspective? In a recent article entitled "What Does Aristotle's Prime Mover Do?" Sarah Broadie has, perhaps unintentionally, provided just such an interpretation. The crux of her position is that it is not the case that the Prime Mover "essentially *contemplates,*" but rather that his function or activity is *essentially kinetic.*[14]

The Prime Mover is responsible for the eternal circular motion of heavenly bodies as "an object of love or desire," that is, in order to realize some objective that must include the very motion it engenders. The movement engendered is a desired end, "something that is enabled through being valued."[15] As the Prime Mover is necessarily aware of this, his activity is both kinetic and noetic, thus becoming a pleasurable activity enhancing the agent.[16] According to this interpretation, the Prime Mover does not "eternally produce movement, but *what* the Mover produces is a movement essentially eternal and all-containing in time and space." This requires that such an end be "understood" in order to be brought into being. Finally, it is not just eternal rotation that takes place, but "an eternal *world-making movement.*"[17]

Broadie further analyzes this point by citing *Lamda* 10 (1075a11 ff.) and Aristotle's analogy of a military commander. What the Prime Mover engenders is world-making motion, comprising many different, independent, and possibly interacting substances. But, as a commander, "he does not expressly dictate the detail that unfolds within the field secured by his influence," so that we can argue that, although the end is prescribed, unalterable, and unchanging (that is, the continuation of the living moving world), it only represents a "prescribed framework."[18]

If this new interpretation is accepted, several points follow, all of which are favorable to an Aristotelian understanding of complex systems theory in general and to Ulanowicz's proposed "ascendency perspective" in particular. First of all, the Prime Mover is essentially (or at least co-essentially) kinetic as a Final Cause, in which case, "eternal world-making" is no longer as mechanistic as is sometimes supposed. It is *essentially* movement or change that is not totally determined in all details, since interaction among independent substances must retain some degree of creative openness. Second, the creative openness I ascribe to Aristotle could account for the systemic feedbacks that are eventually responsible for evolutionary paths and that have hitherto been viewed as excluded from Aristotelian thought. Third, and most important, the existence and continued support of world making, considered as an absolute and final end, would provide additional support for an ethic of respect for the complex life-support systems that make "world making" possible, since the continued, eternal existence of this kinetic activity would remain the indisputable final end.

The moral necessity for ecosystem integrity to *ground* this end is also something that can be corroborated in Aristotelian thought. I shall return to this point in my conclusion. But before that, I shall discuss a number of ecological terms and concepts taken from ecology that manifest a clear Aristotelian origin.

Some Aristotelian Concepts in Ecology: *Ergon*, Excellence, Potentiality, Actuality, Telos, *Eudaimonia*

Most of these concepts are familiar ones, either from ecology or from the notion of ecosystem integrity and the principle that is either explicitly or implicitly based upon it, the principle of integrity. A brief discussion of each of these will help to support the claims of the previous section about the links between complex systems theory, in relation to ecology, and Aristotelian thought.

Potentiality, actuality, and the movement from one to the other have already been mentioned. In true Aristotelian fashion, let us start with *ergon*. Perhaps we can speak of the function of an organism, but can we say the same of an ecosystem? Moreover, can we relate that concept to *eudaimonia*, as Aristotle would in the case of a single human organism? First, the term *eudaimonia* should be translated "well-being" (rather than "happiness"), a notion that appears to capture precisely what an ecosystem in a state of integrity is and does. This concept differs from the understanding of happiness used in modern moral theory. For instance, in the work of John Stuart Mill the term "happiness" represents a preponderance of pleasure over pain across a period of time, and the attainment of such happiness is the goal of utilitarianism. For Aristotle, the concept transcends both pleasure and the absence of pain, although the presence of some goods is required, and involves an unequivocally metaphysical component. In order to understand what it means, one needs to refer to what it is to be a human being and to the nature of the human *ergon* or function, the latter being defined in terms of the former. As such, the definition highlights the intimate connection between structure (or essential being) and function. If the notion of well-being also helps bridge structure and function, the question of the meaning of integrity may be rephrased as the question of what the *ergon* of an ecosystem is.

Integrity as "well-being" or "faring well" is a notion that clearly introduces a combination of physical and metaphysical components, and thus it accommodates both structural and functional aspects of integrity. On the other hand, Kay maintains that a scientist may lay bare and explain any number of changes an ecosystem may undergo, including possible transformations after both usual changes and catastrophic events.[19] What is neither possible nor appropriate, he adds, is to rank these in hierarchical order, or to state which might be the "better" ecosystem. This might be done, if I understand him correctly, only in regard to a single ecosystem, viewed at different times, which could be in turn pristine, well-functioning or healthy, degraded, restored, or whatever. Even in this case, some ambivalence appears to be present in science, as no attempt is made to specify the "value" of an ecosystem except in respect to some human goal. Yet for Aristotle not only may individual humans change and improve or lose (moral) ground, but humans in general may be compared and ranked hierarchically, and the wise ("happy") man can be distinguished from the less "actualized" or excellent. The *Nicomachean Ethics* is devoted precisely to the task of discussing, making explicit, and defending these differences.

The use of thermodynamics to provide a framework to define and understand ecological integrity goes beyond previous approaches; by showing that "all real processes are irreversible, it indicates a direction and an end state for all real processes."[20] This addition is extremely significant: it reintroduces teleology in processes described in solely scientific terms, without appeals to metaphysics, to Aristotelian doctrine, or to any other anthropocentric framework. Here, teleology does not imply a necessary movement from a worse to a better state, even less the existence of an ideal state as an end goal. It simply shows that ecosystems act as wholes, and that they *tend* toward some specific state, without, of course, *intending* it.

The question of the relation between individuals and wholes can also be fruitfully examined from the standpoint of Aristotelian doctrine. What is the value of individuals and the value of wholes in Aristotle?

In true Aristotelian fashion, the first thing to establish is the purpose or end towards which each living thing unfolds. This is not a conscious normative unfolding, in the sense of choosing one end among others, or one value among many. On the contrary, as A. Gotthelf puts it: "Since a naturalistic account can . . . be given of the notion of the good within which Aristotle operates in his biology, it seems to me that the fundamental account of the final cause need not make use of that notion." In Aristotle's biological account, all things move or change according to "locomotive natures" and "qualitative potentials" towards their "mature state" (*akme*). Therefore, it is clearly not an enterprise that needs philosophical defense in the way in which a moral doctrine does. Aristotle's is, rather, a doctrine which is "fundamentally empirical in character, and not an a priori doctrine brought to his investigation of nature."[21]

The good is identified as the achievement of the "mature state," which in turn "is identifiable in terms of the presence of maximal powers of self-maintenance without reference to independent normative criteria." If, for "meta-ethical reasons the good is defined by reference to this same mature state," I think we have identified a good that remains valid outside the ambit of Aristotelian thought. This "good" may not impose on us a *positive* obligation, in the sense that moral agents will be obligated to bring about the mature, stable state of self-maintenance of such an entity; but it does bring a *negative* obligation, that is, an obligation on our part not to prevent that good by unwarranted interference with the various stages through which an entity may pass on its way to its own telos.

Even though the latter does not represent a normative value as such (for it or for the moral agent), the self-maintenance of an organic ecosystem is an indisputable value, the foundation of all other possible values for which one might want to argue. It is, moreover, a value for all life, not just human life, and as such is central to the endeavors of both anthropocentrists and biocentrists. Thus we have reached a foundational good, for the sake of which action can be taken (or omitted) in a metaethical sense. We need not derive an "ought" from an "is"; we may simply observe and accept that this is a naturally unfolding "is" and that the telos appears to be valuable as such. Since it would be hard indeed to argue for a moral position requiring that there should be no life, the existence of a stable foundation for all life appears to be an obvious good or value. Yet one might object that Aristotle's teleology appears to be confined to single organisms. However, this possible objection ignores the whole thrust of Aristotelian physics, ethics, and, ultimately, even metaphysics. Aristotle does not view individual telos as the existential basis for individual self-fulfillment. Rather, what counts is *species* survival; and the modern assertion that ecosystems, too, transcend individuals and support species (as well as individuals), thus fostering and enhancing biodiversity and life, is fully in line with such a view.

The major "flaw" in Aristotelian science is that Aristotle has no conception of evolutionary theory: for him, what exists has always existed, except perhaps for the unusual coupling of animals producing unusual kinds (*Generation of Animals [GA]* 2.4.4.738b32). On the other hand, Anthony Preus has argued that, as species may be classified in terms of the character of the genetic information carried in the chromosomes, Aristotelian science might be to some extent reconcilable with contemporary theory. He believes that Aristotle was indeed "groping for genotypic taxonomy," and some of what Ernst Mayr says supports this position.[22]

What about the charge of environmental fascism as the inescapable consequence of accepting an organic teleology? Once again, an answer can be found in Aristotle: Only when "element potentials" actualize their "irreducible potential for form" in the context of a living organism does such indisputable "value" accrue to the actualized nature. It is, therefore, only when a living organism—that is, an interconnected organic whole or an interconnected system—is under consideration that we can most appropriately reason in this manner. On the other hand, the naturalistic account of the good cannot simply be transferred to a society or government. These are artifacts, although they are, in a sense, made up of living parts, the citizens of that society. There is a vast difference between the relationship between the components of an organism or—for that matter—of an ecosystemic whole and the parts of a society or other social group. The former are diverse in themselves, but fitting only into fixed niches, playing specific roles according to an evolutionarily established harmony, although some species may play a substitute function if required in some ecosystem.[23] This is not true of the latter, who may be optional parts of an optional whole, filling positions within it that are often interchangeable. This is only remotely analogous to a living organism; the variables are too numerous to permit an a priori decision about the possible value of any one element. Citizens may belong to one society or another; within that society, they may move from role to role or not; and finally, the *akme* or finished mature state cannot be identified with ease, if at all, nor defended as foundational for value. An acorn can become actualized only as an oak tree, if favorable conditions prevail, but a group of citizens can form an almost infinite number of societies, both good and bad.

It is only within a stable, healthy natural environment that (a) individual roles are fixed with the exception noted immediately above; (b) component parts as a whole identify (and can interact within) *that* environ-

ment and no other; (c) the "maturity" of the actualized state is potentially recognizable; and, finally, (d) that and no other whole, when it possesses integrity (or at least health) and is naturally functioning, can sustain the very life of its component parts. The relation between citizen and
society is not at all like that; one can live in a socialistic state or a libertar-
ian one. Within either, one might be a leader or a follower and fit (inter-
changeably with many others) a great variety of positions and roles. This
is not true of natural systems; a plant cannot take the place of a fish, nor
can it choose to live submerged any more than the fish can choose to root
itself in the earth (although changes do occur—a switching of roles,
change of prey, or movement into or out of the ecosystem, for example).
The value of the organism when appropriately placed within a "live"
(that is, a functioning, not degraded) ecosystem proceeds according to the
notion of an irreducible potential for form. This potential separates organisms from mere aggregates.[24]

Aristotle in Support of Biocentrism: Being and Eternity

The opening quotation is taken from Aristotle's discussion of why the
generation of animals occurs. Two premises are made explicit that many
of today's moral philosophers read as merely implicit: (1) that "to be,"
generally, is better than its opposite; and (2) living is either equally as
desirable as, or more desirable than, not-living. Aside from arguments
about quality-of-life issues in biomedical ethics, it is only in the literature
regarding future generations that these questions are even raised. On the
topic of future generations, they represent the focus of the disagreement
between different positions. Some of these positions I shall discuss in the
final section. At this time I shall review Aristotle's doctrine of "life" as an
ultimate value and a "good" beyond discussion.

As I have argued, "life, for Aristotle, is primary because it represents the
basis for all other goods and ends. As it is unique in that sense, it provides
the first and best value uniting humans and non-humans, individuals and
wholes."[25] Aristotle takes this to be obvious, and he uses it as a first principle rather than as a conclusion for which he needs to argue. Given our
instinctive as well as our reasoned responses to life questions in general
and the fact that most regulations and laws also take it for granted and
enunciate it as a starting point for all other human rights, it seems that
Aristotle may be generally correct in his assumption. In the *Generation of
Animals* he speaks of eternity and the limits of what is possible for that
which comes into being:

For since the nature of such a kind cannot be eternal, that which comes into being is eternal in the way that is possible for it. Now it is not possible in number (for the being of existing things is in the particular and if this were such, it would be eternal) but it is possible in form. That is why there is always a kind of men and animals and plants. (*GA* 2.1.731b32–732a1).

Of course, what Aristotle believes is that what happens in nature is "for the sake of something," and the telic, eternal unfolding of the universe is also not in question for him. Generation and corruption, growth and decay are all part of this orderly unfolding that supports life and guarantees the eternity of universal kinds, in the face of the limits of particularity. Here he makes no effort to escape, and still less disdains, particularity itself. As Martha Nussbaum puts it:

In the *Parts of Animals* (1.5) he addresses some students who had evidently protested against the study of animals, and their form and matter, asking for something more sublime. He tells them that this reluctance is actually a form of self-contempt: for they are, after all, creatures of flesh and blood themselves.[26]

Thus, long before Aldo Leopold's "land ethic" (1969), we find a clear, unequivocal statement of our kinship to all life, in clear rejection of much of Platonism and—later—Cartesianism. Nussbaum adds: "We could generalize Aristotle's point by saying that the opponent of the return to appearances is likely to be a person not at peace with his humanity." Hence it is a normal part of life as humans to want to understand the laws and functioning of the universe. But it is also part of our humanity to accept our commonality with the rest of life, aside from our position as "external" observers and scientists.

Yet many argue that the ancient Greeks, including Aristotle, perpetuate the split between humankind and the rest of nature because of their emphasis on rationality as the element that separates us from the animals. However, to say that we are rational animals, as we have seen, is not to deny our commonality with nonhuman creatures. Aristotle sees the eternal waxing and waning of natural processes, natural entities, and wholes as part of a desirable and even divine, plan for the universe, without for a moment ascribing intentionality to either individuals or processes.

We can therefore say that living is better than its opposite and that all of nature unfolds "for the sake of" the continuance of life through eternity. Because actual individuals are particulars, and hence mortal, the true and divine aim is for eternity through forms and their universality. Furthermore, for Aristotle "we should always act for the sake of happiness," which includes a number of goods; so the pursuit of other "intrinsic" goods over and above simply virtue will be necessary, since these, too, are components of happiness.[27]

Therefore, not only does a naturally unfolding, physical "is" represent nature's goal, but the continuance of life is both a precondition and a component of our moral commitment to virtue and happiness. Both of these values are, of their very nature, intrinsically good and temporally unlimited.

The advantages of this approach are clear: unfolding over time, not only in the present but also in the future, life and being are part of the universal telos. Rather than adding posterity and the future to a temporally and locally limited moral theory, Aristotle includes them in his theory from the start. These intrinsic goods, however, do not appear to include individual entities. Rather, they apply to wholes, so that their corresponding component parts gain value—and can indeed be considered equally parts of that intrinsically good whole—in virtue of their participation in its functions.[28]

A further powerful reinforcement of the basis for obligations to future generations is Aristotle's theory of potentiality in relation to actuality. In an earlier discussion of the meaning and role of integrity, I indicated that it was wrong to identify an ecosystem in a state of integrity with one that is flourishing or with a "climax" system. I suggested instead that the evolutionary process's unconstrained, natural unfolding was absolutely dependent on the nonimposition of strong anthropogenic stresses. Unstressed, unmanipulated natural systems would in fact be closest to a state of true integrity and hence would possess the utmost capacity for sustaining and continuing the full range of potential evolutionary paths for a specific system at its particular time and location. Only this "optimum capacity" would indicate ecosystem integrity, particularly as no landscape on earth today can be termed pristine or can be deemed to have escaped some anthropogenic alteration.

Aside from his emphasis on the telic nature of all single physical processes and the universe as a whole, Aristotle was the first philosopher to articulate clearly the distinction between potentiality and actuality. In fact, all "matter" is potency awaiting actualization in various forms. Hence we need not have any specific information about the future "actuality" evolving from matter's potency to acknowledge its value as intrinsically good. For example, we need not know that Michelangelo will use it to sculpt his David to attach intrinsic value to a slab of Carrara marble and to understand that it is worthy of respect here and now, without any assurance of its future fate. The same could be said about any presently uncultivated land, or untouched forest, or the embryo of horse or man. Nor is the intrinsic value in this sense separable, except in thought, from the instrumental value of what we consider. All things have a range of capacities that in turn limit their possible function.

But function is for Aristotle a "movement" and hence requires the presence of life in natural entities. Flesh, for example, is not really "flesh" unless it is said to be the flesh of a live animal, and a dead man's eye is not an "eye" in the sense of possessing the capacity to function in the manner that is appropriate to it. I have defended above the relation between parts and wholes as something fundamental to the intrinsic value of integrity; I have also proposed the telic thrust of natural processes in relation to that value.[29] In this section I have argued that the relation between actuality and potency and the foundational value of life look like additional constructive aspects of Aristotelian thought. All these Aristotelian arguments are valuable in support of a holistic environmental ethic and also of our obligation to future generations. In essence, the ultimate telos lies in the functioning of all matter, not only because it is the basis of all that exists, but also because it encompasses the capacity to exist and to develop into all that it can be. Both are then in a sense final causes, and goods that escape all time constraints.

My previous work excluded final causality altogether, despite my reliance on other aspects of Aristotelian doctrine, which I found helpful, on the whole, and even foundational for an understanding of both ecology (in its complex-systems approach) and environmental moral obligation. But, as I argued in the first part of this chapter, recent scholarship appears to support a reconnection between two realms of thought that I had previously taken to be irreconcilable. I have argued that Aristotle's thrust toward a metaphysical understanding of the functioning of the whole physical universe can also be said to support the continued existence, telos, and good of the whole. Hence for Aristotle no conflict exists between the telos of individuals, species, and the whole.

This may appear to be a rather sweeping statement; but recent Aristotelian scholarship moves in the direction of the position I defend, although to be fair, there has been controversy over the question of the possible extension of organic (individual) teleology. This represents a very important point in support of my position, and thus it is worth analyzing in some detail. For instance, John Rist says, "Nature always strives for the better . . . and Aristotle goes on to tell us what this means: being is better than non-being."[30] All nature is "graded," and "that which is best is at the top of the hierarchy," so the principle of final causation comes from the top. Hence, from the Aristotelian perspective, we can view the whole of nature as "motivated" by a series of final causes. "Insofar as each item in motion can 'desire,' it desires to be better, that is, it will desire being rather than non-being, life, rather than non-life, etc.[31] What is implied here is that not only can we speak of individual "natures," each with its immanent telos, or principle of development, but that Nature as a whole (which "does nothing in vain") may have an immanent principle that "must work in a law-like fashion," and this principle and telos transcends individual development.

Rist speculates whether this might be an "echo" of a "world-soul" concept. If the individual's "aspiration is to fulfill oneself, to achieve one's form or purpose," then a parallel "striving" or desire in all of *phusis* (nature) appears to be in line with Aristotle's thought and his doctrine of the Prime Mover. The latter cannot be said to provide a final cause for individuals only. In fact, for Aristotle, as previously noted, it is fair to say that reaching one's physical *akme* or mature state is primarily a *species* achievement; hence, the fulfillment of one's nature in that sense is not primarily for our individual benefit but for that of our species.

Further, in the *Physics* (192A13–15), the "bold metaphor of matter desiring form" can be found. Once again, this applies to all of matter, not to individual parts of it. It represents a holistic "striving," not an individual one. Hence, the world can be viewed as alive in some sense and as embodying a sense of overall (rather than individual) purpose, a good exceeding individual survival and flourishing. As Aristotle puts it: "As in the universe (*en toi holoi*), so (in the soul), God moves everything (*Eudemian Ethics* 8, 1248A25–26).[32]

This statement lends further support to the "new interpretation" of the Prime Mover's activity that Broadie proposes and defends.[33] If she is right, not only may Aristotelian science now be viewed as far less removed from modern, "real" science than has hitherto been supposed, but even biocentric, holistic environmental ethics receives additional support from the ultimate value of the eternal movement that supports creative, interactive, and evolving life.

In conclusion, rather than opposing the insights and arguments of biocentric or ecocentric environmental ethics, an Aristotelian understanding of the universe tends to support philosophical and scientific insights that help articulate an environmental ethic. The recognition of both scale and hierarchy in ecology is central to the understanding of the functioning of natural complex systems. They also help us understand why certain human activities must fall under the scrutiny of moral philosophy today, even if they have not done so in the past, if we are to take seriously the primacy of the harm principle and, in general, the principle of respect for all life.

8

The Greening of Aristotle

C. W. DeMarco

Notorious among the difficulties of Aristotle's "functionalism" is its failure to provide a single example in the nonhuman order of the function of a natural individual. This absence makes one suspect that Aristotle was simply unable to know what he claimed we could know: the nature and function of natural wholes. Examples of the functions of parts of animals abound. It is this feature that has led Pellegrin—rightly I believe—to characterize Aristotle's working biology as a *moriology*.[1] But this is problematic and indicates a lack. There is a lack because primary nature is form, and form is function (*ergon*), so to lack knowledge of the function of a whole being as a whole is to lack knowledge of that being *as* a being. This emphasis on the function of parts displaces the notion of species in biological work. It opens a gap in Aristotelian theory where a keystone should lodge. A tiny turn of emphasis can make good this lack, though it involves some recasting of the sense of "form" and of "nature." This turn is an ecological construal of Aristotelian form. It is this ecological construal of form, I wish to argue, that allows us to understand the function of natural wholes and fills a gap in received Aristotelian theory. Moreover, Aristotelian resources allow us to accomplish this while avoiding the extremes of individualism and holism; suitably modified, the Aristotelian approach is still a viable option in even the most recent and most technical discussions.

Substantial Form and Ecological Function

The substance of this axe is to be for cutting, to be at work cutting well. To be a knife is to be for cutting—a different sort of cutting in a different sort of context. To be a house is to be a sheltering. To be a leaf is also to be a sheltering of sorts, in a different setting. We can say that the function and nature of the teeth of this horse are to chew grasses and grains, and the hooves of this horse are protective coverings for its feet. But what is it to be a horse? To be a horse is to be at work as a horse; it is to be for being a good horse, yes; it is also to be made out of other horses, in a sense, and thus to have a horseysort of flesh and bone. While true, these statements are caught in an inward spiral that risks tautology. Aristotle's four "causes" seem to become intensively self-referential as they approach an essence. Why should this be so? While we can give account of the functions of the parts of houses and horses, we seem to be unable to give account of the function of the horse as a whole, though we can give account of the function of the house as a whole. Why is this? Is it because, as Heidegger and Wittgenstein suggest, the Aristotelian analysis turns on a comparison of nature with art, which comparison collapses, making *natural* teleology impotent and exposing it as a sort of metaphor that strains here to the breaking? Or is it rather the height of profundity to come to the end of explanation with the "being" of the horse so that all we *can* do is stammer that to be a horse is to be at work as a horse and to be made out of horse-flesh and by other horses, and is to be for being a good horse? This stuttering answer is not wrong, just uninformative—less informative than it need be. We can break the vicious cycle of self-reference with a notion of *ecological* function. To be a horse in nature is to enjoy a distinctive ecological function, to be a grazing animal in certain contexts that, lacking horses' grazing function, would not function as it does or should.[2] To be this horse is to have (is, ultimately, to "be") a form that is an operative function; it is to be a distinctive character in a distinctive type of context.[3] Similarly, to be this leech is to be a parasite in a certain sort of wetland, and to be a lion is to be a savanna predator.[4] These functions—grazer, parasite, predator, symbiote, and others such as decomposer, aerator, nitrifier, and the like—are functions that whole living things perform in context. We can specify them with differentia that bond character and context.[5] Characteristic function is ecological, as is the context to which such functions are relative.[6] An ecological understanding of form finds the functions the Stagirite was seeking: the active forms of natural wholes.

Ecological Function and Definitive Purpose

Such prominent functions as predator, symbiote, and so on point us in the right direction, but perhaps are not primary among ecological forms. They involve classifications based on nutritive functions, which might be definitive for some beings in some contexts but not for all. They plainly are useful. But we cannot rest content with this alone. After all, Aristotle had already distinguished respiration and digestion, circulation, and so on long ago, even if he misidentified most of their organs. A satisfactory ecological account of species form must attend to all these functions of the *psyche*, that is, the nature or internal principle of change and stability of a living thing.

In *Politics* 4.4, Aristotle defines "animal" as something that feeds itself and is sensitive and self-moving; he goes on to say that to define an animal, we need to define its parts and the functions of the parts—such as nutritive function and its chewing and digesting parts (which parts themselves have functions). The possible variations on these themes yield the various kinds of animals. Gotthelf speculates that to these items, which he calls "the givens," we must add the *bioi* of the animals, whether they are marsh animals or water animals, for instance, and what they habitually eat.[7] I concur. The basic features of living things are just the functional aspects ("parts") of their *psyche*, or "nature" (their "'nature" as inner source of stability and change), plus certain situated, habitual factors. The use of these notions is quintessential—perhaps not to the "Aristotle" who has been assimilated to Linnaeus, but to the author of the *Parts* and the *Generation of Animals*. I add only that the juncture of the habits and settings plus the functions and their organs is best understood as the juncture of ecological character and ecological context. A notion that conjoins habitat with habit and function is, I assert, a natural cognate of *ethos*. Each natural whole is in substance an ecological character that enacts a function in context. Again: the notion of species form is modified in a way that lets us make sense of the function of natural wholes in context *and* lets us avoid the temptation of construing the relation of natural individuals to their contexts as a part-whole relation.

If ecological function is to serve to unify the components of an entity, it must have enough unity in itself to bind the parts of a living whole in a shared, definitive purpose. This inner unification of function can be achieved in a number of ways. The most originally Aristotelian way to the inner ordering of function is through focused hierarchy. Here, a focal function serves as the primary ecological function that is the definitive good of the thing; it is assisted by the function of the item's parts, which may also have ecological import. These come in an ordered series of internal functions relating to nutrition and excretion,[8] reproduction and rearing, sensation and motility, and so on for the parts of the kind of *psyche* at issue. Some of these are properties in the proper sense: features that are unique to the species yet not contained in its definition; others are features shared with other types. What is a plausible ordering for these functions? It is Aristotle's suggestion that natural heat comes first. D. L. Balme writes, "The fundamental difference between animals . . . is the difference in their natural heat."[9] This notion seems arcane and antique. But it is not. We understand the notion of heat today through a science of thermodynamics. The issue of natural heat for us becomes the question of the thermodynamic properties of the being, that is, how the life form contours heat exchange and how it operates as a self-regulator to maintain its own metabolism in context. An animal, in this capacity, functions well when it channels thermodynamic flows through itself so as to maximize available energy and minimize dissipation. The natural heat of an organism, to a contemporary Aristotelian, is its characteristic way of exchanging energy with the environment and maintaining itself through this exchange.[10] Heat exchange is the telos of this function, and what is preserved through the function is the formed individual, the being in its near matter, in which near matter is embedded the means by which the organism deploys energy to eat, reproduce, and so on. So "natural heat" comes first.[11] It is, on this analogue of Aristotle's ordering, first in a hierarchy of ecological functions, which hierarchy is unique and definitive for the being at issue. Natural heat is that part or function that the others presume and support. Its differentiae provide basic groupings of living things. That is not the way we tend to classify living things, but perhaps we should, as I argue below.

According to Balme, after natural heat comes environment.[12] "[G]iven that each animal has a basic capability determined by its heat, the next determinant is environment and lifestyle, which together explain functions and organs."[13] That is because "nature always assigns each organ solely or chiefly to those that can use it, e.g., tusks, teeth, horns, spurs, and all such parts as are for help and defense" (*Parts of Animals [PA]* 4.684a28). That's Balme again. But since I have already construed "natural heat"in a context-sensitive way, I would have to say that after natural heat come *additional* environmental factors. Among these are reproductive factors such as fittingness of sexual parts (gamete compatibility, as we would say), effectiveness of sexual signaling in context relative to other possible mates, synchronization of breeding cycle, and so on.[14] The various types of reproductive function (biparental sexual, self-fertilizing hermaphroditic, or reproduction by parthenogenic, fission, budding, and so on) all have their ecological virtues and vices.[15] These virtues and vices are context-sensitive. And in all such cases we must remember that "nature makes the organ to suit the function not the function to suit the organ."[16] That holds.

After heat (energy exchange, homeostasis, and metabolism), reproduction, and nutrition, we would need to consider modes of sensation and mobility. Dispersal rates and barrier crossings are facilitated by motility at the right stages of development.[17] Motility gives animals a flexible way of regulating their outbreeding. Inbreeding and outbreeding are two extremes within which all manner of species find their mean, the mean that is right for them relative to their context. We find kinds of species ranging between inbreeders and outbreeders, since the differential between the gametes that produce the zygotes of their next generations depends largely on the amount of outbreeding. The relation of this differential to environment is, roughly, that outbreeders preserve genetic variation and so maximize ecological plasticity (and hence their evolutionary flexibility), but at the price of waste: they produce many comparatively inferior recombinants. On the other hand, outbreeders have found a lucky genotypic combination that permits them to flourish in some specific sort of context, but at the price of an inability to cope with sudden ecological change. "A species thus has the choice between optimal contemporary fitness combined with considerable evolutionary vulnerability and maximal evolutionary flexibility combined with the wasteful production of inferior genotypes. . . . No species can combine the two advantages into a single system."[18] That necessity gives us another way of specifying kinds of species. In general, plants feature greater dispersal and lower flexibility (weeds provide some exceptions); animals, lower dispersal but greater flexibility. Among animals, the genetic flexibility of outbreeders is favored by large, complex, slow-growing animals that produce few offspring but are adapted to a more generalized ecotone. The genetic fixity of inbreeders is favored by small, simple, fast animals that produce many offspring but are highly adapted to specific ecological situations. Hence vertebrates' distribution is determined largely by dispersal barriers, flora's by climate. The lesson for my purpose is that it is possible to be overspecialized or underspecialized: an inclination to excess or defect has long-run consequences for the flourishing and survival of character-in-context.

A good deal of evidence indicates that ecological factors are crucial to determining the kind of species. "Any characteristic ever described as distinguishing species is also known to be subject to ecological variation."[19] Most theorists deny that speciation can be determined by ecological factors alone; that is true, and the proposal advanced here makes no such claim. Moreover, since every species has a unique ecology, if ecology alone could determine species, every species would be a different *kind* of species. That hardly troubles the approach taken here, for the ecological character that expresses the function of natural wholes is the key part but not the whole of species form—and that principal part *does* determine what could fairly be called a "kind" of species. Ecological function is something that cuts across now standard taxa.[20] Species form and the ecological function that is involved in it both refer intrinsically to environment, though in different ways. Aristotelians can make sense of these strong relations through the notions of character and context. And we can draw on this understanding of the relation of character to context to make sense of the notion of ecological function as the definitive good of natural wholes.

Definitive Purpose and Fourfold Determination

It is important for an Aristotelian to identify the functions of natural individuals, despite their de facto lack in the biological works, since we know from the *Peri Psyches* and the *Metaphysics* that the substance of things is a definitive function that is a form of good. Ecological function fits this characterization: it is a definitive function that is a form of good, the good the being enacts in situ. Now, parts of animals and plants, too, are called "substances" by Aristotle (in the *Metaphysics* as elsewhere), but they are not primary substances. For Aristotelian theory to be consistent (as between biological and formal works) and complete (as within the formal works, to have examples of substantial wholes as functional goods), we need an active good that is identical with what the thing does and, in the end, is most what the thing is in the primary sense of "is." Ecological function fills the order.

The proposed account of species form is not, despite its focal appeal to ecological function, an "ecological species concept."[21] The error of ecospecies concepts is to take ecological role by itself as the species form, instead of taking it as the formal side of a formula (*logos*) that is itself but one aspect of a natural compound.[22] In Aristotle's account of biotic form, a natural whole or individual compound (*synolon*) is a composite of matter and form: this-form-and-this-matter. The species form of this composite is the generic version of the same formula: this-*sort*-of-form-and-this-*sort*-of-matter. The species form is not a pure or separate form independent from any reference to matter. For this reason, a designation such as "parasite" or "decomposer"—a function *simpliciter*—is independent from any reference to particular kinds of matter, so it cannot be a species form in the Aristotelian sense. The Aristotelian species form binds a reference to form or function with a reference to matter.[23] I wish to claim that this holds true for the form construed as ecological function: species form is welded *as form* to a certain sort of embodiment. If we try to make the function by itself definitive, we will wind up sorting too broadly and will muddle together quite different varieties of living things (after all, ticks and leeches are both parasites). If instead we try to make the structured matter definitive, we will sort too narrowly and will wind up missing the form and function anyway. On an Aristotelian approach, we need to distinguish form and matter as aspects of a natural whole,[24] and we need to distinguish *on the side of form* a reference to ecological function and a reference to a certain sort of structured body. Both of these references within the species form are generic; neither refers to particular functions or bodies, but to kinds.

The two great stumbling blocks for ecospecies concepts are (1) the existence of different life forms that serve (more or less) the same function, and (2) the existence of otherwise similar life forms that serve different functions. Problem 2 breaks down into cases of the same life form that serve (2a) different functions at different times within a niche, and (2b) different functions at the same time in different niches. In (2b) we find examples of different ecospecializations within single populations and some standard cases of adaptive radiation within a taxon and cladogenesis.

Problem set 1 presents no special difficulty for the account ventured here, since a species is not just a function (predator, grazer . . .) but a situated function compounded with a structured matter. We expect there to be compounds that satisfy the same function, certainly in different sorts of contexts, and even within the same context. Problem set 2a may refer to developmental changes, sexual dimorphism, or variation in function within a geographic range. Some theorists have gone so far as to suggest that different developmental stages of a single organism make for distinct ecological species.[25] From variations as common as size differences to outright metamorphosis, such cases present difficulties for any selective model; the difficulties are not peculiar to ecological models. Selective pressures on tadpoles and adult frogs will differ: energy theorists, cladists, and others must also face these difficulties. These cases do reinforce the imperative to avoid reducing species form to ecological function alone (or to structured matter alone). The proposed model faces the difficulties and heeds the imperative by distinguishing species form and primary form or substance as ecological function.

Another difficulty springs from problem set 2b. It is hard to distinguish, in general, between phylogenetic separation of gene pools, the distinct genetic lineages within a pool, and individual variations within a lineage. The lines are not always sharp or clear. But again, all rival theories face that problem; however, also included in problem set 2b, and more serious for ecological approaches to species, are cases of functional inversion. The toughest case I know is the mollusk that is a crustacean's prey in one locale and that same crustacean's predator in another.[26] Perhaps this difficulty disappears if we make our ecological focus smaller, located groupings such as Damuth's *avatars*. I am not sure that my suggestion that context be built into the definition of materiate form takes care of this difficulty. This case requires more study.[27]

The main point to highlight is that my simple appeals to functions such as "forager," "decomposer," and so on are just that—simplifications, idealizations. Actual cases are typically more complex. Unless a critter sits atop a food chain, it will be not just "predator" but also "prey" in different functional relationships. Moreover, unless we stipulate that trophic relations are primary (or grant reproductive or thermal budgeting or some other ecological dimension an in-principle priority), the ecological function of any life form will be complex. The Aristotelian hierarchy briefed above would take care of this difficulty, but I do not want to suggest that such a hierarchy must always obtain. Fortunately, ecological theory—at least since Hutchinson—has had models to cope with this complexity. Such models typically are state-space models. In such a model, the ecological function of a natural whole, which function is one component in its species form, would be a point in a hyperspace (or "hypervolume") of several ecological dimensions.[28] This point indicates a single dominant function when a hierarchy such as outlined above is in evidence; the point indicates a single focus of complex and overlapping factors when such a hierarchy is absent. Either way, state-space models can square nicely with an Aristotelian approach. Aristotle's own account built in references to "natural heat," reproduction, sensitivity, and other functions. That is because all main powers of the *psyche*, or nature of a living thing, must be taken into account. And unilinear hierarchy is not the only organizing principle that can focus these functions. Sometimes such a unilinear hierarchy will obtain; other times a multilinear hierarchy may obtain; still other times a complex of relations with multiple priorities may be required. The hypervolume model allows us to organize the natural powers of a living thing and preserve the priority of ecological function. The main requirement for an Aristotelian account is that the function be *definitive*. Whether this definitive function that is the form of the being be identified with one of its powers (say, trophic *or* reproductive *or* thermodynamic . . .) or several powers (say, trophic *and* reproductive *and* thermodynamic . . .) uniquely focused in a hypervolume of ecological dimensions is an empirical matter that will depend on the facts of the case. The main point is that ecological function must be definable as the definitive "good" or form of a living being that unifies its material parts and orients its activities.

Table 8.1 depicts some of the main qualifications of ecological form. Species form rests at the center of the chart; this represents its central place at the center of Aristotelian life science. Species form involves a reference to situated ecological function and a reference to a structured matter with a certain genealogy. So distinguishing the components of the species formula we have (1) a reference to function per se and a reference to its nested contexts. That is, we take each of the components of the left half of the species formula abstractly and array (1a) differences in types of function and (1b) types of "realized" niche. So on the upper right-hand side of table 8.1, we have individuals as interactors, species as "natural functional units" (as Damuth says of his avatars) or situated forms, and populations as actually interbreeding groups. Here is the domain of working complexes-in-contexts. Here are realized niches (as opposed to fundamental niches), here are the units that thermodynamic and stoichiometric models seize and cast in their distinctive ways. These are the active and interacting units referred to in life sciences. This is the domain of actuality and activity. The right hand of the species formula prescinded from the left side yields (2a) a genealogy of lineages and a morphological taxonomy and (2b) types of fundamental niche. From this angle, individuals are referred to only in a double indirection, a species is construed as a genic resource, populations are interbreed*able* populations, and the niche is the fundamental niche (which, note, is closely allied to genetic considerations). We have, in short, on the upper left side of the chart, a reference to the domain of *possibility*, possibility constrained by structure (especially structures indicated on the lower left-hand side of the chart), and so a reference to cross-fertile populations that may never interbreed, niches that may never be "realized," and so on. Aristotle already knew that we need both sides of the picture; in the greened version of Aristotelian theory, both sides of the traditional formula require an additional distinction: a reference that binds ecological character and context.

So, for instance, when we ask "What is a carnivore?" we need to be clear which side of the picture we are addressing, and at what level of abstraction. For not all taxonomic "carnivores" (who share a common genealogy and bodily structures) actually eat meat; not all creatures that in fact eat meat (the functioning "carnivores") are taxonomic carnivores. Famously, the eye of the octopus is a functioning "eye" but not a genealogical "eye," because it does not share a common genetic history with the eyes of other animals. So if we ask the question "Do octopuses

Table 8.1
Ecological Form and Some Basic Abstracta

DOMAIN OF POSSIBILITIES	DOMAIN OF ACTUALITIES
Morphological taxonomy/genealogy of lineages	Ecological function *simpliciter*
"Periodic table of niches"	Nested contexts
Cross-fertile populations	Species as natural functional units of interbreeding populations
"Fundamental niche"	"Realized niche"

Ecological form as **species form**
(this sort of function [in this sort of context]
and this sort of structured matter [encoding this genetic history])

=

Ecological form as **form of natural individual**
(this function [in this context]
and this structured matter [with just this genealogy])

MATERIAL AND STRUCTURAL DETERMINANTS	FUNCTIONAL AND ENERGY/EFFICIENCY DETERMINANTS
Internal "Causes"	External "Causes"
Germ line — Structural determinants	Functional determinants
Soma — Material determinants	Energy/efficiency determinants

Constraints	
Genostasis	Phenotypic plasticity hidden from selection
Limits on autocatalysis	Pleiotropy and linkage
Ancestral limits from physical, chemical, mineral domains	Energy budget
Autoselection	Interactive selection

have eyes?" from a perspective situated in the right half of the chart, the answer is "Yes, of course"; the converse answer emerges when the question is asked from the other side. Again, we must be clear about the level and dimension of analysis lest different inquiries remain at cross purposes with each other. The modified Aristotelian picture helps us to make the relevant distinctions and situates them in a natural way.

The lower half of the diagram indicates causes rather than units of varying degrees of abstractness. We can begin with a rough distinction between internal and external causes. Drawing on Aristotelian terminology, I refer to the "internal" causes as matter and structure and the "external" determinants as functive and effective causes. The former two determinants emphasize autoselection, while the latter two emphasize interactive selection. Constraints on internal determinants and autoselection include genostasis, autocatalysis, and various ancestral limits rooted in physical, chemical, and mineral forms. Constraints on external determinants and interactive selection include phenotypic plasticity hidden from natural selection, pleiotropy, and linkage.

Greened Aristotelianism once again provides not only ways to make distinctions that resolve interpretative issues but also an antidote for "misplaced concreteness." If this model is sound, then the primary concretum of life science is not the isolated physiological individual, nor is it the species as a sort of large individual, nor is it an ecosystem construed as a living superorganism. The primary concretum for life science is situated form. Any of the features tagged in the diagram (and of course there are more) are real enough in one way or another to serve as the locus of an inquiry. But abstracta, whether on the formal or the material side, will always fail to be integrated functionally and informationally: if we find a unit of analysis falling on one side or the other of this divide, we can be sure we are dealing with some aspect of a being and not with the real article in its full, functioning concreteness. That is located at the center of the chart.

I am not so bold as to try to advance a rival notion of species that might contest the molecular, paleobiological, or biogeographic notions prominent today. It would be possible, but perhaps not desirable, to restructure the whole polyphyletic inventory of living things around these categories. Instead, I might go so far as to suggest the device of an *ecological prefix*. The prefix would consist of the statement of operative character—the ecological function and context type (thus: savanna predator, woodland decomposer, etc.) appended like an operator to the standard two- or three-term species name. The Aristotelian species formula contains a reference to form and matter. Here, this becomes the joint reference to function with its context type and structured soma with its genealogy. We can take the standard "scientific name" as a conventional reference that specifies (indirectly) the matter, while the ecological prefix would define, as the standard scientific name does not, the substantial form of the natural whole at issue. Ecological form is the *ti esti* of the being, sought but not found by the Stagirite.

Neither Holism nor Individualism

Aristotelian "functionalism" is rightly regarded as a taproot of ecological theory, but Aristotle's own account is really not ecological in character. A primary challenge for any greening of Aristotle—by which I mean an ecological construal of Aristotelian form—is the following. Since Aristotle characterizes the functions of parts with respect to the wholes of which they are the parts, we might be tempted to characterize that in reference to which we make sense of the forms of natural individuals as wholes, and so we might be tempted to construe the individuals whose functions we are characterizing as "parts" of these larger wholes. An ecological holism that construes that in reference to which we make sense of the functions of substances as natural wholes or functioning individuals is too radically un-Aristotelian according to some standard criteria. The purpose of this project is to venture an ecological account of form that is an Aristotelian account. (Such a holism is also, I shall claim below, false.) For the same reason, we must avoid the contrary error of understanding functions exclusively in terms of subindividual components or material pieces and processes of whatever scale.[29] While the greening of Aristotle requires some change in our understanding of "form," I want to claim that this is not a substantial change and that the notion can therefore rightly be deemed Aristotelian functionalism in a way that other ecological appropriations of the Stagirite cannot.

To be "Aristotelian," an account must preserve at least the ontological priority of whole to part, the priority of act to potency, the priority of function to structure, and the priority of end to means. It must show how a characteristic function is the form or nature of a natural individual (one whole living *this*). It must show how this nature is the principle of unity that binds the parts of an individual and makes it one, while at the same time remaining formally identical with the nature of other individuals of the same species. It must, above all, remain substantively teleological. Finally, I want also to suggest—though perhaps this last requirement is too much a product of the mixed nature of my purpose, which is historical as well as systematic—that the proposed change should not automatically and necessarily involve evolutionary considerations. If a proposed modification immediately involved evolutionary mechanics, it surely would not remain an Aristotelian functionalism. And yet it ought to be open to evolutionary appropriation, on pain of contemporary irrelevance.

The ecological construal of the functions of whole living things provides a key that satisfies each of these strictures. It affords a way to understand the function of natural wholes that does not portray the relation of individual to environment as a part-whole relation. The proposed account is neither a holism nor an individualism, but rather an ecological *contextualism*. In this ecological contextualism, a function is the thing's definitive character, and this character is "relative" to context in the sense that certain traits that are virtues in one context at one time (and so building of character) are in other settings destructive of that character. As with the human virtues of character in relation to their political contexts, ecological virtues are, when they are building of character, building of community (here, ecological community).[30] It is perhaps already obvious that I turn for help in construing ecological character and ecological context to Aristotle's ethical and political writings. For it is in these writings that Aristotle takes possibility, relation, and context most seriously.[31] In the end, it is his practical philosophy that rescues Aristotle from a lack in his theoretical philosophy.[32]

Another apparent bit of arcana in the Aristotelian approach is the claim that primary form is nonmaterial (without matter: *aneu hyles*). An ecological form such as "predator" is nonmaterial in the sense that when we consider it by itself, we should not identify it with any one of the numerous bodily structures that make this function possible in different settings. Such a function is, as form, strictly correlative with matter; it always needs some material substrate or other, but considered per se (*haplos*), it is neither identical with, nor even yoked to, any of them. And even when considering *this* predator, we should, by Aristotelian lights, distinguish the function from the matter: the form is not a material part, is no piece of the being. Function "is" only by informing some matter; but as such it is nonmaterial as being a distinct determinant of the materiate whole. I shall elaborate these points in the following section. For starters, think of ecological context in this discussion as the notion of the *niche* of a species,[33] the biogeographic circumstances in which ecological form performs its appropriate function.[34]

While not Aristotle's theory, the proposed account is Aristotelian. The ecological twist preserves the priority of act to potency (since the actual operation of characteristic function is required for the thing to be and be well, and since as potential it does not engage its context). It suggests that the form or nature or substance of an individual is identical to its function—here its ecological function—even while it emphasizes relation, transaction, and exchange in ways Aristotle did not. Yet the account prescinds from turning natural individuals with their definitive ecological functions into parts that subserve some hypostatized superindividual or collective. The model of character and context—where the function from character into context is actual when the engagement is—satisfies the strictures posed at the outset, while it suggests the direction of the solution to some outstanding problems.[35]

Now it is true that this conception of ecological function downgrades the autarchy and finality and completeness of natural individuals. It emphasizes the *pros ti* in a way that the Stagirite himself might have rejected. But Aristotle did not mandate an absolute autonomy or strict atomicity for sublunary composite substances.[36] Moreover, an ecological contextualism preserves the priority of whole to part (here the priority of the functioning, natural individual to the operations of its parts), since there is a function of the whole animal to which the functions of its parts are relative. But the individual life form is not related to its environment as part to whole, but as character to context. It is crucial to appreciate that the functions of the parts of a living individual make sense relative to the function of the whole in a different way than the function of the whole makes sense relative to its contexts. It is not the same sort of relation at a different level; were this true, the parts of animals, living wholes, and environments would all be "substances" in the same sense. To avoid this presumption, one could always stipulate that we use "part" and "whole" in quite different ways when we write of "the parts of this particular animal" and "the parts of a whole ecosystem." But it is less confusing, I think, to say simply that the relation of a natural individual to environment is not a part-whole relation, but a character-context relation.

Holism, Individualism, and the Double Role of Form

Aristotelian functionalism—even in its greened version—is not compatible with all evolutionary theories, though it is compatible with some. The main requirement is that species as such should not change. Items below the species level (e.g., individuals) and above the species level (e.g., genera, families) may change and evolve, but not species themselves, if species are to do the quite definite sorts of metaphysical and logical work that Aristotelian philosophy calls on them to do. A "form," if it is to operate appropriately in Aristotelian logic and metaphysics, must either be or not be, all or none.[37] What fuzziness organisms admit must not obtain at this point. To insist on this feature of form is not at all to insist that no "characters" (in our modern sense) may change, or that there can be no morphological or other sorts of variation, or that there can be no vagueness or fuzziness. The point is that any cloudiness and variations that do obtain must not obtain within the ambit of ecological function. That is, the form—ecological function—must be, so long as we refer to this sort of creature, a constant.

Phyletic gradualism at the species level is destructive of anything one might appropriately style "Aristotelian." But punctuated equilibrium theory, not to mention more radically saltationist approaches, are perfectly compatible. More difficult is the question of species selection. And we must ask: if species are units of selection, must species play this role as undivided totalities? The question is ambiguous. In the current climate of debate, it seems natural to construe this query as the issue of whether species are individuals, whether they are historical, spatiotemporally bounded particulars, and whether they are "interactors" (in Hull's sense) that interface with the environment directly and as organic wholes. The view briefed here is plainly at odds with the species-as-individuals view, and yet I wish to suggest that the answer is affirmative: species form as ecological function is a unit of selection. In fact, since species form sums the being's adaptations and is the locus of interplay with its context, it is the very focus of selection.[38] Species form is, in different ways, "interactor" and "replicator" without inflating into a superindividual, geographically extensive whole and without reducing to particular individuals or a set of such individuals.

The ability of species form to occupy this dual role flows from an ambivalence that Aristotle insists on, an ambivalence that the best evidence to date suggests is still worth acknowledging. First, form is actual only when it is at work informing some concrete individual. It is the what-it-was-to-be, the *to ti en einai*, the active principle of activity that unites a being's parts and orients its operations. And yet, whenever one understands this form, one grasps its function (along with its associated sort of matter); hence, one will necessarily understand form as something generic. There is nothing general or universal or "common" in a living whole, and yet form is intelligible as general. This wolf's ecological function is formally the same as that conspecific wolf's, and yet it is the substance of just *this* wolf in particular.[39] This lets us make sense of the familiar notion that there can be many members of a single species without construing the relation of instance to species as a relation of part to whole and without taking species to be merely mental constructs, or sets (which do no ecological work). A species is not a set or collection—not a "heap" of individuals as the Stagirite would say. A species is not a property or a bundle of properties.[40] And yet it is not a large individual either. The effective determinant ("efficient cause") of this commonality is that species form, in conjunction with the generative parts of its associated matter, reproduces itself. Form, on the Aristotelian understanding, is replicator. (The details of Aristotle's own misunderstanding of this generative process are irrelevant; the point holds.) Selection amounts to differential success in the generation of ecological interactors. The greater the fitness of this ecological form as it interfaces with its environment, the greater its chances of successful reproduction. Form is interactor on the proposal sketched here, since it is at core the ecological function that expresses the organism's adaptations. Form as function is the very site of ecological interaction. Therefore, ecological form is replicator and interactor.

Second, the form is in some sense identical with the individual that is shaped by that form. Aristotle expresses this by saying that there is no otherness between me and my form. My form is essential to me; I could not in principle be another kind of being and remain "me." I am at my core identical with my essence; though I am not only an essence. My essence is not the whole of me. This is true of other living things. Essentialism was and remains problematic and controversial. If something like Aristotle's version is true,[41] however, we can make metaphysical sense of how I might be identical with my ecological function. If ecological function is directly subject to selective pressure, and if I am, in a certain way, identical with my function, then I am in this sense directly subject to selective pressures. Similarly, since to speak of a species is to speak of ecological form "on the whole," and since ecological form is directly subject to selective pressure, species are—rightly understood—directly subject to selection. I want to claim that species form is the primary site of selection. Ecological form is the self-active interactor and self-replicating replicator. It is the peculiar ambivalence of species form that lets a species be a unit of selection without inflating species into a superindividual *or* deflating it into a collection of individuals. A situated ecological function is only actual as individual, and yet the individual is more than its ecological function, and ecological function is more than any individual. The form, too, is rightly said to replicate itself and survive. Species form is the primary "interactor," since it is the situated function that is the very crux of selection.

The Double Role of Form and Evolution

"Every new species is an ecological experiment,"according to Mayr.[42] This suggests how one might think of evolution if, on an Aristotelian approach, form as such cannot change. The demand that form either be or not be is no bar to evolution so long as forms are ecological functions and ecological functions are discrete. Of course, Mayr's approach relies on patriation: According to Simpson, and Mayr following Simpson, "species consist of local populations, each adapted to its local environment, held together loosely by gene flow."[43] It follows, then, that "every species is an incipient new genus, every genus an incipient new family, and so forth."[44] The difference between these purportive levels is ecological and contextual. "The event that leads . . . to the development of a higher category is the occupation of a new adaptive zone. . . . [T]he broader the zone, the higher the category when fully developed; yet the new occupant when first entering the zone will hardly, if at all, differ from the parental population."[45] The reliance of the Aristotelian proposal on context implies neither strict continuity (I have agreed with Mayr that each species is a "discrete unit" separated from other species by a "bridgeless gap," though for different reasons), nor that the forging of evolutionary transitions—especially transitions across the broadest zones—is easy or common.

We have evidence of this in the infrequency of shifts from water to land habitats.[46] Consider natural heat. Epidermal armoring is required to resist drying and high levels of temperature variation; since water is eight hundred times heavier than air, locomotion on land requires more musculature, and ciliary locomotion is useless. Additionally, the excretory system must reduce water loss to a minimum; most water-ecotoned fauna have no need of this essential function. And, as is well known, there are great differences in the needs of respiration, sensory function, and so on, between land and water life forms. Between such diverse contexts, the small variations that Simpson claims to be typical are insufficient. In any case, it is the acquisition of a new structure that permits a new function that will open up a new adaptive zone: a significant evolutionary novelty is a fresh character that fits a new context.

Less dramatic shifts in ecological context require less formidable ecological virtues. "Individual species, genera, and families of many . . . phyla have gone on land, such as certain tubellarians, nemerteans, rotifers, ostracods, nematodes, oligochaets, land leeches. However, all of these are forced to live in a moist environment; none has succeeded in becoming truly terrestrial."[47] Preadaptations are typically prerequisite for such changes. For instance, "the adoption of internal fertilization in some branches of the amphibians and early reptiles . . . was an absolute prerequisite for a truly terrestrial existence. . . . The invention of mastication by some therapsid reptiles was perhaps the . . . invention that gave rise to the mammals."[48]

So even in the evolutionary picture, the Aristotelian dictum holds: "Nature makes the organ to suit the function not the function to suit the organ."[49] It is the ecological character, the principal part of species form, that is the crux of a clear evolutionary picture. Now, new characters and behavior patterns are not morphological and are not genetically transmitted, but functions, habits, and behaviors may have "morphological consequences" and may serve as preadaptations. That is, functions and functional habits are not transmitted, while morphology and structure are, yet this morphology is selected so far as it is a means to the end of a certain sort of behavior in context that serves an ecological function. (The morphology is encoded in the genome, but the behavior is too, as expressive of the selected epigenotype.) Mayr, at least, knows that function and behavior take precedence over structure.[50] In other words, if a new behavior adds to fitness, it will be selected for—not by any Lamarckian mechanism, but because it expresses an ecological virtue, a function that takes character to context and avoids extremes that are, in that context, destructive of ecological character and ecological community.

Structures may suffer transmutation in various ways. A structure may be modified by an intensification of function, by a change in proportion, fusion, losses, secondary duplications, and so on. If a structure can perform more than one function, and if one function can be duplicated or made contextually irrelevant, the operation of the organism can shift. Once the ecological function changes, whether or not the organism's structures remain the same or remain analogously the same, we have a different kind of organism. There is a new kind of organism when there is a new ecological function that serves as the dominant part of a novel species form. "Many primitive fishes . . . had two independent organs of respiration, gills and primitive lungs. . . . In the terrestrial tetrapods, the simple baglike lungs were connected into the highly complex respiratory organ of mammals and birds, and the gill arches and pouches into endocrine glands and accessory organs of the digestive system."[51] Again, on the account briefed here, such changes in function—whether or not the supportive structures change—contribute to changes in kind. A change in kind is, in the central case, a change in ecological function. Mayr asserts, "Cases of drastic changes of function of an organ are found in every phyletic line of animals. To give a complete catalogue would mean listing a good portion of all animal species."[52] Whether changes are produced in these or other ways, we can assert that species emerge when novel form/matter compounds appear. The nature or "essence" of a natural whole (this function [in this context] with this structured matter [with just this genealogy]) is its species form (this sort of ecological function in this sort of context plus this sort of structured matter encoding this genotype), and the nature or "essence" of this species form is the ecological function per se. Greening the Stagirite, I want to claim that this is primary *ousia* and the main locus of selective forces.

In sum, Aristotle already knew that fur, feathers, and scales had analogous functions. Ecologically refitted Aristotelians can attach these to the functions of natural wholes—something Aristotle was unable to do. And evolutionary-minded ecological thinkers can see that scales with time and selective pressure *become* functioning teeth, ovipositors *become* bees' stings, Daphnia antennae *become* working paddles, and arthropoidal legs *become* mouthparts in function. These functions of bodily parts contribute to the total ecological function of a living, natural whole. Whether we find a new structure with a new function or the same structure with new functions, we have the rudiments of a new kind of life form that will live, and live well. so long as its character is a virtue—that is, so long as its definitive good is a successful ecological function in context. This function is the "end," the definitive good of a being that is its active substance, as Aristotelians knew already; in evolutionary work, this ecological function is the primary object of selective forces and the sum of the creature's adaptations. Therefore the form of the being is the primary focus of selection,[53] as well as the genuine unit of the ontology of life science.

Epilogue

Most of this proposal—whether one considers it a "greening" of Aristotle or an Aristotelianizing of some current biology—requires little more than reorganization of contemporary theory. There are a few points, however, where some modification seems to be entrained and over which one ought to pause. Prominent among these points is a marginalizing of the soma–germ line distinction. That distinction appears in the model (see lower left side of table 8.1), but it is not central (either conceptually or figuratively). This is worrisome because it marginalizes at the same time the standard genotype-phenotype distinction that stands at the core of the received view. A few comments must suffice.

It was Weissman who, with the stroke of a single distinction in 1893, dealt a decisive blow to Lamarckianism and at the same time rescued natural selection from vicious circularity. He claimed that the germ line was separate from, and inviolable by, the soma (body). Insisting on complete functional separation means that somatic alterations cannot be transmitted and hence cannot contribute to evolution. It also means that we are not reduced to saying, of the mechanism of evolution, that selection is survival of the fittest and that the fittest organisms are the ones that survive. For we can add that selection obtains when the differential survival of bodies yields the differential survival of the germ line that produces the bodies. This is still circular, but perhaps not viciously so, thanks to the distinction. Weissman's division has come to be enshrined in the genotype/phenotype distinction that is part of the hard core of evolutionary biology (along with the Hardy-Weinberg equilibrium and a few other items). The problem is that the model proposed here hints at a more flexible relation between soma and germ than Weissman's dogma suggests. So where do things stand with Weissman today?

Plainly, genetic sequestering does not obtain where no nuclear boundary holds. Thus, Weissmann's doctrine cannot hold for prokaryotes. And with advanced eukaryotes, the nuclear envelope disintegrates in meiosis, so the nuclear material becomes subject to an increased number of chemical—especially enzymatic—forces. D'Amato has noticed that Weissman's theory does not hold, strictly speaking, for plants; regeneration phenomena show that the soma can produce its own germ line.[55] Buss points out that sequestering of the germ line from the soma is limited to the animal kingdom.[56] Moreover, for many invertebrates, regenerating cells originate in the somatocytes, so Weissman's theory fails to hold with anything like the requisite strictness.[57] Because of the existence of conditions that favor the induction by the soma of genetic changes in vertebrates, Lima-de-Faria (a chromosomal biologist and prominent anti-Darwinian) goes so far as to say that genetic sequestering does not hold for vertebrates, either: environmental factors can control the action of the soma on the germ line.

One need not go so far to see that Weissmann's foundation is showing cracks. A number of recent workers have begun to appreciate this cracking of a longstanding conviction,[58] but I have seen no discussion of how the breakup—or at least decentralizing—of Weissmann's sequester might affect the genotype-phenotype distinction (which these same authors retain as central) or the circularity problem. Hull's beautiful and much quoted definition of selection ("a process in which the differential extinction and proliferation of interactors cause the differential perpetuation of the relevant replicators")[59] turns quietly on Weissman's dogma without comment.

The contributions of the Aristotelian model to this difficulty are:

1. The distinction is decentralized. It still holds when it holds—as it seems to at least for vertebrates, *pace* Lima-de-Faria—but not so much is made to turn on it.

2. The model shows why it is not the case that gene is to soma as form is to matter (pace Mayr, who follows Max Delbrück in construing DNA as the "unmoved mover" and *eidos* of an organism). Ecological function is instead the crux.

3. Unity: ecological form is the unifying function that focuses and unites a number of material parts. It is, as Aristotle says, the "form of the body." It holds individuals together as individuals, even though it is only identical with an individual in a sense. Ecological form reproduces itself in context, though it is only indirectly yoked to a particular genic sequence. Ecological form interacts with the environment and is the locus of selection, though it is not the only "unit of selection."

4. The model is a remedy for misplaced concreteness. The genetic code is not the final concretum for life science; neither are populations.; neither are individuals nominalistically construed. Ecosystems are not full-fledged entities (though as contexts they have unities and integrities of their own), and species are not large individuals, according to the theory. Ecological function is the single concrete source of a number of analytical strands that appear in the different branches of biology: at ecological form, species and individual, genealogy and economy, the "codical domain" and the "material domain" (Williams) intersect. It precedes these strands as the concrete precedes the abstract.

9

Self-Love and the Virtue of Species Preservation in Aristotle

Richard Shearman

In a recent collection of articles entitled *Eight Little Piggies*, Stephen Jay Gould gave us in the article "The Golden Rule" his perspective on what should constitute the basis for an environmental ethic.[1] As can be gathered from the article's title, he believes that the most effective approach to preserving environmental integrity must involve some form of enlightened self-interest to guide our behavior within the natural world that derives from the principle commonly stated as "do unto others as you would have them do unto you." The others in this case would include other species of life on Earth, and not just the human variety.

The occasion for Gould's article was apparently the debate surrounding the construction of several telescopes under the auspices of the University of Arizona on a portion of habitat occupied by the Mount Graham red squirrel. The difficulty in making the case for protecting the red squirrel emerges from its status as a subspecies *(Tamiasciurus hudsonicus grahamensis)* and not a distinct species in and of itself. Thus the question that emerges is how to justify the preservation of an organism fully capable of interbreeding with other red squirrels within the species *Tamiasciurus hudsonicus* (assuming, of course, that building the telescopes would truly threaten the Mount Graham red squirrel with extinction). In other words, what reasons can we muster to prevent the construction of the telescopes in favor of the Mount Graham red squirrel that can surmount concerns pertaining to its taxonomic status?

Gould gives us two reasons to side with the squirrel that trace back to his conception of the Golden Rule. The first refers to the uniqueness of the Mount Graham red. Although it is not a distinct species of squirrel, it is a unique subspecies within what Gould describes as an important species. The uniqueness of the Mount Graham red squirrel derives from its being an isolated subspecies living at the margins of the species range.

It therefore elicits a great deal of scientific interest among those who study evolutionary biology because the conditions of its existence appear to be moving it toward eventual reproductive isolation from the parent species and thus toward becoming a fully separate species of squirrel in its own right.

The second reason does not concern the squirrel itself but rather the value of the habitat within which the squirrel resides. According to Gould, by saving the Mount Graham red squirrel, we may also be saving "a rare and precious habitat of extraordinary evolutionary interest" since it is a remnant patch of a previously more extensive and continuous biogeographical province. It is quite literally an island of Nearctic habitat within a sea of Neotropical desert that was made possible by the perpetuation of a Nearctic microclimate (the red squirrel's habitat) at the higher altitudes found on Mount Graham. Consequently, what makes the site valuable to both squirrels and astronomers is its altitude. For an astronomer, high altitude usually means less atmospheric interference in the attempt to study the heavens. For the Mount Graham red squirrel, it means the availability of suitable habitat that normally would have been eliminated as the Nearctic retreated northward had there not been suitably high mountains that could accommodate the concomitant retreat upwards.

Although it is not my task here to enter into the squirrel-versus-telescope debate or to examine the environmental ethic of Stephen Jay Gould, I do want to examine Gould's rationale for justifying the preservation of the Mount Graham red squirrel (and I presume of other species and uniquely interesting subspecies), since it is concerned with the broader question of why we ought to preserve environmental integrity in general and species diversity in particular. Two characteristics of Gould's article attracted my attention. The first was his rationale for preserving the Mount Graham red squirrel and its habitat. If I understand Gould's argument correctly, the primary justification he gives for preserving both the squirrel and its habitat is based ultimately on their scientific interest. They are valuable, and thus ought to be preserved, because they are inherently interesting as objects of scientific study. A world without the Mount Graham red squirrel or its habitat (or both) would be a scientifically less meaningful place.

The second (related) characteristic deals with his suggestion that an environmental ethic should be derived from enlightened self-interest. Beyond concerns for satisfying our resource needs, the overall implication of this kind of argument is that the scientific examination of the natural world is perhaps not only interesting in itself but also is in our best interest. In other words, we are somehow made better as human beings in the attempt to understand the world around us. And if we behave in a way that diminishes the opportunity to study the natural world or the level of understanding we may have achieved in understanding the natural world (were it not for the destruction of species or habitats), then our lives are somehow made less good.

I do not take Gould to be articulating a particularly unique argument for preserving nature, nor does it appear to be anything new. Gould is capturing what I perceive to be a common theme among those who are engaged in the scientific study of nature, and perhaps especially among conservation biologists and the like, that articulates the idea that the destruction of the natural world for whatever reason precludes human beings from achieving a scientific understanding of how the world works, which is considered to be an inherently good activity.[2] But can we legitimately claim that the scientific investigation of nature leading to an understanding of natural phenomena is a morally good thing to do, and that this can be used in an effort to justify the preservation of biological diversity, as Gould implies?

In this essay I want to examine how the scientific investigation of nature has been meaningfully linked with achieving a good human life and how this embodies a justification for the preservation of species diversity. To do this, I will draw from the philosophy of Aristotle, who perhaps as much as anyone else in the Western tradition attempted to establish the legitimacy of the biological sciences and their relationship to human well-being. But beyond that, I want to indicate how I think Aristotle can be interpreted as saying that we may have good reason to preserve species diversity in a way that goes beyond any consideration of self-interest, at least as that term is commonly understood.

The Life of Contemplation and the Contemplation of Life

As I understand him, Aristotle held that there were two ways that one could lead a good life.[3] The first was to live according to the ethical virtues as represented by the political life. The second was to live according to the theoretical virtues as represented by the life of a philosopher-scientist. As ethically virtuous or political beings, we can become happy only in a secondary way. We will not achieve what Aristotle refers to as "complete happiness," but we will be living a life that is at least an approximation of the kind of activity that makes for complete happiness.[4] On the other hand, as philosophically virtuous or contemplative beings, we can become completely happy, because we will be living a life that is as close as we can get to the absolute standard of happiness (represented by the eternal contemplative activity of God).[5]

At the base of each kind of life is a commitment to excellence that involves living in a manner that is either best for a human to lead (i.e., ethically virtuous) or simply best (i.e., philosophically virtuous). Since contemplative activity is happiness in the absolute, then a human life devoted to such activity was considered by Aristotle to be the best kind of life that humans could hope to attain. An ethical life, while good in itself, can never realize the level of happiness possible for the life of contemplation. Curiously, Aristotle appears to be saying that through contemplation we can transcend the strictly human life as mortal beings and live the life that is happiness *simpliciter*. In other words, we can live the same kind of life that God does, which is a life of pure happiness.[6]

To understand this line of reasoning, it is important to appreciate the teleological foundation of Aristotle's philosophy. With respect to living beings, all life was viewed as an effort to actualize form, or to realize their true nature. Growth and development of an organism, for example, was explained in terms of the end for the sake of which it occurred—a mature and normally active organism. This makes the world full of potentiality and actuality corresponding to the extent form has been realized.[7] Since Aristotle believed that the true nature of human beings was to live a life according to the theoretical virtues (i.e, the life of contemplation),[8] human form can also exist at different levels of actuality as manifested by the extent to which the desire to know or understand the world has been satisfied. And it is only by actively contemplating the "why" of things in the world that we come to fully realize our niche as a natural being by satisfying our desire to know[9] and live the life that is happiest.[10]

The possibility of having knowledge about the world is realized by the world's ultimate intelligibility. Unlike other species, humans are capable of understanding how and why the world works. But to understand the world, we must first make the effort to experience it through observation and study as part of natural philosophy.[11] Herein lies the importance, from a metaphysical perspective, of environmental integrity, at least with respect to the preservation of biodiversity. Without sensible things in the world existing in a way dictated by their nature, it becomes impossible for us to understand the world adequately and thus satisfy our desire to know—the basis for complete happiness.

In studying the world around us, we are engaged in an activity that will give us the wisdom to understand the "why" of things. By doing so, not only will we come to recognize the world's wonderful character, but also we come to recognize who we are as human beings. This is an important point that should not be overlooked, because it is only in our scientific encounters with the natural world that it is made intelligible; and by making it intelligible, we realize our fullest potential as a product of nature. As Lear puts it, through the study of the natural world we come to satisfy the desire to understand—which, through the eternal contemplation of God, constitutes reality. In a meaningful way, human life can be said to be as rich as the world is diverse.[12]

Given that Aristotle associated human well-being with an ability to render the world intelligible by inquiring into the development of life through the observation and scientific study of nature, then I think it is evident why a degraded or diminished natural environment would have been a source of significant concern to him. For by diminishing our ability to encounter the variety of species to be found in the world living according to their nature, we are diminishing our ability to understand the world and thus to become happy.

Biophilia

I also interpret Aristotle to be implying that we as human beings may have good reason to sacrifice our interests for the sake of the nonhuman world.[13] I would therefore like to go beyond the "enlightened self-interest" type of environmental ethic advocated by Gould and begin to consider how Aristotle's metaphysics can lead us to consider the well-being of other species in a way that is not limited to their perceived instrumental value. Since I have not found that Aristotle himself explored such a possibility, I will necessarily be engaged in an extrapolation of Aristotle's ideas based upon my own understanding of his overall philosophical program, particularly of his discussion of friendship and self-love found in chapters 8 and 9 of the *Nicomachean Ethics*.

If there is to be a basis for human moral responsibility toward the nonhuman natural world, then I think we must look to Aristotle's account of how various moral relationships among unequals are to be acquitted, given his belief that nature is hierarchically organized. As a general rule, Aristotle argues that unequals should render in honor or benefits what is in proportion to their superiority or inferiority to each other.[14] Although he was primarily, if not exclusively, concerned with the equality or inequality of human relationships, his formula appears to be applicable at all levels of existence. He says, for example, that honors are to be paid to the gods (and parents) in virtue of our indebtedness to them, for they have given us the gift of life, a gift that we can never adequately repay.[15] If we can also have a good reason to behave in a morally appropriate way to the nonhuman world (other than God) in proportion to what it is due (if it is due anything), then how would this be derived and manifested?

I would like to offer the following speculative outline as a framework for conceiving our moral relationship to other species as members of the biotic community. I want simply to broaden the horizons that Aristotle developed in his discussion of the human good in society. In a sense, I am attempting to accomplish the same task that Leopold set for himself in developing the land ethic in terms of biotic citizenship.[16] Although Leopold maintained that human beings were but plain members and citizens of the biotic community, an Aristotelian approach would surely not be so egalitarian, given the hierarchical arrangement Aristotle perceived to be the order of life. Yet it is clear to me that he considered human beings to be members of a much larger community than that of the polis. We may be political animals and naturally gregarious, but we are animals nonetheless. Our existence goes beyond the confines of society and is inextricably embedded in the broader natural environment.[17]

In our dealings with other people, our obligations seem to be fairly straightforward insofar as we have much in common. But in our dealings with other species or ecosystems, the matter gets somewhat more complicated, as there are many different species embodying different levels of association in various forms of ecological communities. Clearly, our relationship to nonhuman life would not be defined in the same terms as for God or virtuous human beings, but I would argue that there is a basis in Aristotle's moral philosophy for according at least some moral consideration to the rest of the world. My claim will draw upon two Aristotelian assumptions or principles: (1) all life embodies an element of the divine either as a part (i.e., an individual organism) or as a systematic whole (i.e., a species, ecosystem, or cosmos), making it inherently valuable; and (2) contributing to the common good is an important aspect of human virtue.

With respect to the first factor, Aristotle maintains that life is an expression of desire for God in that the prior actuality of form is realized through divine contemplation.[18] Form, in turn, is both the cause of change for living things and the end for the sake of which all living things exist.[19] Without going into detail, let me just assert that I interpret Aristotle to be claiming that in the effort to realize their form at its highest level of actuality, all living beings are drawn toward self-understanding. However, self-understanding is beyond the capacity of most animals because they lack an intellectual faculty. Human beings alone among perishable creatures of form and matter are blessed with mind and are therefore able to engage in rational activity. This was the basis for Aristotle's claims that human beings are potentially superior to other species of life on Earth and that no other creature can ever partake in happiness.

In his discussion of self-love Aristotle clearly states that it is understanding that the self-lover loves most of all, because it more than anything else is "self," being the authoritative and better part of all human beings.[20] So when Aristotle speaks of loving one's self, he is not referring to a selfish or strictly egoistic conception of personal worth. Rather, he is defining the human self in terms of its true nature or form. Therefore, to be a self-lover is to love one's understanding (which is shared among all virtuous human beings) and not one's discrete organismic self.

Yet Aristotle also indicates that understanding is a divine activity, surpassing anything of value in the purely human realm:

> If mind is divine, then, in comparison with man, the life according to it is divine in comparison with human life. But we must not follow those who advise us, being men, to think of human things, and being mortal, of mortal things, but must, so far as we can, make ourselves immortal, and strain every nerve to live in accordance with the best thing in us; for even if it be small in bulk, much more does it in power and worth surpass everything.[21]

This leads to the curious perspective that the peculiarly human life is one that is not really human at all. To fulfill our nature, we must actually transcend it to live a life that is divine. Self-understanding is therefore not so much an understanding of the human self as it is of the divine self. So it is that when we love our self most of all, we are not loving something that is unique to human life—we are loving something that moves all things, including all other species in life (i.e., we express biophilia).

That there is a divine element in all other living things is indicated in Aristotle's defense of his biological studies:

> We . . . must not recoil with childish aversion from the examination of the humbler animals. Every realm of nature is marvelous: and as Heraclitus, when the strangers who came to visit him found him warming himself at the furnace in the kitchen and hesitated to go in, is reported to have bidden them not to be afraid to enter, *as even in that kitchen divinities were present*, so we should venture on the study of every kind of animal without distaste; for each and all will reveal to us something natural and something beautiful.[22] (Emphasis mine.)

On my reading, Aristotle is claiming that all living things embody something divine. Although other living things may not have the capacity to engage in rational activity, there is still something of the divine present in them. This, I think, is a reflection of his conclusion that all life is both dependent upon, and expresses a desire for, God in that all living things strive to partake of the divine insofar as they are able.[23] For most of life on Earth this involves activities like nutrition and reproduction that seek to ensure the perpetuation of the species. Through such activities, mortal beings are assured of eternal existence "not as the self-same individual but . . . in something like itself—not numerically but specifically one,"[24] by continuing the species.

I also interpret Aristotle to be saying that the order of the world as a whole is an expression of desire for God. This is brought out in the *Metaphysics* where he says that all things are connected and share for the good of the whole.[25] And in the *Nicomachean Ethics* he says that all things, whether a man, a city, or any other systematic whole, are identified with the most authoritative element within them.[26] Since reality is constituted by God's actively thinking the world as a whole, then understanding must be the authoritative element that defines existence as such. And since a self-lover loves his understanding most of all, can he not also love the rest of the world that is the manifestation of God's understanding?

I think we have reason to answer in the affirmative, for self-love does not ultimately involve a love of self in an egoistic sense, nor is it a love of human life in an anthropocentric sense. Rather, self-love embodies an active and loving regard toward God insofar as God's thinking the world is the basis for reality. A true self-lover is one who loves the element within himself or herself that is both authoritative and divine. Since all friends of good character not only share, but are guided by, this same element, then we can meaningfully say that a friend is another self. And when we act on our friends' behalf for their own sake or for no other reason than that they should benefit, then we are also acting in a way consistent with self-love.

As previously indicated, understanding is not only the cause of human growth and development (since all men by nature desire to know) and that for the sake of which growth and development occur (since perfect happiness consists in contemplation), but it is also the force that moves all living things. It is for this reason that Aristotle refers to God as the unmoved mover, for God moves things without also being moved. Aristotle is not implying that God created the world or that the cosmos is God's handiwork. Rather, life is sustained by God's thinking the world and is a response to that thinking that has existed eternally. It is God's understanding that establishes the prior actuality of all living things, from part to whole, and serves as both the end of existence and the cause of movement. Even though other living beings are incapable of contemplation (and therefore of happiness), their growth and development are nonetheless driven by the same desire that motivates human beings to live virtuously. It must be the case, then, that all uncorrupted living beings embody some measure of the divine self that forms the basis of friendship. And if this is true, then there is no reason to believe that we cannot also be expected to express some level of friendly feeling or love toward nonhuman nature in a manner appropriate to the circumstances. The implication of this interpretation is that our love for understanding can encompass a love for all things fulfilling their nature from the least appealing of individual creatures to the world as a whole, insofar as each is good.[27]

The goodness of nature traces back to the objective goodness found in the world both as a systematic whole and as embodied in individual organisms. Aristotle clearly locates the basis for the goodness found in the world as a whole in God and the order that God brings to the world:

> We must consider also in which of two ways the nature of the universe contains the good or the highest good, whether as something separate and by itself, or as the order of the parts. Probably in both ways, as the army does. For the good is found both in the order and in the leader, and more in the latter; for he does not depend on the order but it depends on him. *And all things are ordered together somehow, but not all alike—both fishes and fowls and plants; and the world is not such that one thing has nothing to do with another, but they are connected.* For all are ordered together to one end . . . all share for the good of the whole.[28] (Emphasis mine.)

The order of the world is brought to it by God in the same way that a leader brings order to an army. In this description of the goodness of the universe, we encounter the ultimate relationship of part to whole. In the same way that an individual human is defined in terms of his or her relationship to the polis, all other beings are ordered together and defined in terms of their relationship to the whole universe made possible by God. It is this relationship of part to whole that commits Aristotle to giving priority to environmental integrity considered as a systematic whole over that of any subordinate part, whether as an individual or a member of a community.

All things are ultimately dependent upon God because it is through God's thinking that the actuality of existence is secured. By thinking the world as a whole, God is giving actuality to the world as a whole because God thinking *is* the world. That is why Aristotle referred to God as a living being:

And life also belongs to God; for the actuality of thought is life, and God is that actuality; and God's essential actuality is life most good and eternal. We say therefore that God is a living being, eternal, most good, so that life and duration continuous and eternal belong to God; for this *is* God.[29]

Therein lies the basis for Aristotle's claim that the world is a good place. It is objectively good for "life [that is God] is most good and eternal." To have life is to share in the goodness of God.

With respect to the second factor, Aristotle indicates that what is good and pleasant in itself is also good for the virtuous human being.[30] That is why he said that we should have friends. Since Aristotle considered all life to be good and pleasant in itself, then it would seem to be desirable for the good man to associate with. Friends and other living beings are desirable in part because being conscious of things good in themselves is also inherently good and pleasant.

At a more basic level of instrumentality, I take Aristotle to be implying that we should be concerned with maintaining environmental integrity, for life itself is a prerequisite for the good life. We value our existence and find life to be pleasurable and good in itself. But being perishable beings, we must equip ourselves with all the external goods that are necessary not just for living but for living well. An important point Aristotle emphasizes is that none of our needs can be met in abstraction from our environmental circumstances.[31] We are utterly dependent upon what nature provides to even have a hope of achieving happiness, whether our concern is directed toward what Aristotle refers to as goods of the body, goods of the soul, or external goods.[32]

Beyond any instrumental consideration we may actually have toward the nonhuman world, I think it would not be unreasonable to act on its behalf for its own sake without expecting anything in return. Annas interprets Aristotle as saying that we are equipped with feelings of affinity for ourselves and for our offspring, and after the development of reason, we come to extend concern toward others.[33] Although our concern for the well-being of nonhumans may be based, at least initially, more on instinct than reason, our concern can also be explained and defended rationally. In the same way that mothers love their offspring and make sacrifices for them for their own sake, even if their love is not returned, we can also make sacrifices for the sake of nonhuman beings that are the objects of our beneficence and cannot consciously give anything in return.

The cause of such action is rooted in the nature of our existence. According to Aristotle, we are willing to make sacrifices for others because we choose and love the virtuous life.[34] Since a virtuous life is constituted by activity and is in a sense productive of itself, then we love the things we do according to virtue irrespective of the utilitarian value it may generate. In other words, virtuous activity is its own reward because it is the good life and a source of greater pleasure than actions aimed at personal utility. It is from this perspective that Aristotle concludes that mothers may be willing to sacrifice their personal happiness for the sake of their children's prosperity, even if their children give them nothing in return.[35] Within this conception, we can be beneficent to the nonhuman world as an aspect of contributing to the common good without expecting honor in return, given our desire to live in accordance with virtue and keeping in mind that this desire is ultimately derived from the broader environmental context within which the good life is pursued (i.e., a good life is dependent upon a good or sustainable environment).

If it is true that the good of the whole takes precedence over the good of the part, and therefore the good of the environmental context of our existence takes precedence over the good of any component part (including human beings), then I believe there is reason to consider the possibility that human beings may be motivated to sacrifice personal or collective well-being if by doing so they act to sustain the conditions for happiness. Such a situation would arise, for example, if human beings were to live in a way that eroded or threatened the ability to acquire natural resource goods necessary for life or that diminished the ability to encounter other species necessary for the good human life. Virtuous people would be motivated to protect the integrity of the environment because they know that by doing so, they would be protecting the conditions for happiness or self-understanding, without which personal happiness would be unattainable.

Conclusion

Julia Annas stated that the concept of self-love is basic to Aristotle's ethics, rather than peripheral, and that it cannot be restricted to the discussion of friendship.[36] I think her conclusion is quite right, but perhaps it does not go far enough. As I interpret Aristotle's broader philosophical program, I am led to believe that self-love pervades his thinking in all subjects and not just his ethics. Once we realize that self-love is really a love of understanding, then we can begin to grasp the fundamental role it plays in Aristotle's life and thought. I think we can also begin to appreciate why there is a basis in the Aristotelian tradition to be concerned for the welfare of nonhuman beings for their own sake and why we should be willing to do more than exhibit goodwill for the rest of the natural world, even if that means self-sacrifice either as individuals or as a species.

Today we are witnessing the mass extinction of a significant percentage of the world's flora and fauna primarily because of habitat destruction. Although extinction is the eventual fate of all species, the current rate of extinction is many times faster than the normal background rate. In the tropical rain forests alone, the rate may translate into approximately 50,000 species each year, or about 140 species per day.[37] The majority of these species are invertebrates, or what may be described as ignoble creatures; this perhaps explains the relative lack of concern about their demise among most people. Yet, if Aristotle is to be believed, perhaps even they should be respected as a source of wonder and beauty and considered worthy of our efforts to preserve them as a part of human virtue.

10

The Organic Unity of Aristotle's World

Mohan Matthen

Aristotle and the Environment: A Puzzle

A ristotle was very much aware of the changeability of the earth. He spoke of this, for example, in *Meteorology (Mete.)* 1.14, where the subject is the alternation of land and sea, one encroaching on the other, and the "aging" of some parts of the earth. "Because these changes take place in periods of time much longer than our lives, they escape our notice; whole races (*ethnoi*) are destroyed before they can record the process from beginning to end" (*Mete.* 351b8–12, adapted from Lee).[1]

Nevertheless, he said, it is known that Egypt is a deposit of the Nile and that the same sort of thing has happened in Greece, too, for:

> [i]n the time of the Trojan Wars, the Argive land was marshy and could only support a small population, whereas the land of Mycenae was in good condition (and for this reason Mycenae was the superior). But now the opposite is the case; . . . the land of Mycenae has become completely dry and barren, while the Argive land that was formerly barren owing to the water has now become fruitful. Now the same process that has taken place in this small district must be supposed to be going on over whole countries and on a large scale. (352a10–16, Webster)

He knew that these great changes can affect the environment to the point where whole races are destroyed, and he knew even that humans can affect their own environments adversely:

> One of the kings [of Egypt] tried to make a canal to [the Red Sea] (for it would have been of no little advantage to them for the whole region to have become navigable; Sesostris is said to have been the first of the ancient kings to try), but he found that the sea was higher than the land. So he first, and

Darius afterwards, stopped making the canal, lest the sea should mix with the river water and spoil it. (352b24–30, Webster)

All the same, Aristotle was no environmentalist. He showed little concern for the balance of nature being disturbed by environmental events, and he emphatically denied that the changes just mentioned constitute a threat to the natural world order:

> Men whose outlook is narrow suppose the cause of such events to be change in the universe, in the sense of a coming to be of the world as a whole. Hence they say that the sea is being dried up and is growing less, because this is observed to have happened in more places now than formerly. . . . But it is absurd to make the universe to be in process because of small changes of brief duration, when the bulk and size of the earth are surely as nothing in comparison with the whole world. (352a17–28, slightly modified from Webster)

> If the universe is eternal, the same must be true of the sea. Anyone who thinks like Democritus that the sea is diminishing reminds us of Aesop's tales. . . . Whatever made the sea remain at first. . . . clearly the same thing must make it persist for ever. (356b9–20, slightly modified from Webster)

Perhaps this attitude is unsurprising. In Aristotle's time, it was plausible to regard the environmental depradations of humans as "small changes of brief duration," at least when measured by the scale of the earth. Even natural disasters such as earthquakes, floods, and the fall of meteorites, cited in the *Meteorology* and the pseudo-Aristotelian *De Mundo* as evidence of the instability and ontological (or even axiological) inferiority of the earth, did not persuade Aristotle to give up the belief in the ultimate stability of even the sublunary world order. As the *De Mundo* puts it, comparing God with the leaders of cities:

> So it is, we must suppose, with that greater city, the cosmos.[2] God is a law to us, impartial and admitting no correction or change; he is surely a more stable law than those inscribed on tablets. Under his motionless and harmonious guidance all the orderly arrangement of heaven and earth is administered, extending over all things through the seed proper to their kind, to plants and animals by genus and species. (*De Mundo* 400b27–401a1, Furley)

Aristotle does not think that plant and animal species are mutable. Just like the universe and its features, they persist forever, having had, moreover, no beginning in time. Nevertheless, Aristotle did share some of the attitudes of contemporary environmentalists. Today, it is typical for environmentally unconcerned people (nonenvironmentalists, as I shall call them) to evince a localist way of assessing environmental impact. They assume that, in general, the condition of one part of the world is organically unconnected with that of any other: kill this sort of noxious insect off and you will experience a more pleasant garden dining experience; emit large amounts of oxidized carbon and you will get smoggier atmospheric conditions—but is that not worth the money saved by omitting expensive emission controls? Since these changes do not affect the world at large, as nonenvironmentalists believe, they can be evaluated in isolation.

Opposed to such localism, environmentalists tend to think holistically. Damaging one part of the environment disturbs self-regulating cycles in that environment and thus proliferates destruction that generally turns out to be of much greater magnitude than the original damage. They think of the world as something like an organic unity, in which damage to one part constitutes damage to the whole, and hence to every other part. Consequently, it is characteristic of many environmentalist approaches to emphasize properties of the environment as a whole, and to be antireductionist with regard to these properties. (The Gaia hypothesis is an extreme of this, as we shall see later.)

The passages quoted above seem to put Aristotle into the nonenvironmentalist, perhaps even the localist, camp. Events that bring about the demise of races are but "small changes of brief duration"; viewed from the perspective of the heaven, they do not really make a difference. Aristotle was no localist, however. What I want to bring out in this essay is that, on the contrary, Aristotle regarded the universe as an organic whole, and even as something akin to an organism or living body. Consequently, he is in agreement with the antireductionists in the environmentalist camp.

This stands the whole question of Aristotle's environmental attitudes on its head. Once we appreciate the ways in which Aristotle thinks of the world as a single organic whole, we should be surprised by how little he emphasizes the proliferating effects of events in one part of the world and puzzled by the localism of his treatment of environmental changes. If Aristotle is as much a holist as I shall try to make him out to be, how is it that he is so much a localist as well? I shall return to this question toward the end of this essay and try to show how, given Aristotle's orientation toward the problems of explaining the universe, he arrives at the thesis of cosmic imperturbability that we have encountered.

This display of lack of concern for the environment by a holist is instructive. While the relatively insignificant impact of human activities is

a factor here, it is not the only one. I shall argue that holism is not sufficient for environmental sensitivity: something more is required. What
needs to be added to holism is perhaps surprising. It is a kind of reduc-
tionism that is present (I argue) in even the most holistic forms of contemporary ecology (e.g., the Gaia hypothesis) but wholly absent from
Aristotle. Aristotle is a nonenvironmentalist because his holism is not
"bottom-up."

The Universe: A Single Hylomorphic Substance

In Aristotle's ontology, natural substances such as plants or animals possess form and matter—they are, to use the jargon, "hylomorphic" com-
plexes. For our present purposes, the importance of this hylomorphism is
that the properties of such substances are not simply inherited from the
materials of which they are made; for in addition to any characteristics they
might possess as a result of their material constitution, they have, in addition, "system-level properties," which are not merely results of this constitution. An animal, for instance, may possess a rigid body because it has a
skeleton made of bone. But its ability to perceive and move around is a consequence, not of its material constitution, but of its nature as a whole, that
is, its form. (In fact, even the fact that it has a bony skeleton is a consequence of this form, but that is something that need not concern us here.)

In the early chapters of *De Caelo*, Aristotle establishes the basis of his
science of the universe. My aim in this section is to show how in these passages he is committed to a conception of the universe as a hylomorphic
complex, governed as a whole by laws that are not reducible to laws concerning its parts.[3] The argument of *De Caelo* 1.1–4 is a sketch of a demonstration of the existence and properties of the starry element, commonly
known as ether, and of the sublunary elements considered as parts of the
totality. (Aristotle's name for the universe in these passages is literally
translated "The All," which I render as the "the totality.")

Properly speaking, such a demonstration ought to be set out in the
axiomatic form prescribed in the *Posterior Analytics (APo.)*, but here
Aristotle is content to gesture in the direction of such a presentation. The
starting points of any demonstration include principles, known as theses,
that are proprietary to the subject matter being investigated, in this case
the totality, or universe. These theses divide into definitions, which do not
assert that anything is the case but merely identify and demarcate the subject domain, and hypotheses, which make assertions about the domain
thus demarcated (*APo.*1.2.72a18–24). The definitions that demarcate the

subject matter of Aristotle's cosmology are found in *De Caelo* 1.1. Here we find a definition of the totality preceded by definitions of "body" and "a body." Since the totality is understood by contrast with "a body," let us consider these definitions in sequence.

First, body:

> What is divisible into what is forever divisible is continuous, and body is what is divisible in every way. Magnitude is of these kinds: line is what is divisible in one direction, plane is divisible in two directions, and body is divisible in three directions. (*De Caelo* 268a6–8)

Body, then, is not just continuous, but continuous in all three directions. This makes it complete:

> It is clear that there is no progression to some other type, as there is from length to plane, and to body from plane, for in that case this kind of magnitude would not be complete since necessarily every advance is in respect of some defect, and it is not possible for the complete to be defective: for it is in every way. (268a30–b5)

Lines and planes do not exist concretely, but only in the mind of someone abstracting them out of body. Body, on the other hand, is something fully real. The relationship of line to plane and plane to body is one of dimensional completion; the magnitude with fewer dimensions exists only by abstraction from a magnitude with more and depends on the latter (and on the mind of the person who performs the abstraction) for the existence that it does possess. Since body exists concretely, it lacks for nothing that gives it existence; it stands in no need of dimensional completion.

As defined here, body is not an individual thing; rather it is indefinite extension. Individuals are determinate parts of this indefinite extension. They are carved out of indefinite extension in two ways.

First, bodies "in the form of a part" are spatial subregions of indefinite extension, which are "made determinate by contact with what is close to [them]" (268b5–7)—in effect by their place (which for Aristotle is the inner surface of what contains a thing). Here Aristotle is speaking of individual bodies—this body, a body, or bodies in the plural—as distinct from "body." These are defined by reference to the things they touch—in effect, by their spatial contours. Body is simply a mass; bodies are discrete individuals. Bodies possess a modicum of form; volume is a function of a body's spatial boundaries, for instance, rather than of its material composition. In this sense, volume is a "system property." But understood merely as spatially demarcated extensions, bodies have very few system-level properties. In particular, they have no intrinsic unity, unity that is a consequence of the way in which they are organized into a system. The unity they possess comes from the outside, they are divisible simply by imposing new boundaries, and so individual bodies are divisible into other individual bodies. Pointing at an individual body, one might as well be pointing at the many parts that arise from such division: "in a sense, they are many," Aristotle says (268b7–8).[4]

Second, bodies with intrinsic form are to be distinguished from these partial bodies. Animals are individual, not simply because they are externally demarcated, but because their parts work together to produce actions of the whole: nutrition, movement, and so on. It is this unity of functioning, rather than any spatial boundaries, that consititutes their individuality; and for this reason, animals are not divisible into other animals. (In general, no part of an animal is an animal.) Animals are indeed bodies, because they do have spatial boundaries, but they have form other than that which demarcates them from a greater mass.

In *De Caelo* 1.1, the universe is defined by contrast with bodies in the form of a part. Thus, like animals, the totality has intrinsic form: "The totality of which these things [i.e. bodies in form of a part] are parts is necessarily complete, and, as the name indicates, it is so in every way—i.e. it is not complete in one way, incomplete in another" (268b8–10).

The form of the totality is, simply, completeness: "Everything, the totality, and the complete do not differ from one another in form, but if at all then in their matter and that of which they are said" (268a20–22). All three terms mentioned at the start of this sentence say the same thing but say it of different subject matters. "Everything" is usually applied contextually to some limited domain of individuals, and "complete" to the entirety of some limited collection or mass. The term "totality," however, is understood to apply without any such implicit or explicit restriction. As the contrast with partial bodies implies, the totality is simply all the body there is.

The totality is obviously not a partial body—it is not "complete in one way, incomplete in another," but rather complete in every way. It is bounded—Aristotle insists in *Physics* 3.5–8 and *De Caelo* 1.5–7 that the totality of body cannot be infinitely extended. Nevertheless, it is not "made determinate by contact with what is close to it," as partial bodies are, since there is nothing outside itself with which it could come into contact. Thus the form that it has is not imposed from outside but is intrinsic to itself. The fact that the universe is all the body that there is, is what constitutes it as an individual thing, and there is no part of the totality that shares its form and structure: "We are not compelled to assert a plurality of worlds. Such a plurality is indeed impossible if this world is made from the entirety of matter, just as it is" (*De Caelo* 1.9.278a25–28).

From this definition, certain system-level properties of the universe are supposed to follow: its constitution as a system of elements—the sublunary elements that move up and down, and the eternally rotating starry substance (*De Caelo* 1.2–4), its boundedness (1.5–7), its unity (1.8–9) and its eternity (1.10–12).

Aristotle's conception of the totality as complete might strike us today as nothing more than a clever verbal maneuver. He insists that since the universe is perceptible, it must be a hylomorphic complex (1.9.277b27–78a16). This is something that Democritus and other proponents of an unstructured universe could have agreed with, for as we have seen, there is room in Aristotle's ontology for minimal form—this is what partial bodies possess. Democritus could have agreed that the totality is just all the body that there is, without thinking that this committed him to its possessing any intrinsic determinants of structure and functioning. The crux of the matter, then, is: does the totality possess some system-level property that it does not inherit from the accidental distribution of matter in space and that, moreover, stands as cause to some of its features? In effect, Aristotle treats this question as settled by the fact that the totality is described as complete. Since this is a definition, he seems to think, it must belong to the totality necessarily. He then asks what properties an entity might have that would make it necessarily all the body that there is. This is how he arrives at the idea that the universe must be structured in the manner indicated above. This is how empirically determined features of the universe are elevated into necessary truths about it.

These are criticisms that deserve to be followed up in another place. I am not, however, concerned here with the evaluation of Aristotle's arguments about the nature of the universe. The point I wish to draw attention to is this: for Aristotle, the universe is a hylomorphic system, not merely unstructured matter.

What the Universe Is for

Aristotle's universe is a whole that exhibits motion and change in its parts: the stars move around the center without beginning or end, the sublunary elements move toward their natural places. The sublunary world is characterized by constant change: the environmental changes we noted earlier, the annual climatic cycles, and the eternally continuing generation and death of organisms. I should like now to show how Aristotle thinks of this structure as serving a purpose, that is, how it serves the good. This will constitute the second step in my attempt to analogize Aristotle's universe as a biological organism.

The first book of the *De Caelo* might suggest that Aristotle conceives of this universe as a self-maintaining structure. The heavy elements move toward their natural place in the center, the light ones to places relatively closer to the periphery, and the starry element rotates forever at the periphery. The configuration of this structure appears therefore to be held in steady state by the dynamic tendencies of the elements. Taken by itself, however, such a structure would settle into stasis (*Generation and Corruption* [*GC*] 2.10.337a8–15). What accounts for the constant circulation of the elements in the form of evaporation and condensation and for the continuance through generation and death of the plant and animal species?

In one way or another, Aristotle attributes these continuing sublunary cycles to the rotatory motion of heavenly bodies, particularly the sun and moon. Left to themselves, earth and water would find their natural places close to the center of the universe and simply stay there; similarly, air and fire would remain at the outside. However, the heat of the sun causes, by a process that we might call evaporation, two "exhalations," one vaporous, the other windy or smoky. The latter is inflammable; it rises to the top, and it is what we call fire. The former is air (*Mete.* 1.4). Thus, the stasis that we might have expected when water reached its natural place is disturbed and stirred up by the reconversion of water into the two upper elements. These exhalations are balanced by condensation, which returns the upper elements to the earth in the form of rain (1.9). Aristotle thus envisages a constantly maintained cyclical transformation of the sublunary elements, driven by the sun. In this sense, the sun is the mover or efficient cause, referred to in *Physics* 8.4, responsible for the movement of the sublunary elements to their natural places. Because its motion on the ecliptic is a compound of two circular motions, it comes closer and retreats and possesses a duality of motion that is responsible for alternate coming-to-be and perishing (*GC* 2.10.336a33–37b16).

Now, this is a form of explanation reasonably familiar to us. It sounds a lot like high-school accounts of the water cycle and of the seasons, for instance. For this reason, and because the sun plays the role of an efficient cause, we might overlook the role that the cyclicity of the sublunary elements plays in Aristotle's view of the universe, in particular that there are formal and final causes involved in the process. It is these factors that are the subject of this section.

We can discern Aristotle's line of thought clearly in a famous passage at the end of *Generation of Animals* 4, where Aristotle remarks on the determinate length of biological processes: "In all cases, the times of gestation, of coming-to-be, and of life are measured according to nature by periods, by which I mean night and day, month, and year, and by the periods of the Moon" (4.10.777b17–20). He makes it clear that the climatic cycles described above are part of this same "measuring":

> The sea and whatever is of a fluid nature remains settled or is on the move according as the winds are at rest or in motion, while the behaviour of the air and the winds in turn depends upon the period of the sun and moon, so too the things which grow out of them and are in them are bound to follow suit. (777b31–78a1)

All the events measured by periods are part of Nature's plan, that is, of the way the universe is structured:

> Nature aims (*bouletai*) to count the generations and endings by the numbers of these [heavenly bodies, i.e., the sun and the moon], but cannot do so exactly because of the indeterminateness of matter and because there is a plurality of causal principles at work, and these hinder the natural progression of generation and decay. (778a5–8)

This talk of Nature's plan links the discussion to a passage at the beginning of book 2 of the same treatise:

> [Generation] occurs on account of what is better and for the sake of something; the principle is derived from above (i.e. from the heaven) . . . Of the things that are, some are eternal and divine, and others admit admit alike of being and not being. . . . By its very nature, the beautiful and divine produces what is better in the things which admit of it. (2.1.731b24–28)

In other words, since it is impossible for sublunary substances, which are perishable, to participate fully in the perfect and endless periodicity of the stars, they are made to do the best of which they are capable. Organisms mimic eternality by reproducing. The sublunary elements, too, execute imperfectly periodic cycles forever, and these cycles too involve the coming to be and perishing of individuals. This is made explicit in *Generation and Corruption* 2.10:

The cause of the perpetuity of coming-to-be is circular motion. . . . That is why all the other things . . . imitate circular motion. For when water is transformed into air, air into fire and the fire back into water, we say the coming-to-be has completed the circle because it reverts again to the beginning. It is by imitating circular motion that rectilinear motion too is continuous. (337a1–7)

The sublunary imitation of eternity is governed and regulated by the sun, which is there to do this job (336b1–16). The world is so organized that this imitation of eternity may be made possible.

How the Universe Resembles an Animal

I have argued that Aristotle's model of the universe is that of an individual substance with form and matter, an organized, purposive whole, designed so that each of its parts might partake of, or imitate, the eternal as best as it can. I now want to complete my analogizing by suggesting that he thought of this purposive, organized whole in terms appropriate to an animal.

Let us turn first to Aristotle's treatise on the motion of animals. Here he appeals to the fact that lifeless things are moved by something outside themselves: "Lifeless things [like fire and earth] are moved by something else, and the origin of all things so moved are things which move themselves" (*Progression of Animals* 4.700a16–17).

When we trace the motion of lifeless things back to their source, we find that a living creature is always responsible: "If we exclude the motion of the universe, living creatures are responsible for the motion of everything else, except such things as are moved by each other through striking each other" (6.700b11–14).

As we have just seen, the heaven is responsible for the natural motions of the sublunary elements, which are themselves lifeless. It seems to follow that the heaven is a living creature. He says so explicitly in a number of places, for example, *De Caelo* 2.12.292a20–21, *Metaphysics* 12.7.1072b14. The organismic status of the heaven is taken up again in *De Caelo* 2.2. Here Aristotle asks whether it is true that, as the Pythagoreans say, there is a right and a left in the heaven. How should such a question be approached? Aristotle says: "If there is a right and a left, then it must be as a prior principle. These have been treated in our work on the motions of animals [actually, a reference to *Progression of Animals* 4–5] because they are proper to animal nature" (284b11–14).

Later, summarizing the presuppositions of the argument (which purports to show that east is right and consequently that the South Pole is up), he says again:

> Since we have determined that these powers belong to things that have within themselves a causal principle of motion, and that the heaven is alive (*empsychos*) and has such a causal principle, it is evident that it must have an up and a down, a right and a left. (285a27–31)

It is clear, then, that the circular motion of the heaven is in some sense an animal motion. (This conclusion is made even more unavoidable when we reflect that this is not the cosmological sense of "up" delineated in book 1.2.268b22 of the treatise: "By upward, I mean [motion] that is away from the centre." That definition implies an indifference to direction; all radial motion is either upwards or downwards. Here, we get a definition of "up" applied to the heavens alone, not to the universe as a whole. That definition is one appropriate to animals and is discussed in *Progression of Animals* 4.)

Of course, there is a difference between saying that the heaven is treated as an animal and saying that the whole universe is so treated. Aristotle certainly never says that the universe as a whole is alive, but his treatment of the heaven in these terms illustrates his willingness to apply the concept of a living thing to substances that are organized in a certain way. My contention is that when we look at the place that the heavens play in the universe taken as a whole, it is hard to resist the conclusion that the latter is also being treated in the same terms, even if not explicitly so. The key points here are, first, the organization of the whole universe to serve the end of eternity and, second, the role of the prime mover with respect to this totality.

Just like every animal, the heaven too requires an unmoved mover. There is, however, a difference between animals and the heaven. Animals contain within themselves the cause of their own motion (though in a different way they are moved also by the prime unmoved mover). The heaven, however, does not contain an unmoved mover: since it is simple, continuous, and homogeneously moving, it cannot contain one. (The argument need not be rehearsed here: see, however, *Physics* 8.6.259a29–60a19; cf. *Progression of Animals* 3.699a12–26, together with 6.700b30–701a1). Thus they are moved only by the prime unmoved mover. Thus the prime unmoved mover, or God, stands to the heaven in the same relation as does the soul of an animal to its body. Does the exteriority of the prime mover imply that it is not a soul? No, because in *De Anima* 3.5 Aristotle insists on the separability from the body of the active intellect. And in

Metaphysics 12.7, he makes it clear that God moves the heavens by thinking, clearly a close parallel with the soul of an animal that acts, if not by thinking, then at least by the mental activities associated with desire and appetite (*De Anima* 3.10.433a9–12). Thus it appears that if we take the universe as a whole, it has movement of various sorts regulated by an external soul. In this respect, it is completely analogous with human beings.

Let me summarize the last two sections. Aristotle's universe is an organized whole, each part aspiring as best it can to the perfect activity of the God beyond it. There is nothing in the universe that is able, as that God is, to think uninterruptedly without moving. The stars, however, approximate to this activity most closely, since their movement is perfectly homogeneous and without beginning or end. In the sublunary sphere, we have things that perish, so that in order to mimic eternity, they must reproduce. This activity can only be made possible by something that is on the one hand eternal (to ensure the eternity of generation and perishing) but on the other hand has some discontinuity in it (to ensure the cyclicity of generation). This thing is the sun, helped by the moon. Thus the stars are instruments that the prime mover uses in order to regulate and maintain the system of the whole. In this respect, the entire system resembles that found in animals. In these creatures, too, thought and perception control the body, and they do so via the instrumentality of a substance known as *pneuma* (*Progression of Animals* 10 and *GA* 2.3), which is aetherial in character.

The Incorruptibility of the Universe

Aristotle used the paradigm of an organism to conceptualize his universe. This seems to put him in a camp with James Lovelock and those who have followed him in embracing the Gaia hypothesis, according to which "the biosphere is a self-regulating entity with the capacity to keep our planet healthy by controlling the chemical and physical environment." More specifically:

> The Gaia hypothesis said that the temperature, oxidation state, acidity, and certain aspects of the rocks and waters are at any time kept constant, and that this homeostasis is maintained by active feedback processes operated automatically and unconsciously by the biota.[5]

Now, the Gaia hypothesis is closely connected with environmental activism of a quasi-religious sort. Lovelock writes:

Any living organism a quarter as old as the Universe itself and still full of vigor is as near immortal as we ever need to know. She is of this Universe and, conceivably, a part of God. On Earth she is the source of life everlasting and is alive now; she gave birth to humankind and we are a part of her.

There is little time left to prevent the destruction of the forests of the humid tropics with consequences far-reaching both for Gaia and for humans. The country folk, who are destroying their own forests, are often Christians and venerate the Holy Virgin Mary. If their hearts and minds could be moved to see in her the embodiment of Gaia, then they might become aware that the victim of their destruction was indeed the Mother of humankind and the source of everlasting life. (*From Gaia to Selfish Genes*, 40)

Clearly, Lovelock sees environmental depradations as causing harm to the body of Gaia and believes they are wrong for this reason. His appeal to the "country folk" of the "humid tropics" is not based on a concrete vision of damage done to the global environment but on an idea of reverence for the body of Gaia, aka the Holy Virgin Mary.

Why does Aristotle, given his own reverence for the prime mover and the stars, not share this concept? Since he is prepared to think of parts of the earth as aging, why does he not take more seriously the possibility of injuries and traumas to the earth and its seas? Why does he, on the contrary, think of the universe as merely material provided by God for the economic development of humans?

Property, in the sense of a bare livelihood, seems to be given by nature herself to all. . . . Some animals bring forth, together with their offspring, so much food as will last until they are able to supply themselves; of this the vermiparous or oviparous animals are an instance; and the viviparous animals have up to a certain time a supply of food for their young in themselves, which is called milk. In like manner we may infer that, after the birth of animals, plants exist for their sake, and that the other animals exist for the sake of man, the tame for use and food, the wild, if not all, at least the greater part of themn, for food, and for the provision of clothing and various instruments. Now if nature makes nothing incomplete, and nothing in vain, the inference must be that she has made all animals for the sake of man. And so, from one point of view, the art of war is a natural art of acquisition, for the art of acquisition includes hunting, an art which we ought to practice against wild beasts, and against men who, though intended by nature to be governed, will not submit; for war of such a kind is naturally just. (*Politics* 1.8.1256b9–25).

From an environmentalist's point of view, this is a very nasty turn for Aristotle's organismic cosmology to take: the whole organism is declared to exist for the sake of one of its parts. I want to argue that Aristotle's nonenvironmentalism springs from a view of system-level properties fundamentally at variance with that found in Lovelock. In the Gaia hypothesis, system-level properties are chance emergences that can be destroyed if conditions vary dramatically enough. In Aristotle's cosmology, system-level properties are the products of necessity and can in no way be disturbed. They are imposed top-down by the form of the universe, whereas the properties of Gaia emerge bottom-up.

The nature of system properties in Gaia is well illustrated by "Daisyworld," a simplified "parable" of emergent self-regulation. Daisyworld is a planet illuminated by a star that, like our own sun, is increasing in radiant energy output. The planet possesses but one life form, daisies, that thrive at 20°C, die when the temperature rises above 40°C, and fail to grow when the temperature falls below 5°C. The daisies vary in color; some are dark and others light. "The mean temperature of Daisyworld is . . . determined by the average shade of color of the planet. . . . If light in color . . . 70 or 80 percent of the sunlight may be reflected back to space. Such a surface is cold when compared with a dark surface under comparable solar illumination" (Barlow, 17).

When Daisyworld's star was less luminous, only small regions around the equator were warm enough to support daisies, and then only barely. Here dark daisies are favored, because they absorb more sunlight, and hence are warmed to a more favorable temperature. The greater proliferation of dark daisies under these conditions makes the planet itself darker on average, and hence warmer. As the star itself gets warmer and warmer, the situation begins to reverse itself: lighter daisies begin to be favored because they can keep cool. Gradually the planet gets lighter and lighter and thus manages to stay cool enough for daisy life despite the fact that its sun keeps getting warmer. Thus the daisies act as a homeostatic device that regulates the temperature for the sake of their own survival.

However, as the star that shines on Daisyworld grows hotter and hotter, the proportion of dark to light daisies changes until, finally, the heat flux is so great that even the whitest daisy crop cannot keep enough of the planet below the critical 40°C upper limit for growth. At this time flower power is not enough. The planet becomes barren again and so hot that there is no way for daisy life to start again.

The crucial point here is that at the beginning, the connection between the color mix of the daisies and the temperature of the planet was established by chance; it arises from the fortuitous convergence of the color variance among the daisies and, given the temperature of the star at that time, the difference that this color variance made. As things got going, the forces of evolution made the biota into a homeostatic device. At a certain point, external conditions became so unfavorable that homeostasis failed. There is, as Lovelock wants to emphasize, no teleology necessary in order to understand the (temporally bounded) stability of Daisyworld under conditions of increasing radiative heating. There are no system-level causes here to explain the system-level properties, only chance.

Now, Aristotle is not insensitive to the general issue of over-teleologizing the universe. He certainly asks the question of when one ought to infer final causes and when one ought instead to rest with chance. Unfortunately, however, he makes a crucial wrong turn in the consideration of this question:

> Natural things come to be the way they are always or for the most part, but this is never true of the products of chance and spontaneity. It seems not to be by chance or happenstance that it rains frequently in winter, but it does seem so when it rains during the dog days. Nor is it happenstance when it is hot during the dog days, but it is so when it is hot in winter. (*Physics* 2.8.198b35–99a3)

Regularities cannot be the product of chance and spontaneity, Aristotle thinks (cf. *De Caelo* 2.5.287b25–27, 8.289b25–29). This thought led him to a number of profound insights, in embryology, for example, where he insists, as against his more reductionistically inclined opponents, on a role for generative form, an insight that some scientists and philosophers have likened to the discovery of the principle of the genetic code. The same thought also prevented him from seeing that chance events can lead to stable macro phenomena, as in Daisyworld. Aristotle was unable to see that such stable phenomena need not have coherent causes; they can be produced spontaneously. From Aristotle's perspective, the universe is the extreme case of stability: it is an eternal being that exists necessarily, and hence without beginning or end. Indeed he viewed this as a fact that can receive empirical confirmation. He tells us that in Democritus's view, "the heavenly sphere and the most divine of visible things arose spontaneously, having no such cause as is assigned to animals and plants" (*Physics* 2.4.196a32–35). But this contradicts the phenomena, he says, for "they see nothing coming to be spontaneously in the heavens" (196b3–4). (It was, of course, this assertion that made Tycho's observation of a nova and Galileo's discovery of sunspots significant as refutations of the Aristotelian system.)

As we have seen, then, Aristotle invokes the form of the universe as a cause of its stability. This is why he treated environmental change as purely local: such change cannot make a difference to the whole. And, as he does in the biological works, he associates form with what is good, that is, with purpose. This is what leads him to the assertion (quoted above from the *Politics*) that just as an egg is provisioned with food for the developing organism, so the sublunary sphere is made to sustain the economic development of human beings. Ecological system–level properties are extremely important to the environmentalist, I conclude, but so is the consciousness that because these emerge fortuitously they are extremely fragile. When we posit system-level causes for macro phenomena, we obscure the fragility and fortuitousness of the universe. Lovelock's appeal to the Virgin Mary is on the wrong track; nobody would think that she would allow the forests of the humid tropics to suffer.

Part IV

Greek Philosophy after Aristotle

11

Fortitude and Tragedy: The Prospects for a Stoic Environmentalism

Alan J. Holland

The Stoics of the Hellenistic and early Roman periods could hardly have been motivated by the same circumstances and problems that motivate deep ecologists. Moreover, it is all too evident that the *content* of Stoic ethics and the *content* of deep ecology are radically dissimilar. Any attempt to link the two, either textually or subtextually, is certainly misguided from the viewpoint of the history of philosophy and the history of ideas.[1]

This recent verdict gives an indication of the uphill task we face in attempting to bring Stoic insights to bear upon our current environmental problems. But even here, two chinks of light show through. One is the fact that it is only the link with deep ecology that is explicitly denied, for the writer does elsewhere claim to see an affinity between Stoic thought and the social ecology of Murray Bookchin. The other is the fact that part of the grounds for denying a link concerns the difference in our "motivating circumstances"; and this seems a far from sufficient reason. Of course we must be sensitive to our different cultural situation; but the writer overlooks the fact that Stoicism did after all translate from the Greek to the Roman culture. He also overlooks the fact that Stoicism itself recognizes the scope for development and reinterpretation of its "doctrines." This, at any rate, is the tenor of Seneca's letter 33: "We Stoics are no monarch's subjects; each asserts his own freedom."[2] Although Stoicism has the reputation for being one of the most systematic of all philosophies,[3] this should not be taken to imply that it is not also quite an adaptable one.

Methodological Remarks

In any event, neither environmentalism nor Stoicism should be thought of as if it were a single system of thought. Regarding environmentalism, it

151

will only be supposed here that what unites environmentalists is a concern for the nonhuman environment and perhaps a belief that the nonhuman world should be given some moral status. Underlying that agreement is a great diversity of focus, emphasis, and even of fundamental value. Some environmentalists focus on individuals, others on wholes; some attach significance to sentience, others regard this as anthropocentric; some emphasize our affinity with the natural world, while others emphasize its strangeness.

Regarding Stoicism, Diogenes Laertius (hereafter DL), in his *Lives of Eminent Philosophers*, which is the source of a great deal of our knowledge of Stoic thought, gathers all the Stoic doctrines together into his account of the life of Zeno, who is generally regarded as the founder of the school; but it soon becomes apparent that this way of proceeding in no way reflects a uniformity of outlook amongst Stoics.[4] Scarcely is the account under way before we are in the realm of disagreements over the ordering and significance of the division of philosophy into logic, physics, and ethics. Diogenes begins with ethics, he reports, but Apollodorus puts ethics second, while Panaetius and Posidonius begin with physics; Cleanthes has six divisions instead of three, and there is disagreement over whether these are divisions in the exposition of philosophy or in philosophy itself. And so it continues. What *is* agreed, amongst the Stoics themselves, later commentators, and modern scholars, is that Stoic thought underwent substantial development; it is a commonplace to observe the greater emphasis placed on ethical concerns by the later, Roman, Stoics.

In considering the question of possible applications of Stoic thought to our current situation, we shall not be concerned with tracing historical links, nor with causal influences. Nor shall we be concerned, unless incidentally, to establish or deny affinities between certain Stoic doctrines and particular strands of modern environmentalism. In any case, no simple lesson can be drawn from the presence or absence of such affinities, were they to be established. Jim Cheney finds a common tendency in both Stoicism and deep ecology to seek identification with the cosmos, and disapproves of what he finds on the grounds that it neglects the "perception and recognition of difference."[5] William Stephens finds an affinity between Stoicism and the Social Ecology of Murray Bookchin in their "sober rationalism and clarity of thought" and applauds this tendency.[6] Attempts to make such connections are liable to all kinds of methodological objections. For example, Cheney is taken to task by Stephens for relying on Hans Jonas as his sole source for the content of Stoic thought (although it has to be said that Jonas seems to give quite a reliable account). Stephens himself, as will shortly be explained, might equally be taken to task for relying almost exclusively on the Roman Stoics for his evidence as to the content of Stoic thought. But rather than enter further into debates of this kind, we shall be concerned here to raise the direct, first-order question whether Stoicism has anything pertinent to say regarding our current environmental predicament. It is an enterprise somewhat inspired by Bernard Williams's remark that "it is not a paradox that in these very new circumstances very old philosophies may have more to offer than moderately new ones."[7] We shall begin by considering features of the Stoic position that seem to suggest that the enterprise is doomed from the start; we shall show how these "unhopeful signs" can, to a quite considerable degree, be deflected.

Unhopeful Signs

Anthropocentrism

The most unhopeful sign of all is the one that John Passmore highlights in his chapter of *Man's Responsibility for Nature* entitled "Man as Despot"; it concerns the doctrine that "all things are made for man." This doctrine is ascribed by Passmore specifically to the *Graeco*-Christian tradition: "If, then, one can speak of 'Christian arrogance' in supposing that all things are made for men, it must be with the proviso that it is not Hebraic-Christian but Graeco-Christian arrogance."[8] He traces it, even more specifically, to the Stoics (14, 16-18). By way of a preliminary observation, it should be noted that Passmore's chief source for his ascription of this doctrine to the Stoics is the discussion in Cicero's *De Natura Deorum* (*ND*), in which the character of Balbus represents the Stoic position.[9] There are two reasons for drawing attention to this. One is that we might expect a fairly full-blooded or even extreme version of the Stoic position to be advanced in a work such as this for the purpose of setting up a dramatic contrast with the Academic and Epicurean positions, which are also represented. The other, more important, reason is that Cicero's chief source for his account of Stoicism was the Roman Stoic Posidonius, who is known to have been sharply critical of the most authoritative and prolific of the Greek Stoics, Chrysippus[10]—reputed to be the author of more than 705 books (DL 7.180) and quite clearly (but not of course simply because of his output) a philosopher of towering stature. Neglect of the Greek Stoics is understandable, given that we possess almost none of their writings apart from the brief "Hymn" by Cleanthes, but it is not entirely excusable since, as Josiah Gould demonstrates in his monograph on

Chrysippus, it is possible to piece together a passable account of their distinctive positions by a judicious use of ancient secondary sources.[11]

If we now peruse Cicero's text with these points in mind, we find that the claim that the world and all it contains was made for the sake of (gods and) men, although it is affirmed by Balbus (*ND* 2.53), is nowhere attributed to Chrysippus. Moreover, the claim appears nowhere in the comprehensive account of Stoic doctrine provided by Diogenes Laertius, save in one reference where it is *almost* attributed to Posidonius, who is said to define the world as a "system constituted by gods and men and all things created for their sake" (DL 7.138). This view is taken up much later by Marcus Aurelius, who states that irrational creatures are made for the sake of rational ones—and rational ones for the sake of each other (7.55).[12] What Cicero does explicitly attribute to Chrysippus is the view that everything else *except the world* was created for the sake of some other thing (*ND* 2.14). A moment's reflection reveals that this view is actually inconsistent with the claim almost attributed to Posidonius by Diogenes Laertius, affirmed by Balbus, and ascribed by Passmore to the Stoics; for it is quite clearly inconsistent to hold both that everything *except* the world was created for the sake of some other thing and that the world was created for the sake of man. Although it is hardly unknown for philosophers to contradict themselves, a principle of charity (or even discretion) might suggest that we do not without reason convict a philosopher of inconsistency whose command of dialectic was such that it was said of him that if the gods had taken up dialectic, they would have taken up Chrysippean dialectic (DL 7.180). So much for the "Stoic" view that "all things are made for man."

But even the full-blooded doctrine affirmed by Balbus, or the modified version attributed to Posidonius and endorsed by Marcus Aurelius, does not make the Stoic position so unhopeful as it might first appear, in light of the following considerations.

The first reason is hinted at by Stephen Clark when he remarks that "Stoics certainly thought it right to use brutes for good human ends, but would not therefore have endorsed their use to create, or test, cosmetics or minor drugs or luxury foods."[13] To construe the Stoic position as in any way endorsing current anthropocentric practices is to ignore totally the conditions for reasoned action that they also laid down. A wise agent was required always to do what was "fitting"—a technical term referring to actions that "reason prevails on us to do" and that are "adapted to nature's arrangements" (DL 7.108). Only actions of this kind would be conducive to virtue, a disposition that, along with the agents and their action and associated dispositions such as joy, friendliness, and reverence, was the only thing acknowledged to be good (DL 7.94). It is possible to mock the well-attested Chrysippean view that pigs have souls in order to keep their meat fresh for human consumption, or his view that fleas and mice help to discourage laziness and untidiness, respectively;[14] these are nothing but the colorful expressions of his belief in providence. But it is possible also to overlook the corollary that if this is their role, then they had better not be used instead to grow hearts for transplanting into humans, as is currently the fate of (some) pigs, or to grow human ears on their backs, as is currently the fate of (some) mice.[15]

Second, the doctrine that animals are made for designated human purposes is in fact just a special case of the principle that nature has made available for each living thing copious supplies of that food that suits it (*ND* 2.47) together with the means to secure it; providence is said to be directed toward the "safety and preservation of *all*" (*ND* 2.53), and the trade winds are referred to as being of benefit "not for the human race alone but also for the animal and various vegetable species" (*ND* 2.53). Moreover, according to Chrysippus's version of the principle, it is only animals that are said to be created for the sake of man; corn and fruits are said to be created for the sake of (nonhuman) animals (*ND* 2.14). It does not follow that corn is made for man, since it is not self-evident that "made for the sake of" is a transitive relation. (But Balbus may disagree— see below.)

Third, it is indeed affirmed that the whole world as we know it was made for the sake of gods and men (*ND* 2.53). But this is in answer to the question of why the world is *so great* a work as it appears to be ("tantarum rerum molitio"). The claim, in other words, is not simply that the world was made for gods and men but that it was made *as it is* for gods and men. It is because, and only insofar as, neither the plants nor the nonhuman animals would have had a *use* for so marvelous and complex a system, and also because nothing is allowed to be superfluous in a rational and well-ordered system, that it is inferred that gods and men must be the intended beneficiaries. Otherwise, beauty and other features of the creation that only gods and humans could appreciate would have been created in vain.

Fourth, even this claim in fact attracts an important and neglected qualification. It is not in fact asserted unconditionally that all things are made for gods and men. What is asserted is that all the things in this world *that men use* are created so that they may use them (*ND* 2.61). There is a difference between asserting that "everything on earth is for man's use" and asserting that everything on earth that man uses has been made for him to use. The first implies that humans are at liberty to modify the world as they like. The second is compatible with the view that there may be limits to how humans may use the world. In a particularly revealing passage, Balbus remarks that the very shape of the ox's back makes it clear that oxen were not designed for carrying burdens, whereas the shape of their necks makes it clear that they were designed for the yoke; and in the "Golden Age" eating their flesh was a crime (*ND* 2.62). In this connection it is important to observe also that when Balbus goes on to illustrate the bountiful provision of nature, it is primarily with reference to *cultivated* plants (vines and olives) and *domesticated* animals (sheep, dogs, oxen, asses, and pigs); and that when he speaks of animals (mice and ants) as "robbing" humans, a point that draws adverse comment from Passmore,[16] he has corn in mind—a cultivated plant and staple of the human diet and therefore presumably provided for *human* use.

A final point is that humans themselves do not escape the general burden of having been created for some external purpose. This is clear from a remark attributed explicitly to Chrysippus: "Just as a shield-case is made for a shield and a sheath for a sword, so everything else except the world was created for the sake of some other thing" (*ND* 2.14). "Everything" includes human beings, who are said to have come into existence "for the sake of contemplating and imitating the world." Thus the primary relationship in which humans stand to nature is not that it is there for them to use but that it is there for them to seek to understand and follow. "Our motto, as everyone knows," says Seneca, "is to live in conformity with nature" (letter 5); and this is after all a notion that has been used to some effect by a recent environmental philosopher to articulate the environmentalist case.[17]

The Absence of Contract

"'Of course,' they say [sc. the Stoics], 'we human beings have no compact of justice with irrational animals.'"[18] Plutarch, who was also author of *De Stoicorum Repugnantiis (De Stoic. Rep.)*, which aims to lay bare the inconsistencies both in Stoic doctrine itself and between the Stoics' theory and their practice, is a notably hostile witness—although of course his hostility would not necessarily consist in his taking exception to the things a modern reader might take exception to.[19] But on this occasion what he says is confirmed by Diogenes Laertius (2.129), who finds this claim in the first book of Chrysippus's *On Justice*. One of the arguments Plutarch gives for this view is that to deny it would place us in the intolerable position of having either to be unjust or to abandon human life as we know it: "We shall be living the life of beasts if we give up the use of beasts" (*De Stoic. Rep.* 964A). It is interesting to observe that Passmore in fact finds himself in agreement with the Stoics on this point,[20] and even Plutarch concedes that the Stoics must be regarded as correct so far as sea creatures are concerned (970B).

Perhaps the simplest and most direct comment to be made on this feature of Stoic thought is that it is not entirely disabling—that a decent environmentalist position can be constructed without supposing that we enjoy a contractual relation with the rest of the natural world. In fact, there are those who would hold that thinking in these terms is to humanize our relationship to the natural world in an unacceptable way. The danger would lie in using positively the denial of any contractual relation to justify a no-holds-barred approach to the natural world. But we have seen this not to be so. We have seen how human action was subject to the restraint of appropriateness in all its dealings, and we shall shortly see how the Stoics do in fact recognize a sort of community or sense of a fate shared with the natural world. It should be borne in mind that the denial of a contract might have more significance in a world in which contract was the basis of moral relationships; but this was not true of the world in which Stoic ethics was situated.

Self-Sufficiency

One cannot ignore the fact that the Stoics seem to have pushed the theme of the self-sufficiency of the good life to extremes, thus manifesting a tendency that Williams has described as typical of ancient thought, namely, "the desire to reduce life's exposure to luck."[21] Seneca reports with evident relish and approval how Stilbo responded to Demetrius, the sacker of cities, as Stilbo emerged from the ruins of his city, having lost everything, including his wife and children, with the immortal words: "I have all my valuables with me" (letter 9). Whether one finds that response admirable or somewhat chilling, the problem for environmentalism here is that if the good life is attainable no matter what your external circumstances, it is unclear how it could be part of what is required of the good person to care for the environment. The point is well caught by Marcus Aurelius's question whether one can call anything a misfortune as long as it does not prevent one from being virtuous (4.49).

It is important, however, not to misinterpret this "self-sufficiency." It did not involve a retreat into the self but was fully compatible with the most active engagement in public life, as Seneca reveals in his eulogy of Cato the younger (letter 104). Certainly, a full understanding of the workings of the natural world was necessary if one was to accommodate one's own nature to it. Even the famous Stoic endorsement of suicide as "appropriate" under certain circumstances was directed, as Tillich rightly observes, "not to those who are conquered by life but to those who have conquered life."[22] It implied an acknowledgment that there are circumstances in which it is not possible to live a worthwhile life and in which it is fitting, therefore, to seek a worthwhile death. Nor was the pursuit of self-sufficiency any form of escape; on the contrary, it was an expression of a keen awareness of "life's exposure to luck" and a recommendation of how to live life in the face of such exposure. The point was, not to refuse to have anything to do with externals, but simply not to place any reliance in them.

The Attitude to Particular Things

When we lose something or someone dear to us, the Stoics appear to offer a dubious consolation. When your wife or child has died, say to yourself that it is *a* human being who has died, and you will not be disturbed. Or say not that you have lost them but that you have given them back (Epictetus, "Enchiridion" 3, 11).[23] Their loss is like the falling of leaves: even if they do not grow again, they are replaced (Seneca, letter 104). This is no marginal quirk in their thinking but connects directly with the question of how a Stoic is supposed to recognize the natural path that he or she is supposed to follow: "the will of nature is learned from those things in which we do not differ from one another" ("Enchiridion" 26). What this means is that the mark of the natural is the universal. Hence, if one is to act in accordance with nature, one acts in relation to an individual as one would act towards any individual of that type. That way lies dignity, tranquility, and freedom, which is freedom from disturbance— from being dragged where one does not want to go. Thus, the famous Stoic "detachment" is a requirement of virtue, understood as the disposition that makes it possible to act in accordance with nature. The problem with all this from an environmental point of view is that such an attitude appears out of step with the environmentalist's stress on the irreplaceability of the natural world as a reason for valuing it.

Irreversibility

A connected problem is whether the Stoic perspective could possibly explain the difference we feel between reversible and irreversible loss. Marcus Aurelius invites us to consider all loss as nothing else but change (9.35), which effectively obliterates the distinction. The sense of loss, or threatened loss, however, is among the most potent causes of environmental concern. The Stoic response to loss is well illustrated by Seneca's musings on the fire that totally destroyed the Gallic town of Lyons (letter 91). He uses it as the occasion to advise his readers to "anticipate not merely all that commonly happens but all that is conceivably capable of happening." Turning from man-made to natural phenomena, he comments on how mountains are eroded and land subsides and is inundated: "The works of nature suffer. So it is only right that we should bear the overthrow of cities with resignation. They stand just to fall." Seneca believes these remarks will bring comfort; the environmentalist may well be more struck by the lack of urgency that they convey.

Tragedy

The upshot of both the preceding points might be summed up in "dramatic" terms as the absence from Stoic thought of what might be called a sense of tragedy. There would seem to be no room within the Stoic scheme of things for tragedy, whether at an individual or universal level. This arises not so much from their adoption of determinism, although that too might pose a problem, but from the fact that whatever we (humans) do, things are bound to be all right with the world. For a sense of tragedy to be able to unfold, on the other hand, it is arguable that something in the universe or in human life has to be untidy, intractable, irresolvable, or unfair.[24] This can seem to be a problem if one is inclined to see what is currently befalling the natural world as little short of a tragedy. We know what it is like to go to the pantry and discover that we are running out of sugar, and we might even speak of this as a "tragedy"; but we should know this was hyperbole. Some analyses of our environmental predicament do indeed seem to imply that the problem is of this kind—a problem of imprudent accounting—and might not therefore find the Stoic approach wanting. But many would find such analyses inadequate and, echoing William James, might say "it certainly seems like a tragedy." Against the idea that the Stoic approach lacks a sense of tragedy one might plead that one leading Stoic, Seneca, was after all the author of tragedies. But one can build very little on that fact. To the extent that he followed Greek models, the "tragic spirit" might be thought to be borrowed. Some of what he wrote, such as *Thyestes*, was in any case more horror than tragedy. And it is unclear how far his tragedies can be seen as any kind of vehicle for his Stoicism—or indeed how we should recognize if they were. When Hercules in *Hercules Furens* wakes up to the enormity of the fact that he has killed his wife and children, he laments: " I have lost all my goods: reason, arms, reputation, wife, children, strength." The contrast with Stilbo could not be more striking. The second problem, that of recognition, arises from the fact that the Stoic was admonished to "act well the character assigned you" ("Enchiridion" 17); and it could be that the "character" that Seneca thought he had been assigned was that of tragic author.

We have attempted, thus far, to disarm some of the potentially more negative aspects of Stoic thought. We have seen how its privileging of human concerns is at least held in check by its simultaneous recognition of constraints; but we have also seen reason to doubt whether it could quite generate the present sense of environmental "crisis." Let us turn now to the opposing case and consider how some of the ingredients of Stoic thought might positively assist contemporary reflection.

Hopeful Signs

The Value of Nature

It is misleading of Stephens to suggest, as against Cheney, that the Stoics deny the inherent value of things, or to cite in support of such a claim Engberg-Pedersen's statement that "it is because human beings (and animals too) see certain things as valuable that these things are valuable."[25] The Stoics believed that the world (or universe) is a living animal "animans est igitur mundus composque rationis" (*ND* 2.8) and identified it with God—"deum esse mundum" (*ND* 2.17) or, more precisely, as the substance of God (DL 7.148). As such, it is the most perfect and divine thing there could be: not only is nothing better than the world, but nothing better could even be conceived (*ND* 2.7). It would be so regardless of what any human being, prone to erroneous judgment, might think. Engberg-Pedersen's statement can refer only to the so-called preferred items—health, wealth, beauty, and the like—that humans (and non-humans) may value but that are in themselves "indifferent," that is, neither good nor bad.

Stephens is right, on the other hand, to stress the crucial importance that the Stoics attach to reason. But one of the arguments that they put forward to show that the world possesses intelligence is precisely that it is better (i.e., is of higher value) than any of its elements and that since humans possess intelligence and are part of the world, it too must possess intelligence (*ND* 2.12). Moreover, reason is not the unique preserve of humans and God. Or rather, since God is identified with everything, it is because it belongs to God that it belongs to everything—"quid est in his [sc. terrestribus] in quo non naturae ratio intellegentis appareat?" (*ND*

2.47). What *is* true, according to one source, is that although reason permeates the whole world, it permeates some parts more and some parts less.[26] This means, according to Diogenes Laertius, that in some parts it acts merely as a containing force (e.g., in bones and sinews), and in other parts it acts as intelligence (DL 7.139). Thus, reason is present in humans (and God) in a different way. It is humans alone who make use of reason; the rest of the universe merely exemplifies it. Humans are given reason so that they may govern their impulses (*ND* 2.12); nonhumans do not need reason for this purpose, because their impulses never go astray (DL 7.89). A corollary is that humans are also unique in the natural world in that they are uniquely the source of what can go wrong, when their actions stem from erroneous judgment, irrational emotions, or vice. One might sum up the situation by saying that the Stoic analysis would make it perfectly possible to justify the environmentalist charge that humans are uniquely responsible for degrading the environment—both by laying the charge at the door of the only creature for whom this would be appropriate and in its view of the world as a source of value that is ultimately independent of humans and that they might therefore be legitimately charged with degrading, rather than simply using unwisely.

What is undeniable is that although they attached value to the whole world system, the Stoics also believed in a hierarchy or "ladder" of value, with humans somewhere near the top, lower than God but higher than all other creatures. It is not clear, however, to what extent this should count as a disqualification in the eyes of environmentalists, given that those who deny any such hierarchy and promote some doctrine of "biospherical egalitarianism" have quite a hard time convincing fellow environmentalists of the wisdom and practicality of this doctrine.

Interconnectedness

We know of three similes that the Stoics used to characterize the three areas of philosophical inquiry, logic, ethics, and physics: the animal, where logic is the bones, ethics the flesh, and physics the soul; the egg, where logic is the shell, ethics the white, and physics the yolk; the field, where logic is the wall, ethics the crop, and physics the soil (DL 7.40). All serve to underline the inseparability of these areas of inquiry; and all serve equally to reflect the inseparability of the subject matter. We have seen how the Stoics regarded the world as a single living organism. Such unity might count for little if it were accompanied by other dichotomous tendencies, such as the separation of material and immaterial, and the assigning of natural entities to one or the other side of the dichotomy. But the Stoics are notoriously resolute in their materialism and by no means unsophisticated about it. (For example, they find room in their materialism for "somethings" that are not material, such as "sayables," void, place and time, and fictional items.)[27] The strong physical foundation for their materialism is Chrysippus's theory of mixtures, particularly in the idea of a kind of mixture in which the ingredients permeate each other completely while retaining their qualities, as the Stoics held to be true of body and soul, both material items (DL 7.151). Other organismic accounts of the natural world have been put forward since the time of the Stoics, by Hutton and Clements and, most recently, by Lovelock.

It should be noticed how the Stoics avoid the usual criticism leveled at such accounts—that they obliterate the individual—by making the well-being of the individual coincide with that of the larger whole. What emerges is a stance that, to put it no more strongly, at least *prepares* us to see the interconnectedness of natural phenomena and that is, to that extent, consonant with what we now think of as an "ecological" point of view.

Common Origins

All components of the natural world—and the natural world comprises all that there is—are cut from the same cloth: our individual natures are parts of the nature of the whole universe (DL 7.87). As Clark observes: "Stoic ethics culminate in a firm division between the human and the less than human, as well as between the wise and foolish. But it is grounded in natural impulses shared with other animals."[28] This sharing does indeed go all the way down (although impulse does not reach as far as plants), for "nature, they say, made no difference originally between plants and animals, for she regulates the life of plants too, in their case without impulse and sensation, just as certain processes of a vegetative kind go on in us" (DL 7.86). In humans it is said that reason comes along as the "craftsman of impulse." But it should not be inferred from this that the nonhuman creatures of impulse are condemned to a wayward form of existence, for "the impulses of nature are never perverse" (DL 7.89). As Seneca has it: "dumb beasts, sluggish in other respects, are clever at living" (letter 121). Besides sharing "regulation," plants, animals, and humans also share frustrations, as Marcus Aurelius notes: "there is something that is equally a hindrance and an evil to the constitution of plants" (Marcus Aurelius 8.41). Moreover, there are also things that are "appropriate" for animals and vegetables to do: "for even in animals and plants . . . you may discern fitness of behaviour" (DL 7.107). Every existing thing is part of the natural world and therefore a part of the supreme being. One has only to read the discriminatingly hostile introduction to the Everyman edition of the *Discourses* of Epictetus by the late-eighteenth-century translator Elizabeth Carter to see how shocking this idea appeared to a guardian of the Christian tradition. Such divergence between Christian and Stoic thought should not be wrapped up under the heading of "the Graeco-Christian tradition" and made to vanish.

Pain and Suffering

It is a remarkable fact about the *Nicomachean Ethics* that Aristotle has so much to say about pleasure and so little to say about pain.[29] This betrays a very different sensitivity to the problem of suffering among the ancient Greeks than has been prevalent under the utilitarian temper of more recent times. It is necessary to take issue here with Bernard Williams's claim that "there is a 'problem of evil' only for those who think that the world is good."[30] What might be true, only, is that there is a *different* problem for those who think that the world is good and those who do not. In admittedly crude terms, the problem—whether we think the world is good or bad—is what we should do about it. For those who think the world is good, the response to the problem is that we should come to terms with it. This was the position of the Stoics. For them, suffering was one of the "indifferents," neither good nor bad. The problem with the position of those who do *not* think the world is good is that they tend to think that suffering is bad and therefore that almost any measures are justified in combating it. But it is not clear that any form of environmentalism can make headway, or even survive, against a mindset that places supreme importance upon the alleviation or elimination of suffering. The reason, as John Stuart Mill so graphically illustrated, is that suffering of the most extreme kinds is an ineliminable component of natural processes.[31] The conjunction of such a mindset with the technology of genetic engineering could wreak havoc on the natural world as we know it. It seems to follow that environmentalists need to veer towards the Stoic, rather than the Utilitarian line, and focus on how we may come to terms with suffering. At the same time, we cannot be indifferent to suffering but must recognize that it does, and will continue to, pose the most agonizing problems for environmentalism.

But were not the Stoics indifferent toward suffering? This is a misunderstanding. The Stoics classed pain as one of the "indifferents," along with death, disease, ugliness, health, pleasure, and beauty. It is important to be clear that this does not mean that they thought these things of no consequence—a description that attracts quite a different range of examples, such as the picking up of a twig and the question whether the number of hairs on one's head is odd or even (DL 7.109, 104). Nor does it mean that they were indifferent to these things. On the contrary, they held that such things are naturally sought or avoided and are capable of contributing to a worthwhile, or miserable, life. In calling them indifferent, the Stoics intended to signal that these things were neither good nor bad, nor essential for either a worthwhile or a miserable life. Their argument in support of this contention was that what is good (or bad) must have the capacity to benefit but not to injure (or vice-versa); but wealth, for example, could injure a person as well as benefit him; and suffering could benefit a person as well as injure him.

Happiness

The issue of happiness is a corollary of the issue of pain. If, like the Stoics, we suppose that suffering is something that is an ineliminable feature of the natural world with which we have to come to terms, rather than something we can hope to eliminate, the question arises of how this affects our prospects of happiness. If by "happiness" we understand a contented psychological state, as proposed by hedonistic utilitarianism, then it must affect such a state most seriously. For even though we cease to regard suffering as bad in itself, it is hard to see how, faced by the "pain of the world," any human being of any sensitivity could maintain such a state for any length of time. This would only be possible if the psychological state were not only "subjective" but also totally narcissistic. Happiness in this sense, therefore, could be (and is) at most temporarily attained by people who are thoroughly *absorbed* in some project and therefore for the time being distracted from "reality"—whether by some sporting pursuit, aesthetic transport, engaging hobby, or, indeed, love. In place of happiness understood in this sense, the Stoics, like other Greeks, tended to think of the ultimate goal of life as "living a worthwhile life" or "living well"—that, as many commentators note, is a better translation of the Greek term *eudaimonia* than "happiness."[32] The point is that one can sustain a worthwhile life in the face of pain, whether one's own or another's, where one cannot plausibly sustain a happy—that is, contented—one. It is therefore a more realistic, or realizable, goal to propose. Another point of difference is that the utilitarian notion of happiness, that is, contentment, is a naturalistic concept, whereas the notion of a worthwhile life is a normative one. What this means is that the concept of a worthwhile life is open to deliberation in a way that the concept of happiness is not. It thus answers to the intuitive idea that it ought to be possible to deliberate about ends as well as about means.

Conclusion

What has been attempted here is some outline of the prospects for a "Stoic environmentalism." The privileging of human concerns might be thought to hinder such prospects most, but we have found reason to think that this feature of Stoic thought has been given a somewhat inflated significance. At the same time we have recognized elements in the Stoic temper having to do with the Stoics' attitude to loss that do present some difficulty. The positive value that they attach to the natural world could be regarded as undermined by its association with their faith in providence, for someone who does not share that faith. But it is implausible to suppose that they regarded the world as they did *because* of a prior belief in providence and more plausible to suppose that it was their experience of the world that called forth this particular intellectual response. We do not therefore have to think that the removal of providence would automatically empty the world of value. We have seen reason to believe that the very fortitude that the term "stoicism" now conjures up could be put to the service of environmentalism if it makes us rethink our attitudes to pain and happiness.

Supposing that we have succeeded in identifying certain ways in which the adoption, or at least the entertaining, of a Stoic perspective could help us address the environmental problems we face, one might be forgiven for asking what is thereby achieved. For one thing, we may simply find the Stoic perspective unappealing. Bernard Williams, for example, who is certainly not averse to drawing on the resources of ancient thought in addressing contemporary problems, nevertheless appears to draw the line at Stoicism, or at any rate one Stoic in particular.[33] He introduces Seneca's attempt to reconcile a slave to his slavery by telling him that his soul is free as "one of the more repulsive expositions of this attitude," adding the comment that "Seneca and his various associates can let the social world be unjust, because they can, in accordance with one or another of their fantasies, suppose that one can get out of it."[34] Perhaps we have seen reason to think that the Stoic perspective was not as escapist as this assessment would suggest. At any rate, one might cite on the other side the verdict of Paul Tillich, who finds Stoicism—"the way in which some of the noblest figures . . . have answered the problem of existence"—to be the "only real alternative to Christianity in the Western world."[35] What matters, of course, are the reasons he gives for this verdict. Essentially, it rests on his belief that in their response to life the Stoics had found certain kinds of courage, especially the courage to affirm their own rational natures in the face of anxiety and fear. The one ground for complaint that Tillich has against the Stoics is that they failed to confront the problem of guilt. But that is a failure that Williams might welcome, given his sharply critical discussion of certain modern notions of guilt: "In not isolating a privileged conception of moral guilt," he writes, "and in placing under a broader conception of shame the social and psychological structures that were near to what we call 'guilt,' the Greeks, once again, displayed realism, and truthfulness, and a beneficent neglect."[36] With regard to our environmental predicament also, I have tried to suggest that the Stoics have things to say that make a "conversation" with them worthwhile.

12

Plotinus as Environmentalist?

Donald N. Blakeley

This paper is an exploration of the extent to which the *Enneads* supports a "mysticism of descent" as a counterpart and completion of the more dominant erotic-noetic ascent to achieve unity with the One. The possibility of mystical union with the cosmos raises the prospect of a very distinctive ecological or environmental ethic in a philosophical work that is noted primarily for its high ranking of union with the One and contrasting low ranking of embodiment and the existence of the material world.[1]

I intend to show the inadequacy of what amounts to the standard view that Plotinus and the *Enneads (Enn.)* advocate (1) a negative and depreciative evaluation of the cosmos and (2) an exclusivist kind of mystical pursuit for humans, of either an introvertive or a theistic type.[2] Considering the dialectical process of being, the phenomenological descriptions of the experience of being, the response to the Gnostic appraisal of the world, the information provided by Porphyry in his *Life of Plotinus,* one can substantiate that a quite favorable, positive view of the cosmos and a cosmic type of mysticism are included in, and entailed by, the ontology and epistemology of Plotinus.[3]

If the descent of being (or the emanation from the One)[4] is an ever ongoing process that completes its expression of plenitude in the formation of the cosmos, this creates the condition for a unity on the cosmic level that constitutes the basis of an ecophilosophy in the *Enneads.* Such a unity is not shut off from higher-level unities because of continuity with, and dependency upon, the rest of the hierarchy of being. Since humans have access to these unities that ranges from embodied sensibility to *noesis* (and beyond), the epistemic and ethical consequences of existing in the cosmos deserve serious consideration. Although Plotinus certainly does emphasize "the ascent mode" for humans, the more complete structure of mystical and virtuous development via "the descent mode" must also be secured in legitimacy and made explicit in significance. This includes not only social-political-historical affairs but the affairs of nature and the role of humans within it as well.

Objections to Cosmic Mysticism

Three considerations appear to count rather straightforwardly against finding a cosmic (or extrovertive) mysticism in the *Enneads*. One is the negative and pessimistic appraisal given by Plotinus of the material world and embodiment. The second is the hazard of *tolma*, that is, the audacity, arrogance, and self-assertion, in this case, of a (human) soul assuming that it can rightly be independent and find genuine value in worldly pursuits and the affairs of nature. The third has to do with the very idea of mystical unity with the material world. Is it structurally— that is, ontologically and conceptually—possible? Does the material world have the capacity to form a unity with itself according to its material nature—except in some trivial and uninteresting way? Does not any such unity presuppose something that necessarily goes beyond and is other than what (in this case) the universe can realize for itself?[5] If the cosmos requires Soul for any significant unity and organizational integrity, isn't the unity achieved in Soul (by virtue of its powers) rather than in the material universe itself? For a human, if there is any kind of unity with the cosmos, is it not really because of one's soul and not one's body? In this respect, it would seem to be a category mistake and misnomer to suppose that a unity with the cosmos can be realized in some significant way.

I will respond to each of these critical points in what follows, but a brief reference to a closely related study of this general issue will be of interest. I will then turn to reflect upon what types of mysticism appear to have a place in the *Enneads*.

Daniel Kealey on Plotinus

In a recent book on environmental philosophy entitled *Revisioning Environmental Ethics*, Daniel Kealey includes a chapter on Plotinus that is a noteworthy departure from most interpretations.[6] Although he does not find Plotinus himself putting the philosophical structure of the *Enneads* to work in the service of a perspective adequately responsive to environmental concerns, he does find that central features of Plotinus's analysis are supportive of, rather than contrary to, a positive appraisal of the world. By attending, in particular, to the explanation that Plotinus gives of contemplation (*theoria*), eros, and production (*poiesis*), Kealey is able to abstract a list of points that are "particularly relevant to an integral ecological ethic." Referring only to the first and most consequential point, Kealey specifies: "All nature contemplates. This may be the most important tenet for it at once negates the ontological separateness of the natural, human, and divine spheres. All share in and are constituted in the fundamental act of contemplation."[7] By highlighting the common source that determines the basic structure and identity of nature and observing that Plotinus himself must admit that nature is as good as it can be, Kealey is able to show why the world possesses value as a concrete expression of higher principles. An environmental ethic can thus be based upon a consideration of the genuine status and nature of the world, its holistic operation and shared underlying dynamic. "The more that human contemplation identifies with both the natural and divine dimensions of contemplation, the more will humanity both fulfill itself and allow for greater ecological harmony."[8]

Despite the promise of the analysis in the *Enneads*, however, Kealey finds Plotinus's position unsatisfactory because "he is so overpredominantly concerned with the negative return movement of consciousness that he is completely negligent in regards to the possibility that the enlightened sage may have important work to do in the world for which his or her visions of the intelligibles and of the One were as much means as end."[9] I agree with Kealey's analysis of the material that he examines. I, however, would like to proceed by attending more directly to the issue of unity, because I think that it more specifically reveals the richness of the *Enneads* as regards the status of social-political concerns as well as environmental ones.

Cosmic Mysticism and Types of Unity

There is little doubt that Plotinus is a mystic of some sort. It is evident from his writing and from what is known of his life. But how is the mysticism or the "experiences" of unity that are delineated in the *Enneads* to be understood?[10] Writers on mysticism have proposed various classifications of mysticism.[11] The description of the ascent of the soul to its source given in the *Enneads* seems *not* to fit into an extrovert type. Rather than affirm the significant standing of the expansiveness, diversity, and process of the spatiotemporal material cosmos that would include not only the stars, sun, moon, daimons, gods but also more directly human-related conditions such as history and tradition, social-political affairs, family life, individual enterprise, and labor within the world, Plotinus's persistent message appears to be one of escape, flight, detachment, transcendence.[12] The destination for a self is away from the world to a condition of unity with the ultimate indescribable source of all things, a condition where there is a loss of individuation and standing in the cosmos. The world is, by comparison, deficient, incomplete, needy, the least of beings amenable to the good. Embracing the world, from this perspective, is seen to be ontologically degrading, epistemically diminishing and distancing, and ethically bad, regretful, blameworthy, illegitimate, wrong. Who in their right mind, if they could do otherwise, would want to participate in, let alone unify with, such a state of affairs? From this point of view, is it just an observation of eccentricity when Porphyry begins his biography of Plotinus by noting that "Plotinus, the philosopher of our times, seemed ashamed of being in the body"? Plotinus himself even raises the question of whether it would have been better if the material world had not come to be.

But let us explore this option more straightforwardly. The opposite direction from introversion (and ascent) that is possible for mystical unity would involve identity that is consummated by means of achieving unity with the cosmos. The cosmos would be like an extended, expansive body where identity is decentralized, spread out, and penetrating all, so that identities of self and reality would be unified in a field that embraces the totality of material things and states of affairs in space and time. Major features of cosmic mysticism would appear to include the following profile. There would be

1. a sense of the unity of nature, and of one's identity with it;

2. a sense of the cosmos as a living presence, "intimately rooted in life and consciousness";[13]

3. a sense that everything is transpiring in an eternal unchanging present or that the distinctions between time and change and eternity and unchanging are consolidated or interpenetrating without conflict or disparity;

4. a sense that, as a result of the transition from attachment to, to detachment from, ego and world (unity with *nous* and the One), the return or descent to the world and embodiment merits an affirmative appraisal, that it is to be approached as a product and gift worthy of celebration;

5. a sense that individuality, properly appraised, is a site of creative and edifying empowerment that expresses the unifying source (formative power) of all;

6. a sense that such existence in, and unity with, the cosmos has both noetic qualities resulting from the realization of unity and a felt quality of unity (e.g., sympathy) where the distinctions between self and other, within and without, being and process function dialectically and supportively rather than exclusively (in opposition, in competition);

7. a sense that the material world and its unity are real, a work of providence, and worthy of serious regard that may be manifest in a wide range of quite ordinary actions, practices, projects, vocations.[14]

The model for understanding how mystical unity can be duplicated in each hypostatic extension is explicitly set forth in Plotinus's analysis of *nous*. *Nous* is composed of everything intelligible, as differentiated, with every intelligible thing having its individual identity. *Nous* has an identity that is composed of the unity of everything intelligible, as Intellect that has immediate, full, direct access to itself in holistic, indivisible, total identity with itself. It also has an identity that comprises both its unity in identity and in differentiation. *Nous* is many, one, and one-and-many.[15] It is also vitalized and enriched through its erotic aspiration to the One, so that, in turn and as a consequence, it functions as the source of Soul that represents *nous* by means of *logoi*. Soul, in turn, exercises its organizational powers in a bidirectional dynamic of acquisition and generation, of aspiration and descent, to form the cosmos. It has its undescended aspect, its identity and differentiation within itself, and its productive, informing descent into the realm of matter to "create" the cosmos.

I will refer to this model as dialectical because it is composed of three distinct identities (compositions, "moments"), two of which are contrary to one another but both of which are conjoined in the third. In addition, there is a progression from one region of being to another in such a way that the later stages are determined by the structural features present in the prior stage. As Plotinus delineates this dialectical ontology in the case of *nous*, so he continues to employ the basic structure and logic as he delineates the hypostasis of Soul. It is the claim of this essay that it also applies to the cosmos. The cosmos, properly understood, is one, many, and one-and-many. Inasmuch as the factors of *nous* and Soul are the formative forces that determine the structure and process of the cosmos, it is not surprising that this realm will, in its own distinctive and qualified way, imitate the logic and dynamic of these more primal regions of being.

This has direct implication for mystical unity because each level of the emanation process has its "moment" of unity as identity (or identity-without-difference). Mystical unity at its most complete involves a shift to become one (or in identity) with some other. From the point of view of human experience, the self as soul has access to the material realm as well as that of *nous* and the One. Although it is not accurate to say that the self has access to these regions by intentional (subject-object) consciousness, there is no doubt that access to these others is affirmed by Plotinus.[16] The aspiration or ascent of the individual soul is set on this achievement. The self will, in union, become one with the "substance" of the other. Since that substance operates dialectically, with three distinct but interrelated moments, the self can itself be transformed according to the structural features of this other (ontological region). This is most clearly elaborated by Plotinus in his analysis of the relation between soul and *nous* and the transition into unity as identity with the One.[17]

The self, for Plotinus, can engage in this transformation process as it encounters the other levels of being. Its dialectical identity will conform to the specific content of each level. Hence, the identification of the structure and dynamics of being is also an identification of the nature of unifying "experiences" that are responsive to the ontological, epistemological, and axiological nature of the being in question. The three kinds of union are composed of the three moments that comprise the nature of a distinctive level of reality, ranging from the One to the cosmos.

The counterpart to this unity and its formative power is the drive to engender, to apply the power of good and beauty and order into a mode of otherness. It is the proper aspect of *tolma* when a self is attentive and responsive to its appropriate limits and dependencies in the exercise of its resources. If the soul were to lose or forsake its sense of connection and continuity with the higher as it asserts itself into formative action (as an individual embodied life form) in the material world, this would be the excessive, audacious, self-isolating aspect of *tolma* that Plotinus condemns.[18] The drive of *tolma* is, in effect, the descent vector of a properly composed erotic disposition. Rather than lose itself by going beyond its proper bounds, such self-assertion should be a carrying on of the natural, resourceful progression of being.

The erotically disposed Soul begets and cares for its progeny, that is, the space-time-material continuum—the cosmos. So also the erotically disposed individual soul begets and cares for its environment and progeny. The natural disposition and action of a human self involves this bidirectional operation. It is (ideally) able to cover the spectrum of being and be in accord with the dialectical nature and operation of each component. As an embodied human soul, its productive (descent) vector will be expressed in actions, projects, and relations that compose personal, interpersonal, and social-political existence. It will involve a life of virtue in the form of concrete actions and commitments in the routine affairs of normal personal and civic affairs. More broadly, it will include proper appraisal of, and disposition toward, the material world, or cosmos. This is the field of action where principles (*logoi, nomoi*) are assessed in terms of values that cover social as well as environmental ethics. And, according to the *Enneads*, humans can learn to "be" in this field in distinctive differentiated, identity, and identity-and-difference modes.

As it happens, then, Plotinus's emphasis upon the ascent mode functions to make accessible to awareness and understanding the multiple unities that exist for an aspiring self. It is important to note that each vector of the dynamic (of ascent and descent) is operating simultaneously and always. For a self, Soul, *nous*, and the One could not be closer than they are ontologically. Everyday being in the world involves no distance (of time or space) from these realities. But the task of realizing the three moments of these realities is by no means easy. Disposing oneself according to the realization that the transcendent is always also immanent, inherent in, and penetrating every object and state of affairs that come into existence and that there is in each major region of being an identity, difference, and identity-and-difference modality is a tremendous and difficult challenge.

What this analysis means for the issue of unity and identity, then, is that there are three major types of unity that can be realized. They are, in the abstract:

1. unity-with-difference, that is, unity but without identity; there is some sense of individuality and difference preserved even as intimacy and the elimination of many distinctions occur;[19]

2. unity-without-difference, that is, complete elimination of distinctions between self and the One, the two become one without another;

3. unity of identity-and-difference, that is, unity-without-difference is preserved and difference is also affirmed and operative in the life of the mystic. An illustration would be Porphyry's description of Plotinus as "present at once to himself and to others, and he never relaxed his self-turned attention . . . his continuous turning in contemplation to his intellect."[20]

As I understand these three types, there is a sequence such that (3) cannot occur without (2). Unity type 3 should also be understood as the most advanced and complete realization of being. Unity 3 is in touch with the whole spectrum of unities while nevertheless preserving the differentiation of each major unity (vertically) as well as the items of a field at every level (horizontally). For (3), there would be no incompatibility between unity with the One and unity with the cosmos. In fact, if cosmic unity were not realized, the self-identification process would be incomplete and unfulfilled. Unity 2, which is without difference, would not, in this perspective, be viewed as the climax of the epistemic quest or the pursuit of the fullest expression of the Good but rather a focus that is paramount but excessively narrow because exclusive to it. The addition of (3) would be required in order to include the fuller configuration of reality as a whole. This would be the unity and continuity (including difference) that comprises the hierarchy of being.

These types of unity are not prominently displayed in the *Enneads*. Presumably this lack of emphasis occurs because intense focus upon the ascent is needed for persuasive pedagogy, and the unity-without-difference state of being is the supreme edifying presence that is decisive for everything else. Commentaries, expositions, interpretations naturally follow this focus of Plotinus. But if the ideological structure set forth in the *Enneads* actually provides a basis for implications that Plotinus did not himself emphasize or elaborate, as I maintain, then achieving union with the One cannot qualify as the completion of human aspirations. A more thorough delineation is not only available, it is required.

The more expansive view extends the nature of mystical unity to include a unity with the cosmos. It is important to recognize two facets of this extension. One is that the shift from unity-without-difference (2) to unity of identity-and-difference (3) does not abandon or deny unity-without-difference. The second point is that the culmination of the ascent should then be located in the generative response, "the descent" (or emanation aspect), that follows by ontological exigency. What at first may have appeared to be alien and distant—the formation of the cosmos—is actually reconciled and in accord with the primal nature of things. What appears as an unresolvable dualism between the One and all that follows from it can (and should) be experienced in different unities that go from embodiment to soul to *nous* to the One. At each level there is a shift in ontological, epistemological, and axiological content. Each level has its distinctive determinants. But the final and most complete realization of unity will be a type of unity that preserves identity and difference at each level and does so with respect to the whole range of being. Individuation, multiplicity, and change are preserved in the mode of unity as identity-and-difference. The One is preserved in simple identity with itself without rejecting or degrading the fecundity and transformation of its manifestation into multiplicity. The cosmos *is* this One as Other inasmuch as the very nature and form for the cosmos come from the One (via *nous* and Soul). As a result of this complexity in being, the state of "being alone with the Alone" must accommodate itself to the One's resulting identity as Other and this identity as being in unity with itself as identity-and-difference. Focus upon the former cannot result in the neglect of the latter.

Evidence from *Enneads* 4.8

Evidence of the bidirectional (ascent-descent) evaluation and the tension between the "two poles of being" (One-matter) is present from the outset of Plotinus's writings. The sixth treatise in chronological order has received the title "The Descent of the Soul into Bodies" (*Enn.* 4.8). It begins with Plotinus recounting his own personal experiences of awakening into his body after having been in unity with the divine, descending to Intellect (*nous*), and finally arriving at the discursive reasoning (*logismos, dianoia*) and perceptive awareness (*aisthesis*) of the soul (*psyche*). The treatise clearly indicates the historical as well as the ideological context of Plotinus's analysis. Moving from Heraclitus, Empedocles, and Pythagoras to Plato, a dualistic appraisal is given in the most dramatic of images. From the *Phaedo* in particular, Plotinus observes that Plato "everywhere speaks with contempt of the world of sense and disapproves of the soul's fellowship with body and says that soul is fettered and buried in it."[21] The *Phaedrus* describes the embodied soul as disabled, fallen, caught in the terrible conflicting and confusing realm of passions and limitations.[22] At the other extreme, however, the *Timaeus* shows the physical cosmos to be the result of intelligent design and direction. The universe is a good product of ungrudging, abundant, and constant care. This care is evidenced in the structures and formative patterns that render the indeterminate stuff of matter into the best possible world order. Such an effort and its outcome are worthy of appreciation and thoughtful regard.

Such a story line has two seemingly contrary themes: One is of grief, degradation, and alienation as an inevitable result of a transformation process and distancing from the ultimate source that is necessary for there to be a physical world and embodiment. The other theme is of extended care, productive resourcefulness, and ceaseless formative presence that are required for the sustenance of the physical universe. The cosmos is the final scene where the nature of goodness through the activity of soul and the influence of *nous* is expressed to the maximal degree in materialization. The universe is good, as perfect as it can be, and is the objectivization of the nonmaterial forces and factors into space, time, and material form. The natural world is a begotten product and natural and inevitable consequence of erotic-eidetic formative forces that constitute the more basic nature of being through Soul and *nous*.

The case is formulated as follows. First, the "creation" of the cosmos and, as a part of this process, the embodiment of a soul is a decline, degradation, worsening condition. The world of sense deserves the appraisal of contempt in contrast to its origin. Since it is obviously better to be in a higher condition, the best advice is to flee as quickly as possible to the higher. The body to which a soul comes is also despised because of its continual needs and dependencies. Communion with it is disapproved inasmuch as embodiment is a source of hindrance, confusion, temptation, and general limitation.

The position that is delineated in this early treatise comprises the basic case that appears in the later writings. It contains, I maintain, a mixed message that is easily misunderstood and sometimes misleadingly presented by Plotinus himself as he enthusiastically focuses upon and represents the ascent part of the message. But the message can be given a more balanced presentation by attending to both vectors of being. Soul and material are comparatively low in the hierarchy of being. But the One expresses its reality in such a way as to produce the initiative for complete representation in every way to the furthest extent possible. This resourceful drive to maximal delineation and manifestation in effect requires and authenticates soul and materiality. This other direction away from the One must be viewed as a completion or fulfillment process. That *nous* generates and sustains Soul and Soul engages in the generation and sustenance of the material order is a contribution to such a project of fulfillment. Transformation, qualification, or modification of being is certainly involved, but never is there a separation or independence from the ontologically prior sources. The sources are what is being represented in this differentiation process. The progeny cannot be cut off because they depend upon their higher otherness, as essentially, ontologically, structurally akin. The higher otherness expresses itself in every way that it is able by means of the resourcefulness that is available to it. The more balanced description, then, would include both the dynamics of transcendance and engendering. The two vectors and their distinctive activities are integrally linked to each other. Within the scope of the self's discovery of its constitution in the spectrum of being (through the hierarchical levels to the One) is the surge or initiative to a higher identity and unity, but also with the resulting urge to generate and give birth to products that are other than, but imitate, one's own being.

The model, here, is provided most prominently in Plato's *Symposium* and *Phaedrus*. That is, the mixed message is simply a representation of the vectors of being: the returning-to and going-forth modalities. It is love as aspiration and appropriation of the better and love as generation of the good in otherness. In the *Symposium*, the formative productive activities on the human level range from physical reproduction of children to heroic deeds, works of literature, formulation of laws for well-formed political states, to philosophy and the direct tending of souls. The latter vector of descent cannot remain a neglected part of Plotinus's view. What allows for the explicit acknowledgment of the unity that is comprised in the outflow, or emanation, from the One is the return of a self from union with the One to the cosmos and its ongoing affairs. This return for humans involves a field of social and environmental realities that are available in the modes of difference, identity, and identity-and-difference. And these modes will, of course, have features distinctive of this ontological level.

Evidence from *Enneads* 5.3

An illustration of the transition that supports a mystical unity with nature is provided in a late treatise (no. 49) entitled "On the Knowing Hypostases and That Which Is Beyond" (*Enn.* 5.3). After dealing with sense perception (*aisthesis*) as providing data to discursive reason (*dianoia*), Plotinus introduces a distinction between "being in accord with" and "being identical with." We who use reason, he says, will be in accord with it by humans' rational power, but "we ourselves are not Intellect." (5.3.3.32). As he proceeds, a further distinction is observed between two ways that we can be in accord with Intellect: "either by having something like its writing written in us like laws, or by being as if filled with it . . . [by] learning a vision of this kind according to the knowing power, by that very power itself, or ourselves becoming it" (5.3.4.3).

In this transition, Plotinus finds himself now affirming that "a man has certainly become Intellect when he lets all the rest which belongs to him go and looks at this with this and himself with himself: that is, it is as Intellect he sees himself" (5.3.4.30). But this is not the end of the transforming identification process. In characterizing what the activity of the Intellect is, Plotinus writes:

"But it contemplates god," we might say. But if anyone is going to admit
that it knows god, he will be compelled to agree that it also knows itself. For
it will know all that it has from him, and what he gives, and what his power
is. But when it has learnt and knows this, then in this way also it will know
itself: for it is itself one of his gifts, or, rather, itself all of his gifts. If then it
comes to know that [Good], learning by his powers, it will come to know
itself since it comes from there and has received what it can. (5.3.7.1 f.;
bracketed interpolation by Armstrong)

To "know god" would be tantamount to knowing the Good/One in its
power to be other. As *nous* in its manifold nature is the result of the original formative power of the God/Good/One, so the items or gifts (ideas,
forms) that comprise *nous*-as-active become the formative forces that
transmit ideas (*logoi*) to Soul and, through Soul, to the material that
becomes the organized cosmos. Inherent in the cosmos is an image of a
noetic identity that, because it retains something of its original identity,
can be characterized as comprised of traces of being, living, and contemplation. Even though any material thing is other than, and different from,
soul, *nous*, and the One, it will nevertheless possess and participate in
these higher orders insofar as its very identity is determined and preserved by means of these. They must be present and preserved—ontologically, epistemically, axiologically—in order for any material thing to be
distinctly whatever it is. They are expressed in or inform the whole cosmos. As such, they are the structural forces that constitute everything that
exists. And inasmuch as the beyond-being of the One is higher than
speech, thought, and awareness, still "all that is not one is kept in being
by the one, and is what it is by this 'one': for if it had not become one, even
though it is composed of many parts, it is not yet what one would call
'itself'" (5.3.15.12). Plotinus's willingness to use the term "one" in this
manner is an interesting result of the dialectical logic required by indis-
pensable linguistic reference. It also illustrates the continuity and correlation of meaning across the spectrum of being that allows for movement of
reference either up or down the hierarchy; that is, one term finds application at every level, with its meaning determined by its reference on each
level and across the spectrum or hierarchy.

While advancing the more primary link, "since it comes from there and
has received what it can" (5.3.7.8), Plotinus also acknowledges the fundamental basis for the most original unity and identity:

"But how is that One the principle of all things? Is it because as principle it
keeps them in being, making each one of them exist? Yes, and because it
brought them into existence. But how did it do so? By possessing them

beforehand. But it has been said that in this way it will be a multiplicity. But it had them in such a way as not to be distinct: they are distinguished on the second level, in the rational form (*logos*). For this is already actuality; but the One is the potency of all things." (5.3.15.30 ff.)

"But if it has all life, and a clear and perfect life, then every soul and every intellect is in it, and no part of life or intellect is absent from it." (5.3.16.30)

Cosmic Unity and Sympathy

Discourse about such an identity can appear to be paradoxical, contradictory, or otherwise problematical if one misunderstands the dialectical nature of each level of being. In addition, spatial and temporal language becomes problematical when applied to Soul and *nous*. If one focuses upon the mode of unity on the level of *nous*, it is to be understood as the optimal realization of rational reality, as complete intelligibility, without the duality required by consciousness. The union on the level of Soul involves a realization of being, life, and *logos*. This is a specific kind of unity and identity that differs from the noetic. As *nous* is extended to be represented (in otherness and differentiation) in Soul, so Soul is extended to be represented (in otherness and differentiation) in the material world. But in each case, what becomes differentiated does not completely surrender its unity. The unity is either in itself or in the order of being.

The unity that is realized in the material realm Plotinus identifies as *sympatheia* (sympathy). The differentiation of Soul produces a new structural organization involving activity of Soul distributed throughout space and over time. Soul reaches everywhere in material bodies so that wherever matter becomes shaped or formed as body, there Soul is also. Soul sets matter in order (and process). It is natural (as the *ergon*/labor of erotic generosity) for it to be in body, to empower and inform it (e.g., 4.3.9). This is also understood to be an expression of the lawfulness and inherent teleology of the emanation process. Plotinus uses an intriguing analogy: "It is as if a net immersed in the waters was alive. . . . The sea is already spread out and the net spreads with it" (4.3.9.40). The net is explicitly identified as the *logos* (which Armstrong translates as "rational forming principle") that comes by way of Soul. The higher powers in the material world are not, however, *dianoia* but the modified psychic sensibilities indicated by the term 'sympathy.' Although what is encountered in nature is the result of the powers of *logos/eidos* derived from *nous*, this result is constituted in such a way that detection or discernment of the nature and dynamics of things requires a subpsychic respondence of the sort that is appropriate for embodied living creatures—among whom are we humans.

Cosmos as Community

At this point, the link between action, production, and contemplation becomes salient. Plotinus's explanation of these matters (in 3.8 especially) is really a quite amazing illustration of the dialectical and dynamic nature of *nous*. By its presence as life, being, and *logos*, the astonishing implication is that every material thing is a living, meaningful, and intelligible being whose very identity involves contemplation. If every instance of form in existence is the work of Soul and *nous*, it is not altogether bizarre to think of a stone, for example, as a low-grade instance of contemplative life, of ensoulment and inherent intellective determinateness. Soul and *nous* are immanently present and active in the whole universe. Though the cosmos is, by its very nature, dispersed into multiplicity and diversity, it nevertheless preserves a unity in its very being because of the presence of soul and *nous*. Like the net, the unity provided to nature is evident in its limited mode of being, life, and *logos*. This expresses itself operationally as order and regulation in the changing spatiotemporal states of affairs. Inherent in it are principle and law, *arche* and *logos/nomos*.

Plotinus says the cosmos is composed of material forms dynamically interrelated in a community of feeling (4.3.8). It is in sympathetic responsiveness with itself, having internal self-communication; it is interrelated, having continuity, affection, not cut off from itself, bound together in self-correspondence, encompassing all within it (4.4.35). Such unity takes the form of, and manifests itself in, the discernments of sympathy. The cosmos is in living unity with itself while nevertheless being differentiated in its own distinctive materialistic way.[23]

There is, then, a specific type of unity present in the cosmos.[24] One cannot, except by faulty ontology, fail to acknowledge this. In addition, experiential confirmation and recognized participation in this unity are available to human sensibilities. We can know and have access to the unity of identity and difference on the level of cosmos. Even though the epistemic nature of this unity is different from that of the other levels, there is no justifiable reason to discount or downplay the importance of this realization. Mystical unity with the cosmos as a unified being in sympathetic awareness and responsiveness to itself is effectuated in the cosmos, and it is very significant to the genuine and authentic dynamics of nature. For selves as embodied souls who participate in this realm, the realization that the genuine reality of the social and environmental aspects of existence is available in differentiation, in identity, and in identity-and-difference is extremely important. We can come to discern the structure, process, and vitality of the cosmos in each of these major modes of involvement or participation. The existence of other material beings or entities is caught up in, and is affected by, the forces and factors that make up the sympathetic connections and responsiveness of all things.

Since the cosmos has a stable, preserved, everlasting location in the nature of reality, one should welcome the opportunity to affirm and celebrate this legitimate and valuable unity as the highest mode of realization available on this level of being. As we ourselves are gifts and traces from the One and as we preserve the identity of the higher unities within our own spectrum of being, our own embodied living in the world as humans can be experienced as a participation in a cosmic network that is in sympathetic unity with itself.

For Plotinus, there is, in this way, an ecological, holistic perspective that should be acknowledged and represented. The most adept ecologist will be guided by the powers available not only through reason and perception but also by sympathy. It is also the case that the configurations, relationships, and activities of nature will be represented in more cognitively accessible forms in *dianoia* and *nous*. As there is identity in union and difference at each major level of the hierarchy, there is also continuity and a kind of symmetry or correlation (imitation) across the hypostases. It really should be no surprise that even the most materialized form is form nevertheless. As such, the cosmos is a direct contributor to our sense of identity and unity as well as individuation. The cosmos is an important site of unity and, as an expression of the Good, it is not accidental, unnatural, or lacking in value or beauty. The good resides, however, not only in the cosmos but also in our access to, and kinship with, it through the mystical unity of sympathy. Such a description and its implications must be included in the portrayal not only of the environment but also the account of virtuous (individual and collective) living for humans. It would be a shame to suppose that unity with, and absorption in, the One is touted as the most complete realization of human life—although it is undoubtedly of crucial importance. Virtue can be found everywhere, and this certainly includes what may seem to be the hinterlands of the realms of being. Humans, as beings intimately linked with the hierarchy of being, have available in this hinterland a kind of ennoblement and celebratory *ergon* (work, functioning) that comprise an existence in touch with its social and

natural environment. As earthly agents, we can be responsive participants   ⁻
in the ongoing mediation process of gift realizers and givers.

Summation of Claims

It should be clear that the full fruition of mystical unity involves not only
a unity with the One (the absolute, simple, unmanifest, beyond determination) but also a unity that embraces all else that follows from the One,
including the manifold and diverse individuality of the changing cosmos.
Although residing in the world and being embodied can appear to be
alien and a serious impediment when proper perspective and disposition
are lacking, these conditions turn out to be completely right, exactly what
is required, when seen from the perspective of both the ascent and the
descent process of reality. Because the unities that are realized along the
way to the One can be retained in the descent, the mystic's "home" would
simply be this whole reality, living responsibly in each major region, realizing appropriate unity and identity with each, including the region of
embodied earthly existence. As one comes to this world after being away,
absorbed in higher unities, the mystic's identity can be realized and exercised both with the One and, extending through *nous* and Soul, in the
nooks and crannies of the natural and social world. The two "locations"
are not mutually exclusive or necessarily competitive. The spectrum of
identities for the fully functioning self will extend across the whole spectrum of being and involve a series of identities whose unities extend both
vertically (hierarchically) and horizontally (at each level). The life of the
sage (the highest virtue) will involve the realization and affirmation not
only of the legitimate place of disembodied identity (with Soul, *nous*, and
the One) but also of embodiment and being caught up in the changing
material world. This cosmic region of being can be realized in intimate
unity with itself and with us humans as active participants and responsible agents in this realm of the natural world.

Conclusion

The case that I make in favor of a place for a "mysticism of descent" as an
integral part of the ontological structure of reality delineated in the
Enneads has identified and responded to three major objections. To the
first objection—that the material world and embodiment are evil or alien-
ated or degrading and that they are unworthy of serious attention—the

response is that the cosmos comes from the good and shares in its being and value. The cosmos is constructed by its very nature to be responsive to, and in tune with, itself. It has a special unity, and this ontological and epistemic condition of sympathy is important for humans as a source of value and site of value-creation.

The second charge concerns *tolma* and the arrogance of individuation and defiance of dependency upon the One. This is resolved once the erotic-productive nature and activity of Soul are clarified. The cosmos is an active expression of concern for the realization of the highest degree of good that is possible in all states of affairs. Embodiment and materiality can quite properly be the agents and recipients of form. Individuals do not need to be cut off from, and hence isolate themselves (in defiance or otherwise) from, fundamental resources of Soul and *nous*. In effect, cosmic unity involves no denial of the continuity of being and the ultimate dependency upon the One. *Tolma* can be natural and legitimate; it is, in fact, an expression of what Plotinus calls the law of being related to productive resourcefulness. Humans in the world are simply individualized versions of this more general principle at work in all things. This can also be seen as the providential care (*pronoia*) that is inherent to the cosmos and that it has for itself.[25]

Finally, the concern that the ontological character of the material universe is not capable of unifying with itself turns out to be a misunderstanding of the truly dialectical nature and bidirectional dynamic constituting even the affairs of the cosmos. Although the type of unity that is possible on this level is distinctly different from that on the levels of Soul and *nous*, the unity achievable as sympathy is of undeniable value in itself and in its relation to higher levels of being. It presents for humans the maximal epistemic realization on this level, and it would be the basis for the axiological (ethical and aesthetic) evaluation of the cosmos. It affects decisively how a self is to identify itself and understand its embodiment and its relation to the social-political field of action as well as the ongoing affairs of the natural environment.

The *Enneads*, therefore, provides sufficient detail to show that unity with the cosmos is possible, what it is, how it is constituted, and why it is important. The fact that the overwhelming, if not exclusive, emphasis of Plotinus in the *Enneads* is upon the ascent rather than the descent, that there is an important disparity between the metaphysics and its use at the hands of the writer of the *Enneads*, is important but not, I think, insurmountable evidence. The dominant focus upon the specific goal of unity with the One is understandable. Still, it must be acknowledged that dialectical dwelling in unity with the One as well as with the many things, processes, events, beings, persons, institutions, etc., of the material world is not the clearly stated consummation of Plotinus's analysis in the *Enneads*.

Perhaps the restricted focus of his writings is due to the selective intended readership. Perhaps the details of the actual life of Plotinus (as given by Porphyry) provide an additional source of support for the cosmic type of mystical unity. It is not just his commitment to quite open education (including women), or his open household and support of children, or his interest in establishing the community of Platonopolis. It seems fair to say that these aspects of his life could hardly be anticipated on the basis of what is emphasized in the *Enneads*. But the fact that Plotinus is described as himself being able to be present in the rather mundane activities and concerns of a household, as teacher, writer, mentor, friend, and model for many others, while at the same time being engaged in higher-level contemplative activities is of signal importance.

In very general terms, it is perhaps sufficient to establish that not only is there no logical, ontological, epistemic, or axiological conflict between the emphasis upon the ascent and a mystical unity with the cosmos, but there is in fact basic material in the *Enneads* that makes precisely this point inescapable. Characterizations of the cosmos as a "gift of god," "products of the activity of love," "things of beauty and constant care," "the powers of providence" can hardly be set aside. As essentially and not accidentally or dishonorably connected to the One, the cosmos is an expansive expression of the ultimate good. The cosmos is the very location where the good, in its vitality and fruition, is manifest in material form.

This, I take it, is enough to support the legitimacy and importance of a social and political ethic as well as an integral ecological perspective within the writings of Plotinus. Mystical union, which is, in effect, the way of salvation for Plotinus, does require abandoning the world, turning away from the whole cosmic scene. But this educational curriculum leads back—dialectically—to a resourceful kind of dwelling in the midst of earthly affairs. Such a vocation in response to the transcendent, as well as the social and environmental challenges presented by the cosmos, offers not a life of disgrace and alienation but one with suitable edification and accord, a life in unity with all things in the ways that these things really matter.

Notes

Introduction

1. L. Whyte, "The Historical Roots of Our Ecological Crisis," *Science* 155 (10 March 1967): 1203–7.

2. J. B. Callicott, *In Defense of the Land Ethic* (Albany: State University of New York Press, 1989), esp. "Traditional American Indian and Western European Attitudes toward Nature: An Overview," 177–201; Eugene Hargrove, *Foundations of Environmental Ethics* (Englewood Cliffs, N.J.: Prentice Hall, 1987), chap. 1.

3. R. O'Neill et al., *A Hierarchical Concept of Ecosystems* (Princeton: Princeton University Press, 1986); R. Ulanowicz, "Aristotelian Causalities in Ecosystem Development," *Oikos* 57 (1990): 42–48.

4. J. Cheney, "The Neo-Stoicism of Radical Environmentalism," *Environmental Ethics* 11 (1989): 293–325; Laura Westra, *An Environmental Proposal for Ethics: The Principle of Integrity* (Lanham, Md.: Rowman & Littlefield, 1994), 134–42.

5. See Callicott, *Land Ethic*, esp. 177–201.

6. Callicott, *Land Ethic*, esp. 177–201.

7. Callicott, *Land Ethic*, esp. 177–201.

8. Richard Sorabji, *Animal Minds and Human Morals* (Ithaca: Cornell University Press, 1993), 172–74; Diogenes Laertius, *Lives of the Eminent Philosophers* 8:36.

9. Sorabji, *Animal Minds and Human Morals*, 172–74.

10. Sorabji, *Animal Minds and Human Morals*, 107–8; Democritus, frr. 257–59, Diels-Kranz, cited in Sorabji.

11. Callicott, *Land Ethic*.

12. Westra, *Environmental Proposal for Ethics*, 134–42.

13. Martha C. Nussbaum, *The Fragility of Goodness: Luck and Ethics in Greek Tragedy and Philosophy* (Cambridge: Cambridge University Press, 1986), 260; Aristotle, *Parts of Animals* 1.5.654a.27–31.

14. Nussbaum, *Fragility of Goodness*, 260.

15. O'Neill et al., *Hierarchical Concept of Ecosystems*; see R. Ulanowicz, *The Ascendency Perspective* (New York: Columbia University Press, in press).

185

16. S. A. Howe, "The Body Politic: Aristotle, Animals, and Difference" (paper presented at the Society for Ancient Greek Philosophy conference, Binghamton University, Binghamton, N.Y., October 1995).

17. Westra, *Environmental Proposal for Ethics*, 134–42.

18. Howe, "Body Politic."

19. M. Oelschlaeger, *The Idea of Wilderness* (New Haven: Yale University Press, 1991), 55–60.

20. Oelschlaeger, *Idea of Wilderness*, 56.

21. David Ehrenfeld, *The Arrogance of Humanism* (New York: Oxford University Press, 1978).

22. Hargrove, *Foundations of Environmental Ethics*.

23. Thomas M. Robinson, "Parmenides on Ascertainment of the Real," *Canadian Journal of Philosophy* 44 (1975): 623–33; and Thomas M. Robinson, "Parmenides on the Real in Its Totality," *Monist* 62 (1979): 54–60.

Chapter 1: Some Ancient Ecological Myths and Metaphors

1. Plato, *Statesman* 271e, 272a.

2. Plato, *Republic* 2.372a–d.

3. Aristotle, *Politics (Pol.)* 1256b21–27.

4. Aristotle, *History of Animals* 8.20, 603a22.

5. Cf. Robert Graves, *The Greek Myths* (Harmondsworth, England: Penguin Books,1960), 139.

6. Anaximander B1 Diels-Kranz, in *Early Greek Philosophy*, trans. J. Barnes (London: Penguin Classics, 1987), p. 75.

7. Charles H. Kahn, *Anaximander and the Origins of Greek Cosmology*, (New York: Columbia University Press, 1960), pp. 166 ff., esp. 191.

8. It may have been Aristotle who first framed the relationship between humanity and nature as one of warfare, in the *Physics (Phys.)* passage cited above.

9. Empedocles B17 Diels-Kranz, first part.

10. Hippolytus, *Refutation of All Heresies* 7.29.14–23.

11. Empedocles B115.9–12 Diels-Kranz.

12. From Empedocles B128 Diels-Kranz, quoted from Porphyry, *On Abstinence* 2.20.

13. Sextus Empiricus, *Adversus Mathematicos* (Against the professors) 9:127–29.

14. Empedocles B139 Diels-Kranz, quoted from Porphyry, *On Abstinence* 2.23.

15. Actually, the Pythagoreans had suggested that the universe could draw emptiness as a kind of breath from infinite outside itself: Aristotle, *Phys.* 4.6.213b24.

16. Aristotle, *Pol.* 1.2.

17. Aristotle, *Meteorology (Mete.)* 1.14, 352a32.

18. Aristotle, *Mete.* 1.14, 352a29.

19. Aristotle, *Mete.* 353a16.

20. Aristotle, *Generation of Animals* 4.10.777b16–20, 778a5–9.

21. Aristotle, *Metaphysics* 12.8.1074b10.
22. Aristotle, *Nicomachean Ethics (NE)* 1.5.1097b14.
23. Aristotle, *NE* 10.7.1177a27.
24. Aristotle, *Rhetoric (Rh.)* 1.5.1360b14.
25. Aristotle, *Rh.* 1.1360b29.

Chapter 2: Why Greek Philosophers Might Have Been Concerned about the Environment

1. The similarities between men and animals in ancient thought are the subject of an interesting new study by Richard Sorabji (*Animal Minds and Human Morals: The Origins of the Western Debate* [Ithaca: Cornell University Press, 1993]). Sorabji blames the Stoics—and then certain Stoicizing attitudes about the mental inadequacies of beasts emphasized in Christianity by Augustine—for the gradually increasing philosophical alienation of men from animals. As he puts it, the Stoic argument about animals can be summed up as "If they don't have syntax, you can eat them." This is of course an exaggeration, though an interesting one. The philosophers and theologians rather confirmed than formed popular opinion, affording, as commonly, grounds for rationalization to those who thought they needed such grounds.

2. J. L. Mackie, *Ethics: Inventing Right and Wrong* (Harmondsworth, England: Penguin Books, 1977), 15.

3. J. Rawls, *A Theory of Justice* (Cambridge: Harvard University Press, 1971).

4. See more generally G. E. M. Anscombe, "Modern Moral Philosophy," *Philosophy* 33 (1958).

5. T. Nagel, *The View from Nowhere* (Oxford: Clarendon Press, 1986), 104.

6. Nagel (*View from Nowhere*, 230 n. 4) is right to draw attention to the difference a belief or nonbelief in post-mortem survival makes to moral attitudes on many topics: "I suspect that an important factor may be belief in an afterlife, and that the proportion of those who think that death is not the end is much higher among partisans of the [thermonuclear] bomb than among its opponents."

7. I shall speak of Plato rather than of other ancient thinkers at this point because I regard his moral vision as more suited than that of the others to offer comprehensive help in justifying concern for the environment in accordance with a theory dependent not merely on (perceived) self-interest but also on the nature of the cosmos itself. In limiting myself in this way, I do not want to give the impression that Aristotle and the Stoics might not be able to make a significant (though lesser) contribution. I have already implied that on questions of justification, Epicurus is in a position to offer very little—for the same reason that contemporary utilitarianism can offer little as philosophy, though much in public relations.

8. In company with most of his Greek predecessors, Plato (though perceptions were changing in his own day—a fact marked by the first paintings and sculptures of nude goddesses as well as gods) probably thought that male beauty

is greater than female, perhaps believing (a) that the male is more potent (since it could produce a homunculus in the sperm that then need only be nourished by its mother both before and after its birth), and (b) that if human beings are a single species—a fact, as Aristotle remarks in the *Metaphysics*, that was challenged by some—then there must be a single perfect form of that species, and that will be the male form, not only as more potent but as bigger and stronger. (Small males seem to have been thought of as less beautiful than larger ones, and the gods certainly had to be large!)

9. For general comment along these lines, see esp. A. MacIntyre, *After Virtue* (Notre Dame: University of Notre Dame Press, 1981), chap. 1.

Chapter 3: The Philosophical Genesis of Ecology and Environmentalism

1. For a discussion of Haeckel and the early use of "ecology," see Donald Worster, *Nature's Economy: A History of Ecological Ideas* (New York: Cambridge University Press, 1994), chap. 10.

2. R. G. Collingwood (*The Idea of Nature* [Oxford: Clarendon Press, 1945], 4) calls the science of this era "Renaissance cosmology," admitting that it is a less than adequate name.

3. E. J. Dijksterhuis, *The Mechanization of the World Picture* (Oxford: Clarendon Press, 1961).

4. On the different interpretations of "mechanism," see Dijksterhuis, epilogue to *World Picture*, 495–501.

5. See Ernst Mayr, *The Growth of Biological Thought* (Cambridge: Harvard University Press, 1982), 312–13; and Ernst Mayr, "Is Biology an Autonomous Science?" in *Toward a New Philosophy of Biology* (Cambridge: Harvard University Press, 1988).

6. Collingwoood, *Idea of Nature*, 9–13.

7. See Ernst Mayr, "Darwin, Intellectual Revolutionary," in *Toward a New Philosophy of Biology.* (See note 5.)

8. Amos H. Hawley, *Human Ecology: A Theoretical Essay* (Chicago: University of Chicago Press, 1986), 4.

9. See, e.g., Dijksterhuis, *World Picture*, 431–32.

10. Mayr, *Growth of Biological Thought*, 121.

11. Academic American Encyclopedia, s.v. "ecology."

12. Arne Naess, *Ecology, Community, and Lifestyle: An Outline of an Ecosophy* (New York: Cambridge University Press, 1989). See also Charles T. Rubin, review and critique of Naess in *Interpretation* 21 (1993): 73.

13. Naess, *Ecology, Community, and Lifestyle*, 29.

14. See Lincoln Allison, *Ecology and Utility: The Philosophical Dilemmas of Planetary Management* (Teaneck, N.J.: Fairleigh Dickinson University Press, 1991).

15. Louis Dupré, *Passage to Modernity: An Essay in the Hermeneutics of Nature and Culture* (New Haven: Yale University Press, 1993), 72; see also Clarence J.

Glacken, *Traces on the Rhodian Shore: Nature and Culture in Western Thought from Ancient Times to the End of the Eighteenth Century* (Berkeley and Los Angeles: University of California Press, 1967), 475.

16. Glacken, *Rhodian Shore*, 474–75.

17. On historical changes in the philosophical idea of "nature," see Dupré, *Passage to Modernity;* and Glacken, *Rhodian Shore.* See also Dijksterhuis, *World Picture.*

18. Rubin, in his review of *Ecology, Community, and Lifestyle,* argues that "Naess's deep ecology falls into the modern instrumentalist employment of philosophy" (75).

19. *Parts of Animals,* trans. W. Ogle, in *The Collected Works of Aristotle,* vol. 1, ed. Jonathan Barnes (Princeton: Princeton University Press, 1984).

20. For another example of environmentalist concern about the deep-seated chacter of the exploitation of nature and the urgency of the problem, see Laura Westra, *An Environmental Proposal for Ethics: The Principle of Integrity* (Lanham, Md.: Rowman & Littlefield, 1994); cf. Will Wright, *Wild Knowledge: Science, Language, and Social Life in a Fragile Environment* (Minneapolis: University of Minnesota Press, 1992).

For criticism of ecology's distrust of technology and industry, see *Taking the Environment Seriously,* ed. Roger E. Meiners and Bruce Yandle (New York: Rowman & Littlefield, 1993), esp. chap. 10, Robert H. Nelson's essay, "Environmental Calvinism: The Judeo-Christian Roots of Eco-Theology."

21. Robert M. Young, "Malthus and the Evolutionists: The Common Context of Biological and Social Theory," *Past and Present* 43 (1969): 109–41.

22. The scarcity of resources is the explanation for restrictions on population growth; without scarcity (of food, shelter, healthy sexual partners, and so forth) populations would increase, Malthus said, "geometrically." See Peter J. Bowler, *Evolution: The History of an Idea* (Berkeley and Los Angeles: University of California Press, 1984), 162–64; and Young, *Malthus and the Evolutionists.*

23. Plato's and Aristotle's views of nature and nature's stability differ, of course. Aristotle upholds nature's regularity and eternity, but Plato's own position is harder to discern. Nonetheless, whatever varying degrees of stability they see in nature, neither philosopher makes that stability a matter of human responsibility.

24. Plato's *Critias* (111a ff.) tells of ancient deforestation: There was an era long ago when the soil was rich and trees were abundant, but "what now remains compared with what then existed is like the skeleton of a sick man, all the fat and soft earth having wasted away, and only the bare framework of the land being left." *Critias,* trans. R. G. Bury (Cambridge: Harvard University Press, 1981). Critias relates that many convulsions shook this earth, and these convulsions appear to be the natural cause of the decline. He also mentions the use of the trees to supply rafters for the largest buildings (111c6–7), but it is not clear whether human use of the trees played a role in the demise of the land or whether it is mentioned simply to illustrate the great bounty of an earlier time.

25. See Victor Ferkiss, *Nature, Technology, and Society: Cultural Roots of the Current Environmental Crisis* (New York: New York University Press, 1993).

Chapter 4: Platonic Ecology, Deep Ecology

1. The term "Platonic ecology" follows the pattern of such terms as "radical ecology," "deep ecology," "feminist ecology," "spiritual ecology," and "social ecology," which have been coined to describe approaches to the burgeoning field of environmental philosophy. See M. E. Zimmerman et al., *Environmental Philosophy: From Animal Rights to Radical Ecology* (Englewood Cliffs, N.J.: Prentice Hall, 1993); and C. Merchant, *Radical Ecology: The Search for a Livable World* (New York: Routledge, 1992). In the notes to this essay, I will attempt to position Platonic ecology in the context of contemporary discussions of environmental philosophy.

2. See Merchant, *Ecology*, chap. 3, 61–82. The table on pp. 64–65 of that work summarizes the three approaches.

3. For a brief introduction, see Zimmerman's characterization of "deep ecology" in his general introduction in Zimmerman et al., *Environmental Philosophy*, vi.

4. Some environmental philosophers disparage dualism. For example, in *The Idea of Wilderness: From Prehistory to the Age of Ecology* (New Haven and London: Yale University Press, 1991), M. Oelschlaeger claims that in Plato's attitude "lurks the germ of a pervasive dualism and logocentrism, sometimes called Eurocentrism, that since the Greeks has infected virtually all Western philosophy, science, and religion," 57; also see 379 n. 83. Merchant lists dualism as a feature of egocentric ethics (*Radical Ecology*, 65, 69).

5. J. B. Callicott recognizes Plato as an ancestor of an important school of current environmental philosophy. In his introductory essay to the section on environmental ethics in Zimmerman (*Environmental Philosophy*, 3–11), Callicott distinguishes between two basic kinds of environmental ethics: individualistic approaches, such as those that emphasize rights or "moral considerability," and holistic approaches, such as Aldo Leopold's "land ethic." Callicott claims that Leopold and Plato share the holistic approach: see J. B. Callicott, "Animal Liberation: A Triangular Affair," *Environmental Ethics* 2 (1990): 311–38, esp. 324–29. The arguments of this paper support his conclusion.

6. "Forms" is probably the best translation of the Greek *eide*. Although this may also be translated as "ideas," "ideas" is misleading because it suggests that the *eide* are somehow subjective or mind-dependent, which is contrary to Plato's description of them.

The literature on the Platonic Forms is immense and continually growing. Many important issues are still hotly debated, including the question of whether those dialogues most associated with the Theory of Forms demonstrate that Plato himself was a "Platonist," i.e., held the Theory of Forms; see C. Meinwald, "Goodbye to the Third Man," in *The Cambridge Companion to Plato*, ed. R. Kraut (Cambridge: Cambridge University Press, 1992), 365–96. In the present paper, I assume the commonly held view that Plato is, in fact, a Platonist. For good accounts of the Theory of Forms, see R. Patterson, *Image and Reality in Plato's Metaphysics* (Indianapolis: Hackett, 1985), and J. Moravcsik, *Plato and Platonism* (Cambridge, Mass.: Blackwell, 1992). Moravcsik is particularly good at describing succinctly the "evolution" of the Theory of Forms in later dialogues.

7. See *Republic (Rep.)* 5.477b.

8. There is a continuing debate over whether the character Socrates speaks for Plato. This is part of the wider debate over how one can attribute positions to Plato from what is written in the dialogues. Another part of this debate is whether Plato's views underwent significant development; some suggestions as to the sequence in which the dialogues were written are based on theories about such development. On the overall debate, see C. Griswold, ed., *Platonic Writings, Platonic Readings* (New York: Routledge, 1988). In this essay I will assume with the majority of scholars that Socrates probably does articulate Platonic views in most cases. I also claim that Plato's position on the important issues in this essay did not change significantly.

9. See *Rep.* 7.514a–518b.

10. See *Rep.* 6.509d–511c.

11. See *Symposium* 210a–212b.

12. See *Phaedo* 65c–67b. R. Attfield in *The Ethics of Environmental Concern*, 2d ed. (Athens: University of Georgia Press, 1991), 53–54, 58), claims that Platonic thought is ill suited to addressing ecological problems because Plato believes that a person survives the loss of his or her body. But numerous passages in Plato's dialogues (e.g., *Gorgias [Grg.]* 523a–27e, *Phaedo [Phd.]* 107c–115d, *Phaedrus [Phdr.]* 246a–250c, *Republic (Rep.)* 10.614b–621d, *Timaeus (Ti.)* 41a–42d, and *Laws* 10.904a–c) suggest that one's afterlife depends crucially on how well one has lived one's life in the spatiotemporal realm. This opens the possibility that one will punished for one's "ecological sins" in the afterlife, and that view would seem to encourage, rather than to discourage, "this-worldly" ecological concerns.

13. *Phd.* 97b–c.

14. *Phd.* 97c–99c.

15. E.g., *Phdr.* 247c–e.

16. E.g., *Phdr.* 246e, *Ti.* 29d–30a, *Sophist* 265c–e, *Statesman* 269d–272b, *Philebus* 27a28d, *Laws* bk. 10.

17. E.g., *Rep.* 7.530a, and *Laws* 10.899b.

18. *Ti.* 47e. In the *Timaeus*, the Demiurge, or Artificer, (28c ff.) is the godly figure who is described as having the ultimate responsibility for the structure and governance of the physical universe. There is a debate with ancient roots over just how literally one should interpret the Demiurge in Plato's writings; see J. P. Kenney's "The Demotion of the Demiurge," in *Mystical Monotheism: A Study in Ancient Platonic Theology* (Hanover, N.H.: Brown University Press/University Press of New England, 1991), 57–90. Whatever position one takes on that issue, it is quite clear that for Plato the spatiotemporal world is as perfect as it can be because the god (or gods) models it on the Forms.

Oelschlaeger suggests that "Plato's divine Artificer is an intensification of Socratic homocentrism" (58). The truth is probably the exact opposite. The activity of the divine Artificer implies that nature is good and valuable independent of any human contrivance, manipulations, desires, or valuations. The goodness of nature comes from the divine, not from humans.

19. E. Mayr, *The Growth of Biological Thought: Diversity, Evolution, and Inheritance* (Cambridge: Harvard University Press, 1982) argues that Plato is a "disaster" for biology and especially for evolutionary thinking because, among other things, he

eschews observation of the natural world and clings to the idea of a changeless order (304–5). Plato is, according to Mayr, "the great anti-hero of evolutionism" (304).

This seems to me to be an overstatement. First, Plato's thought does not rule out that careful observation provides some cognitively valid description of the world. In fact, Plato's insistence that the spatiotemporal world is modeled on the Forms ensures that the natural world is by and large intelligible, even if it is not completely intelligible as is the world of Forms. In addition, our belief that the most advanced scientific theories of nature are subject to rejection and revision as new data are collected fits well with Plato's view that at best we can only tell "likely stories" (*Ti.* 29b–d) about the natural world. Second, it is certainly true that there is little in Plato that points toward the theory of evolution. But a timeless model of the sort Plato proposes can describe a process of temporal development, one as radical as biological evolution, or even the more radical developmental process suggested by the Big Bang cosmological theory. The entire sequence of temporal and spatial events can be aspects of the timeless model. Such an idea is defended by T. Sprigge in the course of his argument in support of what he calls "the essential truth of what I shall call eternalism, the view that there is a total reality which does not change and in which all moments of time are eternally present as 'nows.'" T. Sprigge, *James and Bradley: American Truth and British Reality* (Peru, Ill.: Open Court, 1993), 478 ff. The position described by Sprigge is not the same as Plato's, since Plato does not conceive of the parts of the spatiotemporal universe as simply identical to the constituents of the eternal model. Nonetheless, Sprigge's discussion points the way to a defense of Plato.

20. Plato, *Ti.* 30c–d. K. Sale approvingly quotes this passage at the very beginning of *Dwellers in the Land: The Bioregional Vision* (San Francisco: Sierra Book Club, 1985), 3.

There seem to be deep affinities between Plato's conception of the spatiotemporal world as a single living organism and the so-called Gaia hypothesis that some contemporary scientists have used to describe the earth. But I do not feel sufficiently well versed in that scientific hypothesis to comment on this issue. See S. Schneider and P. Boston, eds., *Scientists on Gaia* (Cambridge: MIT Press, 1991).

21. See *Ti.* 30a, c–d; cf. *Rep.* 6.419a–421c. Thus the criticism that Mayr makes of Plato's essentialism as emphasizing discontinuity (*Growth of Biological Thought*, 38–39, 87) is not well founded. Mayr's view is echoed by Oelschlaeger, *Idea of Wilderness*, 392 n. 80, and Merchant, *Radical Ecology*, 51 (see her reference to "context-independent entities"). Plato does not view the natural world or even the world of Forms as made up of independent units (see his description of dialectic in the *Sophist* 250e–254b). On the contrary, organicism is a basic pattern in Platonic thought.

22. Mayr, *Growth of Biological Thought*, 38–39; Oelschlager, *Idea of Wilderness*, 391 n. 73; and Merchant, *Radical Ecology*, 57, criticize Plato because they link his emphasis on mathematics to a "mechanistic" worldview. The organicity at the heart of Plato's vision should refute any claims that Plato had a "mechanistic" worldview. The comparisons these authors draw between Descartes and Plato are vitiated by a crucial difference between them: Plato claims that the entire spatio-

temporal world has its own soul (*Ti.* 34a–b), whereas, to quote Oelschlaeger, the "Cartesian picture of the living world [is] *nothing more than inanimate-matter-in-motion"* (391 n. 73, emphasis mine).

23. So the god follows the pattern described by Socrates in *Phd.* 97c–99c: "If Mind rules and directs."

24. Although they are not identical, Plato's outlook is echoed by the view expressed by A. Naess in his interview with Stephen Bodian, "Simple in Means, Rich in Ends" (Zimmerman et al., *Environmental Philosophy*, 182–92). G. Session's comments in his introduction could just as well apply to Plato and his philosophy: "Naess claims that the essence of deep ecology is to ask deeper questions, which, as in the traditional Socratic quest, leads us to the level of ultimate values and commitments, and to the articulation of a total world view." Zimmerman et al., *Environmental Philosophy*, 164.

25. E.g., *Grg.* 466e–468e, and *Meno* 78d.

26. E.g., *Rep.* 2.358e–359a.

27. E.g., *Theaetetus (Tht.)* 172b.

28. E.g., *Rep.* 5.476a ff.

29. See the first and second points of the eight-point program of deep ecology in A. Naess, "The Deep Ecological Movement," in Zimmerman et al., *Environmental Philosophy*, 197.

30. Although Merchant does not classify Plato in her egocentric/homocentric/ecocentric scheme, her remarks elsewhere concerning Plato's alleged mechanistic view of nature (*Radical Ecology*, 50–51, 57) suggest that she would class him as taking an egocentric approach. By contrast, Oelschlaeger seems to put Socrates and Plato in the homocentric (or anthropocentric) camp (*Idea of Wilderness*, 56–58, 65). Although this section explicitly addresses the charge of egocentrism, the arguments of this section also demonstrate that the charges of homocentrism and anthropocentrism are ill founded.

31. See *Tht.* 176a. See below.

32. J. Annas, *The Morality of Happiness* (Oxford: Oxford University Press, 1993), 322. Annas provides compelling arguments against this assumption; see 12, 27, 127, 224–27, 322–23. I have taken the quotation from the conclusion of her examination of the charge of egoism made against Greek ethics: "We can now see . . . why charges of egoism made against ancient ethical theories because of their eudaimonistic form miss the mark completely. The thoughtful person who enters on the path of ethical reflection in the manner of the ancient theories is moving away from self-concern" (322). Unfortunately, she says little about Plato or later Platonists; her book concentrates on the Stoics, Aristotelians (Peripatetics), Epicureans, Skeptics, and Cyrenaics.

33. Other translations have been proposed, such as "human flourishing"; see J. Cooper, *Reason and the Human Good*, in *Aristotle* (Cambridge: Harvard University Press, 1975). But as Annas argues, the correspondence between the terms *eudaimonia* and "happiness," though less than perfect, makes other translations somewhat misleading (*Morality of Happiness*, 453). My discussion of the term follows her remarks concerning the chapter "Ancient Ethics and Modern Morality," 452–55.

34. This is Annas's characterization (*Morality of Happiness,* 453). Moravcsik makes the same point by contrasting the "thin" concept of *eudaimonia* with the "rich" concept of happiness, (*Plato and Platonism,* 109).

35. Annas, *Morality of Happiness,* 453. ,

36. "Insofar as the [ancient] theories give virtue a non-instrumental role in achieving happiness, they are making morality necessary for happiness; and moral demands will lessen the role in the agent's life as a whole on her own self-centered projects, for their status will be determined by moral considerations, not vice versa." Annas, *Morality of Happiness,* 322.

Also see Moravcsik's discussion of Plato's "ideal ethics," especially the two chapters entitled "What We Are and What We Should Be" and "Platonist Ethics: Effecting Reorientation and Sustaining Ideals," in *Plato and Platonism,* 93–126, and 291–328, respectively.

37. E.g., *Rep.* 2 358b–d, 361d, and 367b.

38. H. A. Prichard is perhaps the most important proponent of this argument. See his two articles "Does Moral Philosophy Rest on a Mistake?" and "Duty and Interest," in *Readings in Ethical Theory,* ed. W. Sellars and J. Hospers, 2d ed. (New York: Appleton-Century-Crofts, 1970), 149–62 and 691–703, respectively. T. Irwin is a more recent author who claims that the ethical stance of the *Republic* is ego-centric (*Plato's Moral Theory* [Oxford: Clarendon Press, 1979] 255, 258, 278–9). But, unlike Prichard, Irwin suggests that egocentrism (as he defines it) may not conflict with the demands of morality at all.

39. *Rep.* 2.358b, 367b.

40. *Rep.* 2.360e–361d.

41. I defend this interpretation of the *Republic* in "Do Plato's Philosopher-Rulers Sacrifice Self-Interest to Justice?" *Phronesis* 37, no. 3 (1992): 265–82.

42. The core of Socrates' response is contained in his description of the philosophers, who represent those people who understand true *eudaimonia* (happiness). Socrates says of the philosophers that they value what is just (moral) as the greatest and most necessary thing *(Rep.* 8.540d–e).

43. Glaucon refers to what I am calling different versions of *eudaimonia* as different lives, 2360e; cf. *Grg.* 500c–d.

44. Reason, the "spirited" part of the soul that desires esteem in the eyes of oneself and of others, and the "appetitive" part of the soul that desires a variety of things including objects which satisfy thirst, hunger, and sexual desire, *Rep.* 4.436b ff.; see Mahoney, "Plato's Philosopher-Rulers," 277–80.

45. E.g., *Rep.* 9.582d.

46. See *Rep.* 4.433a–434a, 441d–e.

47. For example, T. Nagel, *A View from Nowhere* (New York: Oxford University Press, 1986) explicitly criticizes the strategy of the *Republic* in a chapter entitled "Living Right and Living Well" (189–207). Also, Plato's "holistic" conception of justice is open to challenge. In an essay entitled "The Conceptual Foundations of the Land Ethic," Callicott defends the "land ethic" against the charge of "environmental fascism," a charge that can be leveled against any holistic approach, including Plato's (Zimmerman et al., *Environmental Philosophy,* 110–34).

48. See A. Naess, "The Deep Ecology Movement: Some Philosophical

Aspects," in Zimmerman et al., *Environmental Philosophy*, 193–212. Again, G. Sessions's remarks concerning the "ecosophy" that Naess articulates in this article could well apply to Plato's philosophy: "Thus, in philosophical deep ecology, there is a decisive shift away from ethics (including 'environmental ethics') and morality and duty, to ontology (a transformed mature self with its corresponding change of perception and understanding) as a basis for right action," Zimmerman et al., *Environmental Philosophy*, 165–66.

49. Some commentators find a contemplative ideal in the Republic based on the remarkable claims that Socrates makes for contemplation in that dialogue. E.g., S. Aronson, "The Happy Philosopher—A Counterexample to Plato's Proof," *Journal of the History of Philosophy* 10 (1972): 383–98. Of course, this position is incompatible with the position I have sketched above. For a further critique of the arguments of these commentators see Mahoney, "Plato's Philosopher-Rulers," 266–73.

50. *Tht.* 172b–177c.

51. *Tht.* 173bff.

52. *Tht.* 176a5–b2. I follow J. McDowell's translation in *Plato: Theaetetus* (Oxford: Clarendon Press, 1973), except I translate *hosios* as "pious," rather than as "religious."

53. In *The Origins of the Christian Mystical Tradition* (Oxford: Clarendon Press, 1983), A. Louth attributes a contemplative ideal to Plato, although Louth believes that there is some tension between the active and contemplative lives in Plato (14–17). B. McGinn, in *The Foundations of Mysticism: Origins to the Fifth Century* (New York: Crossroad, 1991), also seems to attribute a contemplative ideal to Plato, (33–34).

54. *Tht.* 176b2–c3.

55. *Rep.* 6.501b–c and 10.612e–613b; *Phdr.* 247d–256b; *Laws* 4.716b–d. Also see *Ti.* 90a–d.

56. Presumably Socrates specifies "justice . . . with intelligence" to distinguish justice based on insight into genuine values from justice that comes merely comes habit and true opinion without such insight; cf. *Phaedo* 82a–c.

57. See Zimmerman, "General Introduction" in Zimmerman et al., *Environmental Philosophy*, v–x, particularly his remarks on deep ecology and the distinction between radical ecophilosophy and reformist anthropocentric ecophilosophy. The section on deep ecology in Zimmerman et al., *Environmental Philosophy*, 161–250, contains important statements and examinations of this approach to environmental philosophy.

58. This "natural" aspect of human beings is emphasized in *Laws* 10.903b–d.

59. This parallels the "weak anthropomorphic" principle that Zimmerman associates with social ecology (Zimmerman et al., *Environmental Philosophy*, vii–viii).

60. See *Ti.* 72a; cf. *Charmides* 161b.

61. *Rep.* 4.441e.

62. At *Critias* 110c–111d there is mention of deforestation and soil erosion. This passage is discussed by both C. Pointing, *A Green History of the World: The Environment and the Collapse of Great Civilizations* (New York: St. Martin's Press, 1991), 76–77, 143; and Clarence J. Glacken, *Traces on the Rhodian Shore: Nature and*

Culture in Western Thought from Ancient Times to the End of the Eighteenth Century
(Berkeley and Los Angeles: University of California Press, 1967), 121.

63. This was pointed out to me by Thornton Tibbals.

64. I wish to thank Douglas Lind for his very perceptive critical comments on an earlier draft of this essay.

Chapter 5: Environmental Ethics in Plato's *Timaeus*

1. For example, the cosmology attempts to explain such diverse subjects as stellar orbits, brain processes, the relation of heartbeat to emotional states, the physiology of liver function, and the mechanisms of sight, smell, and hearing.

2. In September 1995, the International Plato Society sponsored the Fourth Symposium Platonicum, a five-day conference in Granada, Spain, for scholarly discussion of Plato's *Timaeus* and *Critias*.

3. All further references to dialogues of Plato are to the *Timaeus (Ti.)* unless noted otherwise.

4. For example, Heraclitus had stressed constant change as the fundamental characteristic of the universe. Democritus theorized that all that existed was constituted by, and reducible to, atoms: tiny, unbreakable bits of matter.

5. According to Aristotle, a complete explanation of something, e.g., a natural change, being, or action, would include the identification of its end or purpose (final cause); that which effects the change (efficient or agent cause); its essence, definition (formal cause); and its underlying substratum or matter (material cause). See *Physics* 2.3 and *Metaphysics* 1.3.

6. See Kathleen Freeman, "Heraclitus," 30, 31, 49a, in *Ancilla to the Pre-Socratic Philosophers: A Translation of the Fragments in Diels,* Fragmente der Vorsokratiker (Cambridge: Harvard University Press, 1983).

7. The mathematical formulas for the movements in our solar system are not given. Plato claims that such ratios exist but that one would need a visible model of the planetary system, such as an armillary sphere, in order to work them out in detail (*Ti.* 40d).

8. The image comes from Parmenides, who speaks of "the motionless heart of well-rounded Truth" and of Being as a "well-rounded sphere." Freeman, "Parmenides," 42.1, 44.8, in *Ancilla to the Pre-Socratic Philosophers.*

9. All English quotations from the *Timaeus* are taken from Benjamin Jowett's translation in Edith Hamilton and Huntington Cairns, eds., *The Collected Dialogues of Plato* (New York: Pantheon Books, 1966).

10. Hamilton and Cairns, *Collected Dialogues of Plato,* 1203.

11. Hamilton and Cairns, *Collected Dialogues of Plato,* 1208.

12. Hamilton and Cairns, *Collected Dialogues of Plato,* 1208.

13. Hamilton and Cairns, *Collected Dialogues of Plato,* 1208.

14. Hamilton and Cairns, *Collected Dialogues of Plato,* 1208–9.

15. The term "cosmopolis" comes directly from the political writing of Zeno of Citium (336–265 B.C.E.), considered the founder of Stoicism. It means that human

beings should see themselves primarily as citizens of the universe. Zeno, who postdated Plato (428–348 B.C.E.), lived during the conquests of Alexander the Great, so his notion of citizenship transcends Plato's thought, which evolved within the context of the political structure of the Greek city-states. By using a cosmological model to argue for the ethical foundations of human life, however, Plato anticipates Zeno's concept.

16. I do not depreciate this argument, which may be true and which has immense importance for human living, but simply note that it does not serve as a deductive philosophical argument.

17. *Ti.* 29d, 44d.

18. In Aristotle's terms, we do not have *di' hoti* or *propter quid* knowlege about its origins—that is, knowledge of the reasoned fact—for this would require clear knowledge of its primary causes. Rather, we are limited to knowledge of the fact, *'ho ti,'* or *quia,* knowledge, that such and such is the case about the world.

19. For a thorough development of this type of argument with respect to environmental ethics, see Laura Westra, *An Environmental Proposal for Ethics: The Principle of Integrity* (Lanham, Md.: Rowman & Littlefield, 1994.)

20. Like all human beings, including ourselves, Plato knew the universe was in flux. But in addition to his concept, we bring the understanding of an evolving universe. All species are subject to mutations. The scope of the cosmos is not fully understood, but it appears to follow an expanding pattern. Stars are subject to disintegration. How then can Plato's myth be of interest?

Even in the face of an evolutionary universe, both physics and biology rest on the assumption that change, while not predictable, occurs within a world governed by some fundamental patterns. (Matter and energy, for example, have specific characteristics, even though our understanding of them is incomplete.) Without this fact, any scientific endeavor or success would be impossible.

21. See Thomas Berry, *The Dream of the Earth* (San Francisco: Sierra Club Books, 1988).

Chapter 6: The Ecology of the *Critias* and Platonic Metaphysics

1. Timaeus does indicate that living beings are distributed to the four basic kinds of habitat (earth, air, fire, and water) in accordance with the fourfold division of the Form of "animal." But this division in itself does not indicate an awareness of how life processes depend on habitat.

2. It is not entirely clear to what extent the historical account of Critias is to be understood in light of the metaphysical account of the *Timaeus.* Can we presume that Critias endorses, or even understands the complexities of, Timaeus's account? Although Socrates' praise of Critias is fainter than his praise of Timaeus (20a), there is no reason to believe that Critias gives his account oblivious to the metaphysical teachings that have preceded. After all, he, Timaeus, and Hermocrates were said to have talked over previously what contribution each was to make toward fulfilling Socrates' request (27a–b).

3. See also *Timaeus (Ti.)* 24c–d.

4. Timaeus, unlike Critias, gives only the most perfunctory nod to the deities of the traditional Greek pantheon (40d–41a), relying on reason instead of ancestral teachings. (Environmental philosophers may be interested to note that Gaia is among the deities whom Timaeus mentions in this cursory manner.) Why is there this apparent discrepancy? Perhaps it is because Critias's account is meant to have the political role of a patriotic myth. As such, it needs to be politically informed but cannot undermine the religious foundation of the community.

5. In the *Timaeus* this comes about, not through direct divine steering of our soulds, but through the study of heavenly motions (47b–c), which are identified or closely associated with the noetic activity of the soul of the physical cosmos.

6. At *Ti.* 22d, Critias says that the floods are the means by which the gods cleanse the earth. It is hard to know what philosophical sense this might have. Perhaps it is said in accordance with the political necessity to avoid direct challenges to divine providence, benevolence, and omnipotence.

7. The worth of fertilizers such as manure was, of course, common knowledge among farmers. See J. D. Hughes, *Pan's Travail: Environmental Problems of the Ancient Greeks and Romans* (Baltimore: Johns Hopkins University Press, 1994), 138–39. To my knowledge, none of Plato's contemporaries or predecessors gave any account of why such fertilization works.

8. Critias assumes that the present quality of the soil is an adequate sign of its quality in ages past. That seems to indicate that he does not envisage the possibility of improving soil by adding manure, compost, and the like. Likewise, the text does not mention the possibility of the soil itself losing its excellence or becoming worn out.

9. An alternative translation for *pieira* is "rich." In comparing the land to a sick human body, Plato exploits the double meaning of the term.

10. On deforestation and erosion in antiquity, see Hughes, *Pan's Travail*, 73–90.

11. Plato's recognition of a link between deforestation and erosion is indicated, but not argued for, in Clarence J. Glacken, *Traces on the Rhodian Shore: Nature and Culture in Western Thought from Ancient Times to the End of the Eighteenth Century* (Berkeley: University of California Press, 1967), 120–21; and Hughes, *Pan's Travail*, 73.

12. On this, see Thomas M. Robinson, *Plato's Psychology*, 2d ed. (Toronto: University of Toronto Press, 1995), 132–33; Charles H. Kahn, "The Place of the *Statesman* in Plato's Later Work," in *Reading the* Statesman: *Proceedings of the Third Symposium Platonicum*, ed. C. Rowe (Sankt Augustin, Germany: Academia Verlag, 1995), 54–56.

13. See J. Dillon, "The Neoplatonic Exegesis of the *Statesman* Myth," in *Reading the* Statesman, 364–74. Robinson (*Plato's Psychology*, 136–39) argues against this metaphysical interpretation of the proposed rotations, instead suggesting that "the backward-and-forward rotation of the World Soul epitomizes its 'eternity' as ultimately derivative from the Demiurge and subject to the disturbing exigencies of the bodily." On either account, the *Statesman* myth need not be taken as indicating that the cosmos is increasingly losing its order and perfection.

Chapter 7: Aristotelian Roots of Ecology: Causality, Complex Systems Theory, and Integrity

1. Laura Westra, *An Environmental Proposal for Ethics: The Principle of Integrity* (Lanham, Md.: Rowman & Littlefield, 1994).

2. Westra, *Environmental Proposal for Ethics*, chaps. 2, 3.

3. Westra, *Environmental Proposal for Ethics*, 134–42.

4. Westra, *Environmental Proposal for Ethics*, chap. 2. Cf. K. Shrader-Frechette, "Hard Ecology, Soft Ecology, and Ecosystem Integrity," in *Perspectives on Ecological Integrity*, ed. Laura Westra and John Lemons (Dordrecht: Kluwer Academic Publishers, 1995), 125–45.

5. R. Ulanowicz, "Ecosystem Integrity: A Causal Necessity," in *Perspectives on Ecological Integrity*, 77–87.

6. Ulanowicz, *The Ascendency Perspective* (New York: University of Columbia Press, in press).

7. Ulanowicz, *Ascendency Perspective*.

8. Ulanowicz, *Ascendency Perspective*.

9. Ulanowicz, *Ascendency Perspective*. See also R. Ulanowicz, "Aristotelean Causalities in Ecosystem Development," *Oikos* 51 (1990): 44.

10. Ulanowicz, *Ascendency Perspective*.

11. Ulanowicz, *Ascendency Perspective*.

12. Laura Westra, *Plotinus and Freedom: A Meditation on* Enneads *6.8* (Lewiston, N.Y.: Edwin Mellen, 1990), 134–37.

13. Ulanowicz, *Ascendency Perspective*; see also R. Rosen, *Life Itself: A Comprehensive Inquiry into the Origin, Nature, and Foundation of Life* (New York: Columbia University Press, 1991); and Ulanowicz, "Ecosystem Integrity," 77–87.

14. Sarah Broadie, "What Does the Aristotelian Prime Mover Do?" (paper read at Society for Ancient Greek Philosophy meeting, American Philosophical Association Eastern Conference, Boston, 24 December 1994).

15. Broadie, "Aristotelian Prime Mover."

16. Broadie, "Aristotelian Prime Mover."

17. Broadie, "Aristotelian Prime Mover."

18. Broadie, "Aristotelian Prime Mover."

19. J. Kay and E. Schneider, "Embracing Complexity: The Challenge of the Ecosystem Approach," in *Perspectives on Ecological Integrity*, 49–59.

20. J. Kay and E. Schneider, "The Challenge of the Ecosystem Approach," *Alternatives* 20, no. 3 (1994): 1–6; reprinted in *Perspectives on Integrity*, 49–59. (See note 4 above.)

21. A. Gotthelf, "Aristotle's Conception of Final Causality," in *Philosophical Issues in Aristotle's Biology*, ed. A. Gotthelf and James G. Lennox (Cambridge: Cambridge University Press, 1987), 202–42.

22. Anthony Preus, "*Eidos* as Norm in Aristotle's Biology," in *Aristotle: Essays in Ancient Greek Philosophy*, ed. John P. Anton and Anthony Preus (Albany: State University of New York Press, 1983), 340–63; and E. Mayr, *Toward a New Philosophy of Biology* (Cambridge: Harvard University Press, 1988), 44.

23. Paul Colinvaux, *Ecology* (New York: Wiley & Sons, 1990), 29–32

24. J. Cooper, "Hypothetical Necessity and Natural Teleology," in *Philosophical Issues in Aristotle's Biology* (Cambridge: Cambridge University Press, 1987), 243–74.

25. Westra, *Environmental Proposal for Ethics*, 134–42.

26. Martha C. Nussbaum, *The Fragility of Goodness: Luck and Ethics in Greek Tragedy and Philosophy* (Cambridge: Cambridge University Press, 1986), 260.

27. R. Kraut. *Aristotle on the Human Good* (Princeton: Princeton University Press, 1989).

28. Westra, *Environmental Proposal for Ethics*, 134–42.

29. Westra, *Environmental Proposal for Ethics*, 138–41.

30. John M. Rist, *The Mind of Aristotle* (Toronto: University of Toronto Press, 1989), 123.

31. Rist, *Mind of Aristotle*, 129.

32. See Rist, *Mind of Aristotle*, 129.

33. Broadie, "Aristotelian Prime Mover."

Chapter 8: The Greening of Aristotle

1. Pierre Pellegrin writes, "The entire biological corpus continually refers to animal species as empirically established realities, and furthermore Aristotle's biology seems to be arranged in such a way that 'animal species' should become the central concept in the science of living things. But we will see that it does not happen." Pierre Pellegrin, "Aristotle: A Zoology without Species," in *Philosophical Issues in Aristotle's Biology*, ed. A. Gotthelf and J. G. Lennox (New York: Cambridge University Press, 1981), 96.

2. I prescind from the question of zoos and ranches—horses remain "horses" in these settings, but only because what it is to be a horse remains relative to contexts in which its characteristic function can be exercised.

3. Aristotle says, perhaps humorously, that to be a horse is to be a neighing animal. That is no more the characteristic function of the horse than "featherless biped" is of the human animal. He has, however, no other suggestions.

I say type of context, since the pampas of Argentina, the open fields of the Spanish countryside, and the prairies of the U.S. are all relevantly similar in this regard. The character-context relation is, for thought, a type-type relation. I elaborate this point below.

4. A category like "parasite" may seem to old-fashioned Aristotelians inimical to the dignity of substantial form—but a significant portion of all species are parasites, and we must resist any a priori demand to eschew such strongly relational construals of function.

5. Aristotle's "pale man" problem does not arise here, since the bond between characteristic function and context is not an extrinsic one. I shall argue below that both are involved in the formula of species form.

6. I pass over the matter of biotic communities or networks of mutual aid. See also note 37 below.

7. A. Gotthelf, "First Principles in Aristotle's *Parts of Animals,*" in *Aristotle's Biology,* 167–98. See note 1 above.

8. Excretion is important and too often neglected as an ecological function. Consider that if the whitetail deer did not excrete nitrogenous wastes, the bacteria essential to the regeneration of the deer's foodstuffs would perish and the deer would be out of luck. This coadaptation holds even though the bacteria and the deer are technically in different food chains. See W. B. Clapham, *Natural Ecosystems* (New York: Macmillan, 1973), 73, cited in J. S. Wicken, *Evolution, Thermodynamics, and Information: Extending the Darwinian Program* (New York: Oxford University Press, 1987), 165.

9. D. M. Balme, "Aristotle's Biology Was Not Essentialist," in *Aristotle's Biology,* 300. See note 1 above.

10. D. R. Brooks and E. O. Wiley (*Evolution as Entropy* [Chicago: University of Chicago Press, 1986]) have done the most to advance the thermodynamic conception of biology in general and evolution in particular. Wicken has been the strongest philosophical voice on this scene. His system integrates thermodynamics, information theory, cybernetics, and a sort of structuralism; it is very interesting and very trendy. His association of heterotrophs and autotrophs with heat function is ingenious, and there is much to learn from his presentation. To an Aristotelian, it is unfortunate that Wicken (*Evolution, Thermodynamics, and Information*), in structuralist fashion, moves from defining organisms as "informed AOs" (autocatalytic organizations), or dissipative systems that degrade free energy and sink entropy, to defining ecosystems as AOs (147) and even socioeconomic systems as AOs (144). This leads to a holism of a most radical nature. Indeed, an ecosystem represents "the highest level of autonomy in the biosphere" (168) and is "the primary strategic energy transfer unity in nature" (168), the "fundamental unit of energy processing in the biosphere" (167), a sort of "supersystem" that is construed as a superindividual. In fact he supports Ghiselin's idea that species are individuals, though he finds the word infelicitous (198). Whiteheadians and Peirceans are also tempted to make this move. Among the considerations against it is the ethical difficulty that if each life form is an AO, there should be no ethical difficulty with replacing it with an equally efficient AO (or with not replacing it at all if the embedding AO is left as efficient). In other words, like other attempts to make nature continuous—such as the attempt to turn everything into "energy"— this makes nature homogeneous, so that intervention and manipulation become, ironically, more rather than less defensible. An Aristotelian approach fastens instead on the unique function of each life form.

11. An Aristotelian approach could make "natural heat'" the main thing but could never make it the only thing, for if we construe life forms as essentially dissipative structures, they are no longer substantial natural wholes. As H. J. Morowitz writes, individuals "do not exist per se, but only as local perturbations in [the] universal energy flow." H. J. Morowitz, "Biology as a Cosmological Science," *Main Currents in Modern Thought* 28: 156. It is interesting to note that Morowitz uses the same analogue as Descartes: the vortex—and this despite

Morowitz's claim that the vortex "does not exist as an entity in the classic Western sense" (156).

Thinkers concerned with environmental ethics should also, I believe, be wary of leaning too heavily on thermodynamic considerations. The view lends itself readily to coopting, since it is indifferent to claims of ecological distinctiveness. H. Barnett and C. Morse write: "Advances in fundamental science have made it possible to take advantage of the uniformity of matter/energy—a uniformity that makes it feasible, without preassignable limit, to escape the quantitative constraints imposed by the character of the earth's crust. . . . Science, by making the resource base more homogeneous, erases the restrictions once thought to reside in the lack of homogeneity. In a neo-Ricardian world, it seems, the particular resources with which one starts increasingly become a matter of indifference. The reservation of particular resources for later use, therefore, may contribute little to the welfare of future generations." H. Barnett and C. Morse, *Scarcity and Growth* (Baltimore: Johns Hopkins University Press, 1963), cited in H. E. Daly and J. B. Cobb, *For the Common Good*, rev. ed. (Boston: Beacon Press, 1994), 111–12.

The vanishing of substance into thermodynamic process tempts us to the view that just which shapes the dissipative structures take is indifferent, so long as the flows are "optimized." This invites acceptance of alternative structurings and the view that "natural resources" are material for transformation. On this approach, it becomes easy to agree with George Gilder that we must overcome "the illusion that resources and capital are essentially things, which can run out, rather than products of the human will and imagination which in freedom are inexhaustible." George Gilder, *Wealth and Poverty* (New York: Basic Books, 1981), 232, cited in Daly and Cobb, *For the Common Good*, 109. After all, if nature is just structured energy, alternative structurings and human manipulation of the structurings is relatively unproblematic. As Julian Simon says, "You see, in the end copper and oil come out of our minds. That's really where they are." Julian Simon, interview with William F. Buckley Jr., reprinted in *Population and Development Review*, March 1982, 207, cited in Daly and Cobb, *For the Common Good*, 109. Laura Westra, in *An Environmental Proposal for Ethics: The Principle of Integrity* (Lanham, Md.: Rowman & Littlefield, 1994), tries to resist this outcome by insisting on a principle of structural integrity, but this seems to follow from her preservationist convictions, rather than from any features of her complex-systems model per se.

12. This is only natural, since heat exchange is a relational process. The same organs and processes that function virtuously in one context may turn out to be vices in another. A small autotroph that can respond rapidly to pressures within a narrow range of ecological opportunities will be lost outside that narrow range, while a larger, slower animal may be more adaptable and may function well in that range of options. There is no universal instrument that serves for all ecological contexts.

13. Balme, "Aristotle's Biology Was Not Essentialist," 300 and n. 47.

14. "Most recent classifications of reproductive isolating mechanisms have emphasized a dichotomy between two levels of action: premating and postmating, this division being based on the conservation of gametes, and on the assumption that only those mechanisms operating at the premating level are amenable to the

direct action of natural selection for their isolating effect per se. . . . But this dichotomy may be arbitrary. Hagen . . . found it difficult to separate the lack of hybrid fitness due to ecological incompatibility (a postmating mechanism) which was a consequence of differential parental adaptations, from the ecological isolation of the parents (a premating mechanism)." Murray Littlejohn, "Reproductive Isolation: A Critical Review," in *Evolution and Speciation*, ed. W. R. Atchley and D. S. Woodruff (New York: Cambridge University Press, 1981). Littlejohn, before defending his own radically individualist view, notes the work of Levin, Grant, Coyne, and others in this respect. The distinction between premating and postmating mechanisms has no point for the current discussion, which abstracts, intentionally, from considerations of selective devices.

15. For instance, E. Mayr (*Populations, Species, and Evolution* [Cambridge: Belknap Press of Harvard University Press, 1970]) points out that parthenogenesis permits instantaneous speciation, since a single specimen can colonize a new geographic zone. He distinguishes between five types of ecological specialization: (1) for very narrow niches, (2) broad tolerance for individuals for tolerating environmental extremes throughout the species range, (3) Ludwig effect (polymorphs adapted to subniches), (4) ecotypic variation (within a geographic area, ecological speciation not obliterated by gene exchange with adjacent but differently specialized populations), (5) geographic polytypicism (the formation of geographical races in response to environmental variation over the major part of the species range). Mayr admits that not much is known about most of these mechanisms, particularly (5).

He describes four factors that affect the rate of speciation, given these types of ecological specialization: those that (1) determine effectiveness of geographical isolation, (2) affect shifts into new niches, (3) affect the frequency with which geographical isolates are established, (4) favor genetic turnover within isolates. The capacity to spread (e.g., the dispersal stage in the life cycle of an angiosperm) is affected by rivers, mountains, vegetation zones, climatic barriers, and so on. Every species reacts differently to these barriers. and "no reliable method is known for measuring dispersal ability" (336).

16. Aristotle, *Parts of Animals (PA)* 694b13–14; cited by Gotthelf, "First Principles," 192.

17. This item has evolutionary import as well, since any factor that reduces dispersal may facilitate speciation. See Mayr, *Populations, Species, and Evolution*, 339.

18. Mayr, *Populations, Species, and Evolution*, 339.

19. Mayr, *Populations, Species, and Evolution*, 249.

20. See my remarks on the ecological prefix, p. 109. Both the base and the prefix have their difficulties, to be sure: the standard problems of taxonomic relevance and precision (problems of the genuineness of the subspecies, problems about sibling species and conspecific monotypes, "races"—we would still have "continental" versus "insular" patterns of variation, and so on). If ecological function is a character-context vector, the prefix must refer to both, thus: deep-trench predator, or coral-reef scavenger. It is the functive prefix that gives the *ti esti* in the Platonic-Aristotelian sense; the base that gives the standard species name, orient-

ed to the so-called biological species concept, has its own devices to its own purposes.

21. Turesson took "Linnean species" construed ecologically to be "ecospecies" and distinguished this from the "ecotype" that is an ecological unit arising as a result of the genotypical response of an ecospecies to a particular habitat. The difficulties with Turesson's ecotypes are well known. Valentines tried to distinguish ecospecies into two types, but it was to no avail, and the idea fell into disrepute. Few have been willing, since the 1950s, to try to rejuvenate the notion.

Fisher, Wright, Turesson, Hutchinson, and Simpson are the most prominent contributors to an ecological species concept. One must add Dobzhansky ("each species is . . . an adaptive complex which fits into an ecological niche") and Mayr, who makes ecological factors prominent in his population concept. My approach is also influenced by Sober, who makes rather different use of notions such as "predator." Van Valen has also been working, in an analytic tradition, to define an ecological species concept. ("A species is a lineage . . . which occupies an adaptive zone minimally different from that of any other lineage in its range and which evolves separately from all lineages outside its range.") E. Van Valen, "Ecological Species, Multispecies, and Oaks," *Taxon* 25 (1976): 233–39.

22. Because the species concept proposed here is not, despite the focal place of ecological function, an "ecospecies concept," it does not imply that each species must have a fixed ecology or a definable demand on its resources. It can admit that even though "a species does not have a typologically fixed 'demand' on its environment . . . so that [t]here is no such thing as *the* ecology of a given species" (Mayr, *Populations, Species, and Evolution*, 341), the relation between organism and environment "seems sufficiently important to serve as the basis of a classification of kinds of species" (242). Of course, Mayr's own approach fastens on population-dynamic factors such as sex ratio, vagility, extent of panmixia or interbreeding, and so on (recombination index, chromosomal cycle, etc.), so that a species is a "reproductively isolated population" or an "aggregate of interbreeding populations" (249). Nonetheless, a neo-Aristotelian advocate should take heart from Mayr's assertion that each species is a "discrete unit . . . separated by a bridgeless gap from every other species" (247). Mayr makes good use of ecological considerations. He writes, "A species is an independent genetic system that has the properties of being reproductively isolated from and ecologically compatible with other sympatric species" (247) An incipient species "in order to complete the process of speciation, must acquire sufficient differences in niche utilization to be able to exist sympatrically with sister species without fatal competition" (247).

23. For this reason, species form also is not metaphysically primary, according to Aristotelians; that is a different point.

24. More elaborately, in Aristotelian thinking, we first isolate the living individual from its surroundings, then distinguish its circumstantial variations from its essentials. The living whole in its essentials, formal and material, is the composite, or *synolon*. Since within the composite whole we can discern formal and material aspects, we can, finally, identify the principal function that is the primary *ousia* of the being. On the approach ventured here, even this characteristic func-

tion that is the principal part of an aspect of one side of a living whole carries a reference to ecological context and so is neither fully autonomous nor unqualified.

25. See, e.g., F. Briand and J. E. Cohen, "Community Food Webs Have Scale-Invariant Structure," *Nature* 307 (1984): 264–67.

26. A. Barkai and C. McQuaid, "Predator-Prey Role Reversal in a Marine Benthic Ecosystem," *Science* 242 (1988): 62–64, cited in G. C. Williams, *Natural Selection: Domains, Levels, and Challenges* (New York: Oxford University Press, 1992), 120.

27. I do not wish to suggest that exceptions automatically invalidate empirical proposals (even conservation laws, the strictest rules known to our science, admit of exceptions). I only wish to notice that this case presents the greatest challenge to the approach advanced in this essay.

28. Once this is so, the dream of a "periodic table of niches" (see E. R. Pianka, *Evolutionary Ecology* [New York: Harper & Row, 1983], 281–83) might be made pertinent to this account of the ecological function of actual organisms. Such a periodic table of ecological niches would, if possible, not classify species forms outright but would array differences in a key component in the definition of natural wholes.

29. I include here, not just a focus on the functions of parts such as one finds already in Aristotle, but also the attempt to identify Aristotelian "form" with some such part; Max Delbrück's identification of Aristotle's form with DNA is an example of this last. Mayr follows Delbrück in this curious error.

30. There is a sense of "part" in which a natural living whole is posterior to one part—the ruling part of the soul (in humans the principal part of the rational part of the human soul, which is *nous*—the simple grasp of the simple), but those are parts of the form; the parts to which wholes are prior are their own parts, material and composite parts. That there is a dominant or principal part allows us to distinguish one among the many functions of a being and take this as its single essence. (For instance, the form of a human being is her *psyche*, which is the invariant aspect of the compound whole, and it is the rational part of this aspect of the whole being that is her definitive part; indeed, a part of this part of the soul—theoretical *nous*—is the ultimate function in which our highest good consists.) I discuss these senses of "part" and "whole" in "Plato's Ghost: Consequences of Aristotelian Dialectic," in *The Crossroads of Norm and Nature*, ed. M. Sim (Lanham, Md.: Rowman & Littlefield, 1995), 151–74.

31. I discuss an evolutionary appropriation of ecological form in the Aristotelian style in the final two sections of this essay.

32. An environment as a context is a network or constellation of other organisms (and an inorganic setting) faced by a life form as a single background. Contexts are not individual wholes, but they have integrities of their own and may appear as more or less unitary systems; they have their own locations, their own histories, and their own distinctive types. These contexts fall most broadly into land, air, and water types (with transitional cases: marshlands, etc.) that admit of variations. What in evolutionary thinking are called niches are just these contexts considered as opportunities for exploitation and adaptive radiation. So it is not surprising that they possess parallel types and variations. "Even though

each species in a related group occupies a different niche, these niches are, on the whole, quite similar. Such niches are only subdivisions of a single 'adaptive zone,' as Simpson would call it. The adaptive zones, particularly the major ones, are occupied by distinct types, such as rodents or bats, birds or snakes, sharks or eels. Each of these adaptive types is characterized by a unique set of attributes. It requires a singular combination of genetic, physiological, and morphological properties and a unique constellation of environmental conditions to enable an animal to invade a unique major adaptive zone." Mayr, *Populations, Species, and Evolution*, 373.

33. I elaborate this point in sec. 3 of an article, "Goodness and Community," currently in preparation.

34. In Aristotelian politics, there are decisive respects in which the context (the polis) takes precedence over the individuals. Similarly, there are respects in which ecological contexts take precedence over the individuals they embed. But these are not *ontological* respects. Hence the proposed, Aristotle-inspired ecological contextualism need not reject "ecosystems approaches" to the problems under consideration but only the *philosophical* claim that such systems are ontologically on a par with, or prior to, the individuals who compose them. There are inquiries with purposes that make a focus on contexts and networks of relations mandatory. But we should not confuse these different purposes or the different sorts of priority they involve.

35. The notion of "context" is used in a variety of different ways. One notion used by some biological theorists, one that does not draw on political usage, must be kept sharply separated from what I propose here. William Wimsatt (and Sober and others following Wimsatt) refer to context as a set of external determinants and context dependence as exhaustive determination by those externals. For this reason Wimsatt regards the context dependence of a factor as decisive evidence against that factor's counting as a unit of selection, since it fails to have enough independence to serve as a locus of selective pressure. Ecological function, I shall argue, is context sensitive, and yet the primary focus of selection. The approach sketched here is, I believe, perfectly compatible with the refinement and reformulation of Wimsatt's criterion (the "additivity approach") in E. A. Lloyd, *The Structure and Confirmation of Evolutionary Theory* (Princeton: Princeton University Press, 1994).

36. There are in fact a number of niche concepts deployed in recent discussion. The notion goes back to Grinnell and (later) Elton. The most frequently encountered version in the biological literature is Hutchinson's. My usage of "niche," which I take to be cognate with ecological "context," is, like Hutchinson's, something like microhabitat or the "habitat niche" of Allee. But Hutchinson tends to exclude behavioral factors. Odum's notion stresses behavior so much that, for Odum, niche is the organism's "profession"—that is close to ecological role or characteristic function as I use those terms here. The best introduction to notions of niche is chap. 7 of Pianka's *Evolutionary Ecology*.

37. I do not really broach here the matter of biotic communities or networks of mutual aid. Such mutualisms develop, according to J. N. Thompson (*Interaction and Coevolution* [New York: Wiley & Sons, 1982]) when there is an environment

with either high or low levels of disturbance and organisms with an intermediate survival ability, because under such conditions even a small reciprocal advantage can affect survival and/or growth rates considerably. A situation of low antagonism plus high environmental stress yields much the same result. The investigation of biotic networks is important for this project, but it is crucial to note that the contextualist approach endorsed does not mandate that an ecological context be describable as a full-blown mutualist community, much less a unitary, integrated, self-sustaining system. A context might have a very loose and open-textured sort of organization and vague boundaries and admit of only a problematic sort of identity. So loose an organization does not suffice to compose a community or strict mutualism, but does suffice to constitute a context. That is all the view briefed here requires.

38. If these features serve as criteria of what counts as an "Aristotelian" theory, then the account in Laura Westra's outstanding effort *An Environmental Proposal for Ethics* is not really "Aristotelian," despite her appeals to the Stagirite. Westra's proposal is holistic; she portrays ecosystems as primary and integral, so that human beings are "parts of a living primary reality" (10). I have argued that, if we do construe natural wholes as "parts" of larger entities, then we use "part" in a different sense than we use "part" of the components of natural wholes. (Aristotle surely uses "part" in these different senses, but we must be clear about the equivocation.) There are good ecological reasons why Westra might propound a "reduced role and status of individuals including humankind" (70); my few remarks here focus on whether Westra's holism based in complex-systems theory is Aristotelian in light of the minimal criteria I suggest in the essay.

Second, teleology in some sense is pivotal in Westra's account ("the question of the meaning of integrity may be rephrased as the question of what is the *ergon* of an ecosystem" [45]). But not all teleology is *Aristotelian* teleology. Westra appeals to Mayr's notion of teleonometry (48); however, I would argue that complex-systems theory is (in Mayr's terms) teleomatic, not teleonomic. The end state of a complex system is either an equilibrium or some other sort of attractor that is itself complex and sensitive to its initial conditions. Since neither teleonomic nor teleomatic is Aristotelian teleology, Westra's argument from the "teleology" of complex systems to "Aristotelian teleology" (69) is a nonsequitur. Another shift comes on pp. 135–36, where Westra claims that, since Aristotle moves from individual to species form, her move from individuals to ecosystems "is in line with Aristotle's own thought" (136). Westra is right to point out that the Stagirite's account is not really individualistic, but the moves are not comparable, because the lack of otherness between a natural individual and its species form in Aristotle's account has no counterpart in Westra's proposal. We should avoid individualistic readings of teleology that reduce it to a conatus for self-preservation. But we should also resist holistic readings of teleology that assimilate the specific functions of natural wholes into the thermodynamic "ends" of complex systems.

Third, Westra's model gives priority to potency over act. Integrity is an optimal *capacity* for ongoing development and change. Since integrity must not be identified with any specific end state of a system, it must be a nonspecific potential for change and development. This comes out most sharply in her Hollings figure 8, where the undifferentiated "hypothetical point of origin" marks the spot: point "C" on the figure 8 is a system's maximum capacity for alternate developments and patterns (48, cf. 50, 51). Even the optima (points "A") of which a system is capable contain within themselves the seeds of their own destruction and "constructive disruption." This is *kinesis*, not *energeia*; it is the act of potency as potency—and in this case, not even of some specific potency. The endwardness of ecosystems is teleomatic and not fully teleological, and potency is prior to act in Westra's account.

Fourth, though Westra strives admirably to balance functional and structural considerations (in her I_2 and her I_1, the structural integrity that divides into I_a and I_b), I believe that the complex-systems approach really must give priority to structure. Westra aims to balance them in some passages (e.g., 37, 40) but admits in other passages (e.g., 41) that structure takes priority. These structures are dynamic. But talk about the "dynamic" character of systems and their "process" character does not suffice to justify an appeal to function *in an Aristotelian sense*. The priority of structure also emerges in a blurring of the difference between natural wholes and sub- and superindividual systems, which are regarded in systems theory as entities in the same sense, so that natural individuals are ecosystems for their components and are themselves components in larger systems. (Westra's usage is subtle on this point: she claims both that the paradigm case of a living system with integrity is a living organism [35] and that "ecosystems are not single organisms" [45]). Still, Westra's proposal is unabashedly holistic; she envisions an ecosystem as "not just a plurality of intersecting processes and functions. . . . It is also a unity, a whole, *as I am*" (43, emphasis mine).

None of this yet argues truth or falsity. If Westra is right that integrity "in the ecosystemic sense" is necessary and if I am right that this is non-Aristotelian, then we must simply reject Aristotle. That is a different point. Perhaps Westra is right to assert that, in light of her holism, other views—including the ones I style Aristotelian— are like the "shadows" that float before the prisoners in Plato's cave (52).

39. For an elaboration of the point that even the human composite is not fully "substantial" by the criteria of finality, self-sufficiency, completeness, and the like, see my "Plato's Ghost."

40. By "form" here I mean the form of the species form, the primary form that corresponds to Aristotle's primary *ousia*. The compound individual has a form, which is the species form. The species form itself has a "form," one that makes no reference to any particular sort of matter. When I write simply "form" instead of "species form," I mean this form of species form. This is ecological function as the principal aspect of species form that itself is an aspect of a natural whole.

41. I do not wish to say that species form as ecological function is *the* unit of selection, since it seems that selection operates at a number of points; but I do wish to suggest, in a preliminary way, that it is the primary focus of selection. Most authors admit that the physiological individual is a unit of selection. The best evidence for the gene's being a unit of selection is the existence of "outlaw genes" that replicate themselves while making no phenotypic contribution. Dawkins discusses this point extensively. The best discussion of species selection I know is found in Lloyd, *Evolutionary Theory*, chaps. 5 and 6.

42. The traditional way of saying this is that formal identity is not the same as numerical identity. My form is numerically identical with me but formally identical with all others of my species. The distinction lets us preserve the ontological ambivalence essential to species form.

43. In contrast to contemporary approaches, Aristotle distinguishes essence from properties and qualities. A thing does not "have" an essence, it "is" an essence. A lioness *is* (in the most fundamental sense of "is") her ecological function; there is nothing more fundamental that might "own" the function. We can, in a derivative sense of "is," say that her body "has" the function, but not as a property or quality and surely not as a bodily part.

44. We must not confuse Aristotle's version of essentialism, in which a substance is an essence, with what Quine and others call "Aristotelian essentialism," in which an extensionally identical particular possesses certain properties necessarily. Aristotle's version actually *contrasts* the necessary properties (if any) of a thing with its teleological essence.

45. Mayr, *Populations, Species, and Evolution,* 373.

46. Mayr, *Populations, Species, and Evolution,* 341.

47. Mayr, *Populations, Species, and Evolution,* 353.

48. G. G. Simpson, 1953, cited in Mayr, *Populations, Species, and Evolution,* 353.

49. B. Rensch, *Evolution above the Species Level,* (Chicago: University of Chicago Press, 1960.)

50. Mayr, *Populations, Species, and Evolution,* 357.

51. Mayr, *Populations, Species, and Evolution,* 360. Most such changes come in cascades. Each stage in the cascade sequence opens up new possibilities and reinforces the series in the cascade. I like to call this the *ecological multiplier* (with reference to the "multiplier" of economic theory after Keynes). Today, we are all familiar with examples of the ecological multiplier. The rise of angiosperms facilitates the rise of insects, which facilitates the rise of insect eaters and parasites, and so on.

52. *PA* 6946b13–14, cited in Gotthelf, "First Principles," 192.

53. Mayr, *Populations, Species, and Evolution,* 364.

54. Mayr, *Populations, Species, and Evolution,* 363.

55. This point cuts right to the heart of the "units of selection" controversy, since the form of the natural whole is in a sense identical with the individual and in a sense identical with the species. Once the definitive function of a life form is identified, further haggling about universals and particulars, about species and individuals, is pointless. For more on the peculiar status of form in Aristotle's metaphysics, see my "Plato's Ghost."

56. F. D'Amato, "Cytogenics of Plant Cell and Tissue Cultures and Their Regenerates," *CRC Critical Reviews in Plant Sciences* 3 (1985): 73–112; cited in A. Lima-de-Faria, *Evolution without Selection: Form and Function by Autoevolution* (New York: Elsevier, 1988), 258.

57. L. W. Buss, "Evolution, Development, and the Units of Selection," in *Proceedings of the National Academy of Sciences USA* 80 (1983); cited in Lloyd, *Evolutionary Theory,* 66–67.

58. R. D. Barnes, *Invertebrate Zoology* (Philadelphia: Saunders, 1980); cited in Lima-de-Faria, *Evolution without Selection,* 331.

59. See, e.g., N. Eldredge, *Unfinished Synthesis: Biological Hierarchies and Modern Evolutionary Thought* (New York: Oxford University Press, 1985); and Lloyd, *Evolutionary Theory.*

60. D. L. Hull, *The Metaphysics of Evolution* (Albany: State University of New York Press, 1989), 96.

Chapter 9: Self-Love and the Virtue of Species Preservation

1. Stephen Jay Gould, "The Golden Rule," in *Eight Little Piggies: Reflections in Natural History* (New York: W. W. Norton, 1993), 41–51.

2. Although it might be argued that the scientific investigation of environmental destruction also represents an inherently interesting project, this argument does not satisfy those who consider the loss of species diversity to be not only a scientific tragedy but also a moral one, since our understanding of the community of life is as yet incomplete.

3. This argument is developed more fully in chap. 3 of Richard Shearman, "*Oikos* and *Eudaimonia:* The Human Good in Nature" (Ph.D. dissertation, State University of New York, Syracuse, 1993).

4. For a discussion of complete happiness, see Richard Kraut, *Aristotle on the Human Good* (Princeton: Princeton University Press, 1989), particularly the sections on "Complete Virtue" and "Imperfect Virtue" in chap. 4.

5. As Aristotle says in *Nichomachean Ethics (NE)* 108.1178b22–24, "the activity of God, which surpasses all others in blessedness, must be contemplative; and of human activities, therefore, that which is most akin to this must be most of the nature of happiness."

6. See *NE* 10.7.1177b27–1178a1.

7. See *On the Soul* 2.5.417a22–417b1.

8. *NE* 10.7.1178a2–9

9. *On the Soul* 2.5.417a28–29.

10. *NE* 10.7.1177b27–1178a8.

11. See *On the Soul* 3.8.432a4–9.

12. Jonathan Lear, *Aristotle: The Desire to Understand* (Cambridge: Cambridge University Press, 1988).

13. To say that we can "sacrifice" our interests for the sake of others, whether human or not, is probably misleading. For Aristotle, when a virtuous person acts for the benefit of another, that action simply emerges as an aspect of virtue. "Sacrifice," therefore, does not seem to capture the kind of activity that Aristotle has in mind when he discusses the actions in which virtuous people engage for the sake of others.

14. *NE* 8.13.1162b4. See also *NE* 8.7.1158a24–28.

15. *NE* 8.14.1163b13–18.

16. Aldo Leopold, *A Sand County Almanac: With Essays on Conservation from Round River* (New York: Ballantine Books, 1966).

17. This is made evident in the *Politics*, particularly in bk. 1.

18. See, e.g., *Metaphysics (Metaph.)* 12.7.1072b14–15, 18–20, 1072a21–27.

19. See *Physics* 2.2.194a28–31.

20. *NE* 9.8.1168b29–34.

21. *NE* 10.7.1177b30–1178a1.

22. *PA* 1.5.645a15–23.

23. *On the Soul* 2.4.415a30–b1.

24. *On the Soul* 2.4.415b6–8.

25. *Metaph.* 12.10.1075a15–24.

26. *NE* 9.8.1168b31–33.

27. I do not interpret this as saying that everything in the world is good and thus everything in the world is to be loved. It is to say that insofar as each thing we encounter in the world of everyday experience is a manifestation of the Good (i.e., lives according to its nature), then it is to be respected in a way appropriate to the circumstances. For example, we should love good people (not all people) because they are good, not because they exist. It is their understanding that is the basis for our friendship, not their existence. Good people have properly fulfilled their nature by living a life according to virtue. Unlike most, they have organized their desires so that they desire nothing amiss and do not live contrary to their nature.

28. *Metaph.* 12.10.1075a11–25.

29. *Metaph.* 12.7.1072b26–31.

30. *NE* 9.9.1170a20–22.

31. This is most clearly evident in bk. 1 of the *Politics.*

32. *NE* 1.8.1098b11–14.

33. J. Annas, "Self-Love in Aristotle," in *Aristotle's Ethics,* Spindel Conference, Memphis State University, 20–22 October 1988, supp. to *Southern Journal of Philosophy* 27 (1989): 3.

It would appear that Aristotle is not quite right, in that we also seem to be equipped with feelings of affinity for many other animals as well. In a discussion of neotony, Stephen Jay Gould (*The Panda's Thumb: More Reflections in Natural History* [New York: W. W. Norton, 1980]) discusses how people are naturally drawn to some animals, particularly when the animals are young. Apparently, some animals elicit the same kinds of parental feelings that babies do; this explains the age regression of cartoon characters like Mickey Mouse.

34. *NE* 9.7.1168a5–9.

35. See *NE* 8.8.1159a31–32.

36. Annas, "Self-Love in Aristotle," 13, 15.

37. John C. Ryan, "Life Support: Conserving Biological Diversity," Worldwatch Paper 108 (Washington: Worldwatch Institute, 1992).

Chapter 10: The Organic Unity of Aristotle's World

1. With the exception of passages from *De Caelo,* where the translations are my own, quoted passages are from the Oxford Translation (for example, Webster), with

some changes. Where noted, I have also used Aristotle, *On the Cosmos*, trans. D. J. Furley, Loeb Classical Library (1955); and Aristotle, *Meteorologica*, trans. H. D. P. Lee, Loeb Classical Library (1962).

2. Here compare the army metaphor of *Metaphysics* 12.10.

3. This section draws on material previously published in Mohan Matthen and R. J. Hankinson, "Aristotle's Universe: Its Form and Matter," *Synthese* 96 (1993): 417–35.

4. The classic definition of a mass term is that it denotes something every part of which is also denoted by it. For example, every part of everything denoted by "gold" is also denoted by "gold." By this criterion, "body" is a mass term on both its readings.

5. The quotations are taken from *From Gaia to Selfish Genes: Selected Writings in the Life Sciences*, ed. Connie Barlow (Cambridge: Massachusetts Institute of Technology, 1993), 3, 10.

Chapter 11: Fortitude and Tragedy: The Prospects for a Stoic Environmentalism

1. William O. Stephens, "Stoic Naturalism, Rationalism, and Ecology," *Environmental Ethics* 16 (1994): 285.

2. Seneca, *Letters from a Stoic* (Harmondsworth, England: Penguin Books, 1969).

3. A. A. Long and D. N. Sedley, *The Hellenistic Philosophers* (Cambridge: Cambridge University Press, 1987), 1:160.

4. Diogenes Laertius, *Lives of Eminent Philosophers*, vol 2., trans. R. D. Hicks (London: Heinemann, 1925).

5. Jim Cheney, "The Neo-Stoicism of Radical Environmentalism," *Environmental Ethics* 11 (1989): 322.

6. Stephens, "Stoic Naturalism," 285.

7. Bernard Williams, *Ethics and the Limits of Philosophy* (London: Fontana, 1985), 198.

8. John Passmore, "Man as Despot," in *Man's Responsibility for Nature*, 2d ed. (London: Duckworth, 1980), 17.

9. References are to Cicero, *De Natura Deorum*, trans. H. Rackham, Loeb Classical Library (1933).

10. Ludwig Edelstein, "The Philosophical System of Posidonius," *American Journal of Philology* 58 (1936): 306, 323.

11. See Josiah B. Gould, *The Philosophy of Chrysippus* (Leiden: E. J. Brill, 1970).

12. Marcus Aurelius, *The Meditations*, trans. Maxwell Staniforth (Harmondsworth, England: Penguin Books, 1964).

13. Stephen R. L. Clark, "Enlarging the Community: Companion Animals," in *Introducing Applied Ethics*, ed. B. Almond (Oxford: Blackwell, 1995), 318.

14. Passmore, "Man as Despot," 15.

15. "Is This the Work of Man or Nature?" *Independent*, 20 November 1995, sec. 2, pp. 2–3.

16. Passmore, "Man as Despot," 14.

17. See Holmes Rolston, "Can and Ought We to Follow Nature?" *Environmental Ethics* 1 (1979): 7–30.

18. Plutarch, *On the Eating of Flesh*, pt. 2, in *Moralia*, vol. 12, trans. W. C. Helmbold, Loeb Classical Library(1957).

19. Passmore, "Man as Despot," 126.

20. Plutarch, *De Stoicorum Repugnantiis* (On Stoic self-contradictions), in *Moralia*, vol. 13, trans. H. Cherniss, Loeb Classical Library (1976).

21. Williams, *Ethics and Limits*, 197.

22. Paul Tillich, *The Courage to Be* (London: Fontana, 1962), 23.

23. Epictetus, "Enchiridion," in *The Moral Discourses of Epictetus*, trans. E. Carter (London: Dent, 1910).

24. Cf. Williams, *Ethics and Limits*, 164–65.

25. Stephens, "Stoic Naturalism," 283, quoting T. Engberg-Pedersen, *The Stoic Theory of Oikeiosis* (Aarhus, Denmark: Aarhus University Press, 1990), 40.

26. Hans von Arnim, *Stoicorum Veterum Fragmenta* (Leipzig: Teubner, 1903), 2: 634.

27. Long and Sedley, *Hellenistic Philosophers*, 1: 163.

28. Clark, "Enlarging the Community," 319.

29. See Aristotle, *Nicomachean Ethics*, trans. J. A. K. Thompson, rev. ed. (Harmondsworth, England: Penguin Books, 1976).

30. Bernard Williams, *Shame and Necessity* (Berkeley and Los Angeles: University of California Press, 1993), 68.

31. John Stuart Mill, "Nature," in *Three Essays on Religion* (London: Longmans, 1874), 17–18.

32. See A. Kenny, *The Aristotelian Ethics* (Oxford: Clarendon Press, 1978), 204n2; Martha C. Nussbaum, *The Fragility of Goodness: Luck and Ethics in Greek Tragedy and Philosophy* (Cambridge: Cambridge University Press, 1986), 6; and J. Barnes's introduction to Aristotle, *Nichomachean Ethics* (see note 28).

33. See the preface and postscript to Williams, *Shame and Necessity*.

34. Williams, *Shame and Necessity*, 115–16.

35. Tillich, *Courage to Be*, 20–21.

36. Williams, *Shame and Necessity*, 88–95.

Chapter 12: Plotinus as Environmentalist? Mystical Unity and the Cosmos

1. One could, I suppose, maintain that an ecological or environmental ethic is inevitably built into any view of the world, even of those that find only derivative, indirect, instrumental value in it, e.g., value relative to human interests.

2. It is possible that the information set forth by Plotinus in his efforts to address a certain range of concerns will itself support claims and judgments not

treated at length or given prominence by Plotinus himself. I do think that the issue of the status of the material world is one where it is important to be aware of the possible disparity between the interests of Plotinus and what the explanations included in the *Enneads* may allow, support, or entail.

A. H. Armstrong and John Rist are important sponsors of a theistic mystical interpretation of Plotinus. W. T. Stace places Plotinus in the introvertive mystical category. It must be noted that there is a serious dispute about the extent to which a monistic interpretation is justified, as well as a challenge to the meaningfulness of theistic mysticism inasmuch as the term "theism" must be applied to the One as beyond being, nonpersonal, nonconscious, nonintentional, etc.

3. Closely associated forms have been identified as extrovertive, nature, integrative, mysticism. Although these terms are used differently by analysts of mystical experience, I will assume, for the purposes of this essay, that they are sufficiently overlapping to be helpful in locating the distinctive features of Plotinus's position. I delineate major features of this cosmic mysticism later in this chapter.

4. The technical-appearing term "emanation" is actually expressed by such terms as *prohodos, diexhodos, aporreo, ekreo*.

5. For an important contribution to this issue, see Gary M. Gurtler, *Plotinus: The Experience of Unity* (New York: Peter Lang, 1988).

6. Daniel A. Kealey, *Revisioning Environmental Ethics* (Albany: State University of New York Press, 1990). A beginning on this is also made in a brief article by Michael Wagner, "The Contribution of Plotinian Metaphysics to the Unification of Culture," in *Philosophy and Culture: Proceedings of the Seventeenth World Congress of Philosophy*, ed. V. Cauchy (Montreal: Montmorency, 1988), 5:192–95. It is, I think, significant that A. H. Armstrong finds it necessary to emphasize the importance of the cosmos in Plotinus's apprehension of divinity. But Armstrong refers only to the place of the cosmos in the ascent mode. Although he does, in concluding his article, refer to the descent mode in "participates in an universal movement of return," the next sentence clearly exhibits his focus and direction. "According to Plotinus we seek God by enlarging ourselves to unity with all he brings into being and find him and leave all else for him only after and because of that enlargement." A. H. Armstrong, "The Apprehension of Divinity in the Self and Cosmos in Plotinus," in *The Significance of Neoplatonism*, ed. R. Baine Harris (Albany, N.Y.: International Society for Neoplatonic Studies, 1976), 196.

7. Kealey, *Revisioning Environmental Ethics*, 69.

8. Kealey, *Revisioning Environmental Ethics*, 69.

9. Kealey, *Revisioning Environmental Ethics*, 84.

10. If the required condition for experience is the distinction between subject or consciousness and objects (of whatever sort), then the constitutive states of complete mystical unity will not qualify as experiences. But insofar as the states are epistemically accessible in some fashion and can be retained for reflective evaluation or cognitive adjustment, some extended use of the term "experience" would appear to be justifiable.

11. See, e.g., R. C. Zaehner, *Mysticism, Sacred and Profane* (New York: Oxford University Press, 1961); R. C. Zaehner, *Concordant Discord* (Oxford: Clarendon Press, 1970); Walter Stace, *Mysticism and Philosophy* (New York: J. B. Lippincott,

1960); William J. Wainwright, *Mysticism* (Madison: University of Wisconsin Press, 1981); Stephen Katz, *Mysticism and Philosophical Analysis* (New York: Oxford University Press, 1978); Stephen Katz, *Mysticism and Religious Traditions* (New York: Oxford University Press, 1983); Stephen Katz, *Mysticism and Language* (New York: Oxford University Press, 1993); Robert Forman, ed., *The Problem of Pure Consciousness* (New York: Oxford University Press, 1990); Richard Jones, *Science and Mysticism* (Lewisburg, Pa.: Bucknell University Press, 1986); Richard Jones, *Mysticism Examined* (Albany: State University of New York Press, 1993); William James, *The Varieties of Religious Experience* (New York: New American Library, 1958); Ben-Ami Scharfstein, *Mystical Experience* (Baltimore: Penguin Books, 1973); Nils Bjorn Kvastad, *Problems of Mysticism* (Oslo: Scintilla Press, 1980); Richard Woods, ed. *Understanding Mysticism* (New York: Image Books, 1980); Evelyn Underhill, *Mysticism* (New York: Dutton, 1961); Evelyn Underhill, *The Essentials of Mysticism* (New York: Dutton, 1960); D. T. Suzuki, *Mysticism: Christian and Buddhist* (New York: Collier, 1962); Rudolf Otto, *Mysticism East and West* (New York: Meridian, 1957); F. C. Happold, *Mysticism* (Baltimore: Penguin Books, 1970).

12. See, e.g., *Enneads (Enn.)* 1.4.7.14 f., 1.4.16.22.

13. The first three traits are identified by William Wainwright as characteristics that occur with particular frequency in the extrovertive type of mysticism. The quotation in point 2 is part of Wainwright's formulation of Walter Stace's position (*Mysticism*, 34). See Stace, *Mysticism and Philosophy*, 62–81.

14. Although points 4–7 can be viewed as elaborations of points 1 and 2, I include them as providing both general information and information that is distinctive of Plotinus's position.

15. The ascended identity of Socrates, for example, is one distinctive individual component of *nous*; is totalized in the holistic identity-as-unity of *nous* knowing and being itself as full intelligibility; and is also unity as one and many.

16. An undescended soul, which remains in *nous*, would be an obvious illustration of this dialectical transformation of identity, of continuity across regions, of difference, and as providing a basis for reconfiguring identity (and unity) within each region.

17. The dialectical nature of Soul is its identity with itself, its being manifest in innumerable souls as difference, and its being All Soul in identity and difference.

18. On this issue, see Joseph N. Torchia, *Plotinus, Tolma, and the Descent of Being* (New York: Peter Lang, 1993).

19. For interpreters such as A. H. Armstrong and John Rist, this first type of unity is the maximum possible for humans. The unity-without-difference is, for them, to be understood as unacceptable ontology, bad logic, and misdescription. Experientially or epistemically there may be a loss of distinction between self and other (One, God), but this is not an ontological unification or identity. This allows for the preservation of individuality of self and the integrity and absoluteness of the One. Since these are characteristics of theistic mysticism, Plotinus turns out to be a theistic mystic. See, e.g., A. H. Armstrong, *The Cambridge History of Later Greek and Early Medieval Philosophy* (Cambridge: Cambridge University Press, 1970); and John Rist, "Back to the Mysticism of Plotinus: Some More Specifics," *Journal of the History of Philosophy* 17, no. 2 (1989): 183–97.

20. Porphyry, *Vita Plotini* (Life of Plotinus) 8.19 ff. See an excellent analysis of this portrayal in Frederic M. Schroeder, *Form and Transformation* (Montreal: McGill–Queen's University Press, 1992),91–113. The distinction is operative in various places in the *Enneads*.

21. *Enn.* 4.8.1.25 ff. Quotations are from A. H. Armstrong's translation in *Plotinus*, 7 vols., Loeb Classical Library (1966–88).

22. As previously noted, Porphyry begins his biography of Plotinus as follows: "Plotinus, the philosopher of our times, seemed ashamed of being in the body." Are we to say, according to the proper diagnosis in the "Manual on Dialectical Classifications," that Plotinus is stuck on the ascent mode, suffering from a compulsion for the identity state of being? Does Plotinus require some help from a Plotinian therapist?

23. In addition to *Enn.* 4.3.8 and 4.4, see 4.5–4.9.

24. Such an integrated holism can make sense of "sympathetic magic," planetary influences, and other noncritical and naive "wisdom of hidden powers of the universe," etc.

25. That virtues in human affairs and nature are only "vestiges of nobility" (4.4.44.25) should not be understood completely negatively. The redeeming features of such nobility are also present in these areas.

Index

About the Contributors

MADONNA R. ADAMS is assistant professor of philosophy at Pace University, New York City, and director of the Center for Applied Ethics of Dyson College of Arts and Science. She has published articles in the areas of women's studies and spirituality.

DONALD N. BLAKELEY received his Ph.D. from the University of Hawaii and is professor of philosophy at California State University, Fresno. He has published a number of articles on ancient Greek philosophy and is presently working on a book comparing Plotinus and Chu Hsi.

C. W. DEMARCO received his Ph.D. from Vanderbilt University in 1991. He specializes in metaphysics, especially in relation to language, and has presented papers at national and international conferences on ethics, aesthetics, and other topics. He lives in Stillwater, Oklahoma.

OWEN GOLDIN is associate professor of philosophy at Marquette University. He is the author of *Explaining an Eclipse: Aristotle's* Posterior Analytics 2.1–10 and coeditor, with his wife, Patricia Kilroe, of *Human Life and the Natural World.*

ALAN J. HOLLAND studied philosophy at the Oxford University and is currently senior lecturer in philosophy at Lancaster University, UK. He is editor of the interdisciplinary journal *Environmental Values* and coeditor of a forthcoming volume on animal biotechnology and ethics.

TIMOTHY A. MAHONEY received his Ph.D. from the University of Pennsylvania and is currently an assistant professor in the Department of Philosophy and Humanities at the University of Texas at Arlington. He has published several articles on Plato's ethics, his primary area of research.

MOHAN MATTHEN is professor of philosophy at the University of Alberta. He has published articles and edited collections of papers on ancient

229

philosophy, philosophy of biology, and philosophy of mind. He is currently working on topics in ancient science, particularly the cosmological views of Aristotle.

MAX OELSCHLAEGER is a professor in the environmental ethics program at the University of North Texas. His recent books include *Caring for Creation; Postmodern Environmental Ethics;* and *Texas Land Ethics,* with Pete Gunter (in press).

ANTHONY PREUS is professor and chair of philosophy at Binghamton University. Among his publications are *Science and Philosophy in Aristotle's Biological Works* and *Aristotle and Michael of Ephesus on the Movement of Animals.*

JOHN M. RIST was until December 1996 professor of classics at the University of Toronto. His publications include *Plotinus: The Road to Reality, The Stoics,* and *The Mind of Aristotle.*

THOMAS M. ROBINSON is professor of philosophy and classics at the University of Toronto. His publications include *Plato's Psychology, Contrasting Arguments: An Edition of the* Dissoi Logoi, and *Heraclitus: Fragments.*

RICHARD SHEARMAN received his Ph.D. in environmental science from the State University of New York, College of Environmental Science and Forestry, Syracuse. He is currently an assistant professor in the Department of Science, Technology, and Society at Rochester Institute of Technology.

DARYL M. TRESS is assistant professor of philosophy at Fordham University. She has published papers on ancient philosophy and ancient science, and her most recent work, *Ancient Philosophy* (forthcoming), concerns Aristotle's notion of the child.

LAURA WESTRA is associate professor of philosophy at the University of Windsor. Among her publications are *An Environmental Proposal for Ethics: The Principle of Integrity* and *Faces of Environmental Racism* (coeditor P. Wenz), both published by Rowman & Littlefield.